P9-CSE-950

The World After Oil

THE SHIFTING AXIS OF POWER AND WEALTH

BRUCE NUSSBAUM

SIMON AND SCHUSTER NEW YORK

Published by Simon and Schuster
A Division Simon & Schuster Inc.,
Simon & Schuster Building
Rockefeller Center
1230 Avenue of the Americas
New York, New York 10020
SIMON AND SCHUSTER and colophon are registered trademarks of
Simon & Schuster Inc.
Designed by Karolina Harris
Manufactured in the United States of America

1 3 5 7 9 10 8 6 4 2

Library of Congress Cataloging in Publication Data
Nussbaum, Bruce.
The world after oil.

Bibliography: p.
Includes index.
1. Economic forecasting. 2. Twentieth century—Forecasts. 3. Twenty-first century—Forecasts. 4. Technological innovations. 5. Energy development—Forecasting. I. Title
HC59.N958 1983 338.5′443 83-413
ISBN 0-671-44571-5

FOR LESLIE

W.D.M.

ACKNOWLEDGMENTS

Inspiration, information and insight for this book have been provided by many dozens of people. For those who prefer remaining anonymous, I offer a collective "thank you."

Special thanks go to those people who over the years reminded me of the need to take the "long view," and look at the "big picture." One of the hardest things for journalists to do is to pull away from the daily event. We are trained to anticipate and cover breaking news, not to analyze general trends. I have been fortunate to know several people who think in terms of decades, centuries and eras, as well as themes, issues and policies. They include Charles Tilly and Eric Wolf at the University of Michigan, and Gordon Williams and William Wolman at my professional home, *Business Week*.

The following have also contributed significantly, offering ideas and information that I have used in my own way and for which I am totally responsible: André Sharon, Geoffrey Bell, Lawrence G. Franko, Yves Laulan, Alan Stoga, J. Paul Horne, Ken E. Mathysen-Gerst, Yves Oltramare, Rimmer de Vries, Anne P. Mills, Karl Van Horn, Barry Gelman, Phil

Skolnick, John Hennessy, John Pearson, Jack Pluenneke, Ed Mervosh, Robert Dowling, Ronald Taggiasco, John Templeman, Lewis H. Young, Bruce Cameron, Rand Smith, Ben Weberman, Peter Friedland and Robert Stolorow.

Alice Mayhew, my editor, believed in the importance of the book from the very beginning and her belief carried me through the "dark months" of writing. Her suggestions were enormously important to the structure and focus of the work.

Elizabeth McKee, my agent, was far more than a literary "broker." Her line-by-line reading of the chapters and her mountain of suggestions enhanced the analysis tremendously.

Every writer knows the personal price paid as part of his trade. I drew very heavily on the strength, humor and patience of Leslie Beebe during the months of writing. Leslie's shared drive for individual achievement and creativity kept her in my corner at all times—a geographical fact that was a constant pleasure.

One final tribute to that skunk-filled little island, Martha's Vineyard, which somehow insinuated itself into the very beginning and very ending of this book.

CONTENTS

INTRODUCTION

The origin of this book goes back to a return flight from Zurich in 1979. As a journalist, I was covering international finance. It was a great beat at the time. The smell of catastrophe, be it war, plague or money crisis, excites any good journalist, and that odor was definitely in the air. Gold was soaring, people were fleeing the dollar, and the good Swiss were making their usual profits by providing safe havens for the cash hoards of panicky Arab sheiks, European barons and American oral surgeons. The whole postwar international system was tearing itself apart in those years, and anyone with big money was seeking some kind of sanctuary.

Tracing just where that cash was flowing was part of my job. In Zurich and Geneva, it became clear that the Swiss money managers were funneling most of this "capital flight" into precious metals, government-guaranteed bonds, real estate and diamonds. In short, an enormous chunk of the world's capital was being put into small things that could, literally, be stuffed into your pocket if you were forced to run like hell or into shopping centers outside of Houston. Not much was being invested in what we normally call productive enterprises that provide jobs and profits and economic growth. The world was stalled, collapsing in on itself as people fled for the financial caves of hard assets and government IOUs.

There were a few Swiss, however, who were putting their clients' money into something everyone else was avoiding—the stock market. Not the American stock market, mind you, but the Tokyo exchange. Of the dozens and dozens of professional money mavens in Switzerland, two or three were actually investing in companies that they thought would grow and prosper in the future.

I was shocked by this aberrant behavior. Bankers are lemmings at heart and seldom act outside the running pack. Swiss bankers are even more fearful than most. What were these people up to? During the long flight home I began asking myself how they could be investing for the future, when everyone else was busy running from the present? And what kind of future were they betting on that would expand so fast and provide their clients with handsome profits?

I have tugged at that thread of a question over the past four years and discovered that the Swiss were really betting on a new Genesis—the virtual destruction of our entire way of life and the creation of a new twenty-first-century society built on its ruins. In the late 1970s, while the world was teetering on the edge of collapse, they were investing in certain types of high-technology companies that we now quickly recognize—Fujitsu, Matsushita, and Hitachi, the Japanese electronics firm that the FBI, in a "sting" operation last year, caught buying stolen IBM computer secrets. These money mavens were onto the greatest story of our lives; for the first time in three hundred years, the political and economic axis of the world is shifting away from the Atlantic Ocean to the Pacific Basin, changing not only the international balance of power among nations but also the intimate details of our personal lives.

What the Swiss could not know, however, was how painful the transition would be for the world as a whole and for each of us individually. They could never have guessed that their investment strategy was premised on the death of entire industries, the eradication of millions of jobs, the creation of a new army of "de-skilled" unemployed. Nor could they have guessed that the passing of the Industrial Era and the rise of the Age of High Technology would mean the shattering of NATO, the disintegration of the Common Market and perhaps the demise of the Soviet empire as we know it.

This book is a personal vision of what is happening to us as we pass through the cauldron of destruction and creation on our way to the future, a future not decades away, but right around the corner. It is not a picture of some high-tech Pollyanna playground so common among futurologists. This book is not about a "boom." It is a practical, clear examination of what is actually taking place, not a misty-eyed dream of what could happen. It takes as its first premise that the world of tomorrow will be constructed by what powerful people are doing today—people running governments, multinational corporations, banks, unions.

What struck me most about Swiss investment was that none of it was going into the traditional smokestack industries of steel, cars and chemicals. All of the money was heading into Japanese companies producing electronic things or automation devices. When I dug into the deeper meaning of what these robots and computers were doing to our way of life, I realized that they were, in effect, heralding in a brand-new twenty-first-century society. It will be a world of tremendous promise, fantastic wealth, speedy social change and quick personal advancement. It will also be a place of broken dreams, wrecked labor unions, lost skills.

Even worse, it can easily become a political incinerator as nations fight for the technological heights of the 1980s. Only a handful of countries will succeed in smoothly making the transition out of the twentieth century and into the twenty-first. There will be many losers, and their decline will unravel the alliances and institutions that were built on the ruins of

World War II. In the years immediately ahead of us, the issues of peace and war will once again be seriously debated in a way not seen since the 1930s.

For America, the twenty-first century has already begun. It holds incredible promise, yet promises incredible pain. A new high-tech Pacific frontier is already pulling economic and political power away from the traditional heartland of the nation, the Midwest and Northeast. And while Washington struggles with a nascent second "war between the states," the culture and way of life are being totally transformed.

For us, twenty-first-century life will be as different as the pre-car, pre-TV, pre-telephone nineteenth century was from today. The workplace is about to be completely revolutionized. Mind power, the mental ability to create, will finally replace labor, the physical ability to assemble, as the most valued skill among workers. Indeed, the very concept of "work" and "workers" will change. The prototypical workplace of the 1980s will soon consist of individuals sitting behind computer terminals and analyzing words and data, rather than teams of people putting things together on an assembly line or typing pages on a machine. Robots, not laborers, will be assembling finished parts made by other robots. And this will occur by 1985—not 2000.

A new set of social statuses will follow. Access to higher levels of data banks and information will come to determine the true status of individuals in the United States. The greater the access, the higher the status. "Are you a level ten or only a level six?" will replace such questions as "Are you a manager?" or "Are you a line worker?" Information will replace manufactured goods as the most valued commodity in the economy. By the middle of the 1980s, information processing will surpass car manufacturing as the largest industry in the country. And so inundated will society become with this data deluge that people with the skill to interpret and manage the flood for others will rise to the top of society and perhaps hold it hostage.

Just as important, the building of an American twenty-first-century society will without doubt be one of the most turbulent developments ever experienced in the history of this nation. The shift to manless factories run by robots may well produce a massive *superlumpenproletariat* of unemployed workers, minorities and immigrants. And it will be not only the working class that will suffer. Countless millions of Americans will find it difficult to make the transition to a high-technology society. Many will suffer from "cyberphobia," or the fear of computers. By the year 2000 the misfits of the new high-tech era could easily climb to 30 percent of the working-age population, if Washington does nothing to retrain them.

Even the people who do succeed in finding their niche in twenty-first-century American society will find that the tremendous opportunities opened to them by new technologies will have to be matched against a new horror—the loss of privacy. The image of an America made up of millions of electronic cottages spread across the landscape with people sitting in their living rooms happily at work in front of their computer terminals is nothing but a short-sighted fantasy. Even today, as the telecommunications revolution sweeps through the nation's offices and businesses, the very first questions anyone asks are "How safe is my computer?" "Can anyone look into my files?" "Who knows my secret password?" The years ahead will spawn an entire new wave of crime. Indeed, crimes of the 1990s will be radically different from today's concerns. Computer crime in particular—tapping into private electronic files—will soon become the most troublesome crime of the future. And it will trouble foreign governments and domestic corporations as much as the heads of households.

Understanding the cold reality of what the future is bringing is but the first step in knowing how to interpret what is happening to us today. The massive shift in the international balance of power and the mammoth tilt in the regional axis of American society are the direct consequences of a seismic change in history. The deathbed agonies of Detroit, the anti-Americanism in Europe, the stealing of computer secrets by the Japanese are all part of the same race through time to the future. This is my chronicle of that story.

1

THE LOCOMOTIVE TECHNOLOGIES

•

EVERY ERA, EVERY CENTURY HAS TWO OR THREE DOMINANT technologies that define it. They pull the entire society into the future. In ways unseen by the people living from day to day, these technologies determine what work people do and where they do it, the number of children they have, the clothes they wear, the house they live in.

During the past 110 years of the Industrial Era—roughly, from 1860 to 1970—electrical machines, chemicals and steel formed the core technologies of our lives. Combined with the assembly-line mode of production, these technologies gave us automobiles, plastics, textiles, tanks and napalm. This was the "century" of heavy industry.

These technologies, created in the late nineteenth century, lasted well into the twentieth. Developed in a period of cheap labor, cheap raw materials, and above all, cheap energy, they are now obsolete. To compete in the world economy, to generate new industries and new jobs, a whole new series of technologies is now being called forth.

As in any one period of time, dozens of "advanced" technologies today exist side by side, each pregnant with potential.

In recent years, we have been flooded with books about the future, books describing fantastic new wonders. Gigantic mirrors in orbit to collect the sun and send electricity back to earth; nuclear fusion that uses sea water as fuel; deep ocean currents that generate electricity—all are part of this fanciful prognosticating.

In reality, only a tiny handful of new technologies come to influence the societies around them. Right now none of the futurists' dreams is realistic. A cold, pragmatic look at the world will show that for any technology to be successful today, it must have at least three characteristics:

1. It must be an energy sipper that not only uses less energy but also makes new things that use less energy.
2. It must have an immediate and pervasive impact on our lives, affecting us where we work and where we live.
3. It must increase productivity and efficiency by using less labor and fewer raw materials—both of which are high-priced items in the world of the 1980s.

Today there are only three technologies that meet these requirements: robotics, bioengineering and telecommunications. Each in its own way will soon have a revolutionary impact on America. Two of the new technologies—robotics and telecommunications—are but the latest stages in the evolution toward computers. While we rush to put Ataris, Apples and IBMs into our homes, corporations are moving to install computer-based automation and communications. The switch away from labor-intensive "smokestack" heavy industries toward electronics and computer-controlled work is one of the great developments of our lives.

The other, of course, is the change in the economic foundation of Western life from petroleum-based chemistry to genetically based biology. By taking the chemical, pharmaceutical, textile and food industries away from a process that uses up resources that can never be replaced in our time to one that can be generated again and again by living organisms, we are taking a gigantic step into the future.

These three technologies, robotics, bioengineering and telecommunications, are not the dreams of tomorrow; they are the realities of today, and they are already beginning to change our lives. By 1990, they will have transformed the entire world we live in. They are the true locomotive technologies of the eighties.

But technology, to work, must find its proper niche in the right society at the correct time. It must fit into the "hot mix" of economic and political tides coming together at just that moment in history. The mere existence of technologies means nothing in isolation. In Germany in the late nineteenth century, everything coalesced as Bismarck unified the German nation with blood and steel. In America, a Northern victory over the agrarian South ensured an industrial expansion. In Tsarist Russia, however, a feudal society smothered imported technologies with suffocating tradition.

Today, nations around the world are scrambling to remake themselves through new technology. They are competing with one another to create the newest industries and offer the most advanced goods on the global markets. Only those countries that can find the right mix of social policies capable of nurturing the new technologies will succeed in their drive to claim a piece of the future. Only they will dominate the new balance of power that will exist in the world by the beginning of the twenty-first century.

•

ROBOTS—STEEL-COLLAR WORKERS

In the small village of Oshino, near Mt. Fuji, sprawls a giant building put up by Fujitsu Fanuc, one of Japan's new high-tech companies. There is very little light in this factory. There is none of the fluorescent glare so typical of plant floors. The entire area, two football fields in size, just glows dimly. Something else is also different here. The air-conditioning is turned way down, and the air is stale, full of metallic smells.

Light and air are not needed in this place. It is midnight at the base of Mt. Fuji, and the Fanuc factory is working on the "ghost shift." There are no people here—none at all. No voices, no sneezing, no coughing, no laughing. Just the sound of machines.

During the day, 100 people are employed—63 to assemble the finished parts, 19 to care for the machines, 4 inspectors to check on quality, and 14 managers and clerks. But from five o'clock in the afternoon through the night and into the morning there isn't anyone there; just robots and machines making more robots and machines, which will turn out yet more robots. The factory operates twenty-four hours a day. Set up in January 1981, this plant makes one hundred robots a month. Soon it will make four hundred.

Even now, the one hundred "day" people are only one fifth the number that a conventional factory normally employs to do the same work. By 1986, when Fujitsu Fanuc will bring out a new robot that will put together the parts machine-tooled during the night, the 63 workers who assemble those parts during the day won't be needed either. Only three or four managers and clerks will be employed, plus the robot caretakers. A handful of people, dozens of "cells" of robots and machines, all linked by computer, will produce and manufacture around the clock. The unmanned factory is coming. It already exists in Japan.

While the spread of the unmanned factory is still a few years away, the industrial robot—the heart of the automated factory of the future—is not. At this very moment, a new labor force is emerging from the Fujitsu Fanuc factory and others like it around the world. These steel-collar workers don't take coffee breaks, ask for raises, come in on Mondays with hangovers, or complain about unsafe working conditions. They couldn't care less whether or not the air is stuffy or the light isn't just right.

Robots are being introduced around the world at an incredible pace, and they are generating a workplace revolution more important than even the assembly line that was captured and caricatured in Charlie Chaplin's *Modern Times*. When that revolution finally spends itself by the end of the 1980s and robots take over from people on the factory floor, more than just the system of production will have changed. The international balance of power will no longer be the same. The nation with the largest number of robots will almost certainly be at the top of the new global power pyramid. For not only will robots generate a quantum leap in productivity and thus allow goods to be made better and cheaper, but the robot industry itself will soon become one of the largest, most profitable and most important industries in the West. Robot making and robot exporting will become, by 1985, one of the handful of twenty-first-century high-technology industries that dominate our economies, much as autos, chemicals and steel dominated the 1960s and 1970s.

In an era of high-priced energy, robots mean higher productivity, lower costs, and even better quality. Compared with people, robots produce more things in a given hour of work. In the past decade, U.S. productivity—measured by the amount of goods and services produced in a given hour—has fallen so low that fewer and fewer "made in America" items can compete anywhere around the world. At the same time, Japanese productivity has soared. The Europeans have done a bit better, but not much. Only the robot and the entirely automated factory of the future that it heralds can save the United States from its productivity quagmire—and a permanent decline of power.

The first modern robot ever produced came out of America in 1961. Joseph F. Engleberger, the "father" of modern-day robotics, took a jointed mechanical stick patterned after a human arm and stuck it onto a computer, producing the "Unimate."

But then nothing much happened. By 1970, there were a

couple of dozen experimental robots in use around the world. But they were expensive toys, the playthings of scientists and science fiction writers. It took the price explosion of the 1970s to make the robot revolution possible. An inflationary firestorm cut the value of the dollar in half and raised the prices for all commodities, including the cost of labor. Led by an enormous jump in energy prices, costs of production skyrocketed. Steel and aluminum prices soared, and every petroleum-based product, of course, ranging from plastic Bic pens to polyester suits, shot up. Labor costs were no exception. Wages soared in the U.S. in the 1970s; in many industries, nominal wage levels, including tons of "perks," doubled during the decade. With such huge new costs of production, the prices of all goods took off like rockets. Remember the old VW Beetle in 1969 when it sold for $1,800? By 1980, its successor, the not-much-bigger Rabbit, was going for nearly $10,000—an increase of more than 450 percent. That price reflects not only a soaring inflation, but a declining dollar as well. The only solution to combating that gigantic inflationary binge is to make more things in a shorter period of time using fewer and cheaper materials.

This became clear in the late 1970s—but not everywhere. No one knew it at the time, but the first high-tech robot war in the international arena quietly began about a dozen years ago. The battleground was in the world auto market, long dominated by America. The incredible rise in the price of energy made the *macho* behemoths of the 1950s and 1960s totally obsolete on American roads. No one could afford big cars anymore. The Japanese, of course, realizing that small cars made the most economic sense in the age of high-cost energy, began to produce and export them to the United States by the millions. Detroit was very slow in coming around, and was nearly destroyed by its delay. Only massive pressure on Tokyo by Washington in 1981 to curb its exports saved Detroit, and even now Detroit remains in jeopardy. AMC has become a mere marketing agent for France's Renault. Chrysler lives as a result of Congress's policy of subsidizing giant corporations. Ford remains in trouble. Only GM appears to be surviving, although at a shrunken size.

But while today businessmen and politicians grudgingly admit that the Japanese were brilliant in their marketing strategy of producing chiefly compacts and subcompacts, they are still turning a blind eye to the hidden part of the Japanese automobile miracle, the secret that is being repeated today in other products—robots.

•

ROBOT FEVER

The first robot built in Japan was a copy of an American model. Kawasaki Heavy Industries licensed the technology from Unimation, the company founded by Engleberger. This was in 1968. At that time, the robot was still a great toy; it did fantastic things, but only for a fantastic price. People—human labor—were a lot cheaper in Japan in the late sixties before the oil crisis. In fact, it cost about twelve times as much to buy and use a sophisticated robot in 1970 as it did to employ a single worker for a year. It wasn't much different in the United States or in Europe. But with the energy-induced inflationary boom of the 1970s, the relative price of robots began to look a lot better. Helped by the budding microelectronic revolution that took off in the 1970s and made computers smaller and cheaper year after year, the actual price of robots began to tumble. But only the Japanese took notice. By 1975 the relative cost of robots had fallen from 12 times the cost of a man to only 4.8. By 1978, the ratio had plummeted to 3.7; by 1982, it was beginning to disappear. Moreover, these numbers had the robots working only a single shift. Add in a second or third shift, as in the Fujitsu Fanuc factory, and robots can pay for themselves within a year. Everything after that is profit. The steel-collar workers had suddenly come of age.

The Japanese auto industry realized this incredible technological breakthrough first. From zero in 1970, the auto industry began buying as many robots as companies could make. The Japanese auto makers became the largest consumers of robots in the world, and by the end of the seventies they had six times as many of these machines as their American competitors. Thousands of robots began making precise and perfect welds on millions of cars during those years. The Japanese suddenly found that not only were they saving money, sharp improvements in quality were being made as well. There were no "Monday" cars that fell apart. There was no worker at the end of the assembly line with a sledgehammer to bang ill-fitting parts into place.

By 1980, it took only two thirds as many Japanese working only two thirds as many hours to produce the same number of cars that Detroit was putting out. And Fiat, Renault and Volkswagen were even further behind. This gave the Japanese an incredible cost advantage, over American producers, of $1,000 to $2,000 per car, and that advantage still remains.

The results are plain to see. Over 200,000 American auto workers are now jobless, and most of them will never see the inside of a car plant again. The American auto industry produced 13 million cars in 1978. In 1980, it made only eight million, and in 1982 it manufactured five million. The Japanese captured 27 percent of the domestic United States market before Washington forced Tokyo to cut back. If it hadn't acted, the Japanese could probably have grabbed one half of the market. In Europe, only strict protectionism prevented the Japanese from dominating. Even so, the Japanese have taken 10 percent of the much-vaunted German car market, 30 percent of the Belgian market and 30 percent of the British market. By using illegal nontariff barriers, only the French have been able to keep the Japanese out of their domestic auto market. This was in Europe, the land of small cars. Robots and the incredible increase in productivity they create have made the Japanese auto industry unbeatable in any free market.

But this is already history. The promise of such enormous productivity gains in the post-OPEC era is leading to an absolute explosion of the robot industry. The United States, Japan, Europe and Russia are scrambling to create, produce, import or steal the most advanced robots in the greatest quantities possible. The fight for leadership in robotics is taking on a sense of battling for national survival—and indeed it is. There is no single technological advance that is more important today than robots in determining which nation will win the fight for the technological heights in the 1980s—and come out on top in the new balance of power of the 1990s.

So far, Japan is way out in the lead. Indeed, Japan is so mesmerized by robots that its press describes the obsession as "robot fever." Japan is quickly moving to apply the lessons learned in the "auto wars" with the United States and robotize its entire society. The Japanese are absolutely convinced that robots hold the key to national economic survival in the twenty-first century. The entire country is being mobilized. Newspapers and TV are full of stories about the miracle of robots and the need to keep ahead of the United States and Europe if Japan is to survive and prosper in the decades ahead.

Right now, according to Paul Aron of Daiwa Securities Company, an expert on Japanese robots, Japan has more robots installed than the rest of the world combined. It has about 13,000 robots in its factories, compared to only 4,000 in the United States and about 2,500 in Europe. But more importantly, Japan is producing robots at a much faster rate than the United States. Aron estimates that in 1980, Japan made over 3,000 robots, compared to only 1,300 for America. And he projects that by 1985, Japanese companies will make 32,000 robots—ten times the current level, while U.S. corporations produce 5,200, or four times their 1980 level. If that trend continues, by 1990 Japan will be putting out nearly 57,000 robots annually in a multibillion-dollar industry while the United States struggles along making 22,000 robots a year. But even these numbers are extremely conservative. It might well be that actual production of robots turns out to be in the hundreds of thousands a year. No one really knows.

Demand for robots is so incredibly high in Japan that only about 2 percent of them are exported—and half of that goes to the Soviet Union. But factories are going up all the time. In early 1982, Kawasaki announced that it was building the biggest robot factory in the world outside Kobe—a $76-million giant that will be putting out several hundred robots annually when it opens in 1983 and nearly 3,000 robots a year in 1987. The year 1983 will be a crucial one for Japan and the world economy. At that time, Japan will have enough factory capacity in place not only to satisfy domestic demand for robots but also to begin exporting them in quantity. Exports will make up 20 to 30 percent of all robot production at that time, and unless American companies gear up to satisfy America's own burgeoning demand for robots, the entire market may go to the Japanese in much the same way as in TVs, VTRs, semiconductors, steel, shipbuilding and, of course, autos.

Dozens of companies make robots in Japan. Until recently, only a handful of U.S. companies produced them. Cincinnati Milicron and Unimation together still manufacture half the robots in this country. But this is about to change as the giants of American industry bring out their own proprietary robots secretly built over the years. In early 1982, IBM announced it was going to be selling a sophisticated tactile robot with "fingers" able to grip and feel objects. IBM may even open up its own robot manufacturing plant in 1983 in Boca Raton, Florida, the site of its 5,000-person Advanced Manufacturing Systems division. At the same time General Motors is talking with Fujitsu Fanuc and other robot makers about marketing its own version of the robot spray painter—a robot so huge that it can paint an entire car at one time. Other U.S. corporate giants are just now beginning to get into the robot act. Westinghouse has set up an $8-million Productivity Center, where robot applications are being studied, and will begin selling equipment for the ballooning factory-automation market. Bendix was to introduce two new robots in 1982, and United Technologies is going to sell an automated welder.

•

ROBOTS ARE CONSERVATIONISTS

Incredibly, the robots behind the success of the Japanese auto makers are really pretty stupid, quite blind, deaf and senseless. They are the very first generation of steel-collar workers in history, and these robots look a lot more like a dentist's drill than R2-D2 of *Star Wars*. In fact, they haven't changed much in design from the first robot built over twenty years ago. A jointed armlike structure, a motor and a computer that serves as a memory are the basic parts for 90 percent of the robots now in place around the world.

What these primitive machines do offer, however, is precision, predictability, flexibility and, sometimes, brute strength. In an eerie way, the fact that they are not alive is a big help also. Just consider the energy savings on light, air-conditioning and heat in the Fujitsu Fanuc factory.

It is no accident that upwards of 60 percent of all robots now used in the United States, Japan, and Europe do just one thing—spot-weld steel auto parts. Most small-car bodies are made up of about four hundred major parts pressed out from sheet metal that have to be bonded together by about four thousand spot welds. Before the introduction of robots in the 1970s, workers would spend eight-hour days hauling heavy welding guns to the exact same spot on car frame after car frame, continuously moving down the line, to make those spot welds. It was boring, sometimes dangerous work, with sparks flying everywhere from the searing metal. After a few hours, it would be pretty clear that the welds made at the end of the shift were going to be a lot worse than the welds made at the beginning of the day. The auto makers had to pay high wages to get people to do this work. During the 1960s in America, when the auto workers were the aristocracy of organized labor, the spot welders were near the top of the pay heap.

Robots changed all that. In the 1970s, companies began manufacturing robots that made spot welds on a car frame at exactly the same place in exactly the same way hour after hour, day after day, around the clock. The accuracy was beyond anything that a human could achieve, and the endurance was unmatchable. Mechanical arms tipped with welding "hands" would reach out, sear the metal parts together, and retract. These robots made welds at a faster clip than the people they replaced and highlight the benefits of repetition, precision and endurance. Another type of first-generation robot, the spray painter, shows how they can increase productivity in one other very significant way: robots are conservationists.

This time, it isn't necessary to cross the Pacific to illustrate a point. General Electric is one of the handful of U.S. companies that are making a full commitment to robots throughout its vast manufacturing empire. In 1980 alone, GE spent $5.1 million for 47 new robots, which saved it nearly $3 million in labor and material costs in just twelve months. By the late 1980s, GE will have one thousand robots working in its Major Appliance Business Group, which manufactures all its kitchen and laundry appliances, and hundreds more throughout the company.

One of the machines GE is using is a Norwegian robot called the Trallfa. Trallfas spray-paint anything, and these particular robots are used to spray adhesive material onto refrigerator-cabinet interiors. One Trallfa does the work of two people. The savings, of course, are huge, but they do not stop there. Just as important, the Trallfa uses 10 percent less adhesive material. And even that is not the end of it. On top of the 10 percent saving, the robot sprays the material much more uniformly than humans. People talk to one another at work on the line. Their arms get tired. They itch, they scratch. With men using big spray guns, the stuff tends to glob up in corners. Not with Trallfas. Spray-painting robots use nearly 20 percent fewer materials than people—they conserve resources in a resource-short world.

GE saves 30 cents per refrigerator with the Trallfa robots—and the quality of the job is much higher as well. In early 1980, there was a growing fear that the Japanese would soon invade the American appliance market in the same way they came to dominate consumer electronics. That fear is now quickly fading. Robots—and the productivity gains they are introducing—are saving the day for GE and for this one American industry.

The leading edge of robot technology has now advanced to the point where these steel-collar workers can do spot welding, spray painting, lifting and loading, and even handling parts in machine-tool plants like the Fujitsu Fanuc factory. They are spreading throughout the industrial landscape at a blinding speed. But these robots are merely the first-born of an automated army of workers. They are extremely limited.

To move from infancy to maturity, robots will need one more crucial attribute—artificial senses such as sight or touch. The world is at the brink of the next stage in the evolution of robotics—a second-generation steel-collar worker. The goal is the creation of a machine that assembles parts made by other machines. The date is 1990. The geopolitical and social consequences are immense. The nation that first develops the second generation of seeing robots will have an incredible edge in manufacturing goods at the lowest possible prices and the highest possible quality. Dumb robots are already changing the workplace and the world. Seeing robots will mark the final victory of the steel-collar worker over flesh-and-blood laborers and herald in twenty-first-century society.

The current first-generation robots have to be coddled like some blind infant giants. Everything must be fed to them in just the right manner and lined up in exact precision on the assembly line or in the parts box for the robots to work. Without "eyes" the robot blindly repeats the exact-same task time and again. For example, if the two thin sheets of metal on a car body that need to be welded together do not come down the assembly line perfectly aligned, the robot will reach out its arm and torch the spot where the sheets should be. That might turn out to be a door handle. The assembly line has to deliver the sheet-metal parts to a specific place in a particular orientation. If it doesn't, the robot will make the spot weld anyway and not even realize that it has blown the job.

Robots with eyes or fingers and a better computer "brain" are not bound by these limitations—and they will be able to work a lot more like ordinary people. They will be able to adapt to slight changes in the production procedure. They will be able to tell if a part is arriving down an assembly line out of sequence or damaged. They will be able to "jiggle" a part to get it into place, move a section of a car body to align it correctly or even stop the whole assembly line if there is an impending emergency.

The next step in the evolution of robots is to advance the artificial eyes and brains to the point where they can begin to put together parts on the assembly line. IBM and Texas Instruments have a few such robots already at work in their own factories, putting together computers and semiconductors, but neither one is yet willing to put it on the open market. They want to keep the technological advantages and the productivity gains to themselves for the moment. TI uses twenty-four robots to assemble calculators and appliance controls. But it is only a matter of time before both go into the robot business. In Japan, electronic manufacturers are now only second to automobile makers in using robots, and most of them use these very early assembly robots.

•

UNMANNED FACTORIES OF THE FUTURE

Whoever wins the race to breed the next generation of "smart" robots will take a commanding lead in developing the unmanned factory of the future. For it is the seeing robot that can change its actions and adapt to a changing environment that is at the heart of what the Japanese call the flexible manufacturing complex, or FMC, and the Americans describe as the flexible manufacturing system, or FMS. With sight and sophisticated computer brains, robots will form the heart of a totally automated factory run by computers. The era of computer-aided manufacturing—CAM—will be launched and with it, the first major technological breakthrough of the twenty-first century. These factories will offer productivity gains so great and product quality so high that no plant run solely by human workers can ever hope to compete.

No one knows exactly what the unmanned factories of the future will look like. Each plant will be customer-ordered. At the very least, the factory will include assembly lines and various types of robots and machine tools controlled through minicomputers right on the shop floor. This entirely automated workplace will in turn be connected to larger computers run by supervisory personnel in a continuous hierarchy all the way to the president of the corporation. The true unmanned factory will be a manufacturing facility with the executive suite directly connected to the factory floor in one integrated computerized system. The highest officials of a company will be able to monitor and control what is taking place on the assembly line in factories around the country—even around the world.

The key to this unmanned factory is flexibility. Gone are the days of Henry Ford, when assembly lines turned out millions of black Model-T Fords—one exactly the same as another. Consumer tastes are now so specialized and electronic products have such short life cycles that everything is becoming customized. Standardization is definitely out. Just think of the dozens of car models made by GM or Toyota. In the past, each time a model changeover occurred, the entire production line had to be shut down and new machinery brought in. An enormous amount of time and money was wasted as highly paid labor was laid off for weeks and months at a time. In a similar way, this occurs with every product from TVs to typewriters. Each time something new comes down that line, everything has to stop. And with production runs of fifty or fewer occurring three quarters of the time on the factory floor, the waste is enormous. With fixed assembly lines and soaring costs for new capital equipment, the cost is fantastic.

Robotized factories will end all that. One automated assembly line recently introduced at a machine tool shop in the United States cut labor by 30 percent and increased the use of the machinery by 45 percent. CAM systems can increase productivity up to 400 percent and cut labor and material costs by incredible amounts.

•

THE EUROPEAN CHALLENGE IN ROBOTS

The United States is not alone in competing with the Japanese in robotics. There are a number of European companies that are now producing robots more advanced than either the American or the Japanese. For years the Japanese have gone to Europe to license and then copy robot designs. And now U.S. companies like General Electric are also importing and licensing them by the hundreds.

Surprisingly, the Swedes, the Norwegians and the Italians make the most sophisticated robots in Europe, not the Germans. When GE decided to get into the factory-of-the-future business very fast by licensing designs before its own robots were developed, it turned abroad for help. In 1981, GE began licensing an arc-welding robot from Hitachi. But GE could have gone to Sweden. Many people in the industry swear that Hitachi's robot is only an adaptation of an original Swedish design. In fact, Asea Inc. of Sweden is one of the foremost robot builders of the world and it specializes in building very fancy arc-welding robots. The Japanese insist that their robot is quite different from, and much better than, the Swedish machine. Yet they do admit that Asea came out with the first such arc welder years ago and that Hitachi used it to develop its own model. Asea's biggest customer is West Germany, which takes more than half of the seven hundred robots the company now produces every year. Several German companies—such as Kuka Mann, Volkswagen and Daimler-Benz—do make robots, mostly spot welders, but so far only the Russians have been interested in buying them.

GE is also licensing the Allegro robot from an Italian company called DEA, of Turin. The Allegro is a very early prototype assembly robot. Westinghouse, GE's rival, is turning to Olivetti for its assembly robot, the Sigma. Olivetti is shipping about forty Sigmas in the next year or two for Westinghouse to offer as part of its over-all sales effort in selling the components for the unmanned, automated factory of the future.

But the ability of certain European countries to make technologically advanced robots does not ensure their widespread use. The United States makes the most advanced robot in the world now in commercial use—the T3—but only a few of these models can be found on factory floors, because of their high cost and extreme complexity. In Europe, the technology exists to produce the best robots found anywhere, but the application of robotics on a massive scale is even more limited than in the United States. To be sure, there are exceptions. Renault, Volkswagen and Fiat have some of the most automated plants anywhere, with plenty of spot-welding robots scattered around assembly lines. But Europe has yet to display the ferocious drive to robotize and automate its entire manufacturing process that is so much a part of Japan's drive for economic supremacy. Europe, with perhaps only one exception—France—shows little evidence that it knows that it is in a race to build twenty-first-century societies. And while it is as technologically advanced as America and Japan in robotics, it is not applying that technology to radically change its economic base. For that reason and others, Europe is falling further and further behind Japan and the United States in the international balance of power.

•

ROBOTS DON'T DRINK

One of the great wild cards in the robot race is the Soviet Union. By some counts the USSR is already number two, ahead of the United States, in installed robots. But most of those six or seven thousand machines are very unsophisticated. Only about two thousand have electronic controls. Moscow's push for robots has exactly the same force behind it as Japan's or America's—the need for greater productivity. "Robots don't drink" is the most familiar comment among Russian automation experts, and it expresses the keen disappointment with Russia's labor force, which has perhaps the lowest productivity level among all of the industrial nations of the world. With absenteeism three or four times higher than in the West, an unmotivated work force and an epidemic of alcoholism, the Soviet authorities are turning more and more to robots to solve their industrial problems. None other than Leonid Brezhnev in 1981, in his speech at the 26th Congress of the Communist Party, specifically mentioned the mobilization of twenty-two ministries to build 40,000 robots over the next five years.

Right now Russia is about five or ten years behind the West in robotic technology. One of the basic problems is that the Soviet Union is backward in microelectronics and computers—the heart and brains of all robots. To make up for this backwardness, Moscow has been turning to both Japan and America for robots. Unimation has shipped dozens of its spot-welding Unimates to Russia, many of them winding up at the infamous Kama River truck plant, built with heavy United States involvement, that turned out vehicles used in the invasion of Afghanistan. Unimation recently signed an agreement with Nokia, the biggest private corporation in Finland, to build Unimates. Nokia will be able to sell in Scandinavia, but most of the robots will probably go for export to the Soviet Union. And Kawasaki, which builds Unimates under license, also exports Unimates to Russia. It sent 26 Unimates to Russia in 1981. When Kawasaki completes its newest robot factory, the largest in the world, 30 percent of the production will go for exports, and many of these will wind up in Russia. So enamored are the Soviets of the Unimate that they have turned to reverse engineering to make copies of the U.S. robot. The Soviets now have the K-690, which is simply a Unimate that was broken apart, studied and remade. They aren't fancy, but they are better than workers who drink, stay at home and care little for what they put together on the line.

In Japan, America and parts of Europe, robots are already beginning to make and assemble cars, TVs, computers and airplanes, and they are doing it faster, better and cheaper than people. In a few years' time, steel-collar workers will displace not only blue-collar workers on the factory floor, but also white-collar managers and clerks in offices. The steel-collar revolution will have a greater impact on life in the United States, Europe and Japan in the 1980s than any other technological change. Robots promise to bring about an era of riches unmatched in the past fifty years. But they also threaten to bring about a modern-day Luddite rebellion by a new army of *superlumpenproletariat*, who feel threatened by the marching machines. Robots offer tremendous promise for the future, but like all new technologies, they will bring great pain as well.

Unlike earlier phases of automation, when machines replaced human labor in one sector of the economy and left others to absorb the slack, the current march of the steel-collar workers is hitting all industries at the same time. There is no place to soak up displaced workers, no place to run. Even the service industry, so effective in generating millions of jobs during the 1970s, will be hit. The Japanese are working on a

"McDonald's" robot that will cook hamburgers, serve Coke and make change. And you can buy a "butler" robot right now from Neiman-Marcus that mixes drinks. An army of "techno-casualties" may well be brought forth by this new technology —men and women disemployed, with no abilities, no skills for the future. Who takes responsibility for retraining these dispossessed, who supports them as they seek out new jobs, indeed, who makes sure that jobs are there—these will be the crucial social questions of the twenty-first century.

•

BIOENGINEERING—"BUG" FACTORIES

For decades, America had the reputation of being the world center for automotive engineering. Germany, no slouch when it came to cars, was also known as the center for project engineering—designing and building huge steel plants, petrochemical "crackers," hydroelectric dams. But the days of annual changes in car models are gone. The smoking ironworks are closing. The era of mechanical engineering is passing. The time of bioengineering is about to arrive.

Bioengineering is a powerful, pervasive technology that will cause massive changes right down to the core of American society. It will transform the pharmaceutical, food and chemical industries. It will profoundly alter mining and may end the energy business as we know it. It will change how long we live, how we live, and whom we live with. It promises to take our culture, which is now based on using up nonrenewable raw materials, and put it on an entirely different foundation, propelled by renewable, living resources. By creating new life, bioengineering will transform all life. The first nation to learn the alchemy of this new technology will gather to itself new sources of economic and political power not seen on earth for generations.

Bioengineering in a general way has been with us from the beginning. Breeding animals, developing new strains of grains, growing yeast for bread and making yogurt are all ways of manipulating genes. It has taken thousands of years to breed cows, horses, and our friendly dogs and cats. Wheat, corn, barley, grapes, rice have all been altered. Without manipulating them, there would be no tacos, no Wheat Thins, no beer, no wine, no cheese, no sake.

•

DESIGNER GENES

But these traditional methods are extremely limited. They are terribly time-consuming, with change taking place over many generations. They require the entire living organism to change, even if the object is to alter just one trait. They are inexact, because animals and plants are complex. As a result, they are very expensive.

Bioengineering is different. It is precise, sharply focused. It requires only a short time for the procedure, very little energy, and perhaps most important of all, it holds the promise of creating radically different living things tailored to demand. "Designer genes" is more than a joke; they may soon be a reality.

Bioengineering is basically gene splicing, the taking of a single gene from one organism and transferring it to another. The gene itself is the basic blueprint of all cells, all living matter. Like software programs that tell computers what to do, the gene is a code that commands the cell how to operate and what to produce. In the simplest procedure, scientists find one organism that produces something they want—alcohol, for example. They then extract the gene responsible for ordering the cell to make alcohol, and they stick it into another organism known for its fast growth. The second "bug" then follows the instructions of the newly installed gene and becomes a miniature factory that makes alcohol. It is grown or fermented in large quantities, and the alcohol is drawn off. With the right kind of large-scale, continuous fermentation process, a "bug" factory can be built that manufactures commercial quantities of alcohol that can then be used as a fuel.

Such a factory is not an ivory-tower fantasy. One is nearing completion right now, and several others are already on their way. The National Distillers and Chemicals Corporation is building a $100-million plant that will make forty million gallons of ethanol annually for fuel. The company is using a new life form, a genetically engineered yeast created by Cetus Corporation, a West Coast biotech company, to produce the ethanol. It will be operating by the end of 1983.

•

DESIGNER COWS

Just a short time ago, the manufacture of alcohol by super-yeasts would have been the type of thing to catch the fancy of a biochemist, not a businessman. Ethanol, along with methanol, ethylene glycol and dozens of other basic "building-block" components that go into our plastic world of Baggies, polyester suits, Naugahyde chairs and Tupperware, are normally made out of petroleum.

We often forget that petroleum not only is used as a fuel, but it is a major raw material, a "feedstock," that is broken down into dozens and dozens of simpler parts, which are then reconstructed to make a huge number of the plastics and chemicals we use every day.

When the price of oil was at its early-1970s low of $2.10 per barrel, it made all the sense in the world to build massive, multibillion-dollar "crackers" to separate the gooey liquid. The price was right for both the raw material and the huge amounts of energy needed to break the petroleum into simpler components. Now the whole cost structure is all wrong. The price of petroleum used as fuel to run the huge crackers has gone through the roof, and the cost of buying the same petroleum as a raw material has jumped in exactly the same way. Any new process that can offer to generate the "polys" and "glycols" of the petroleum-cracking process at a lower price is clearly going to be favored.

And that is exactly what is happening to bioengineering. Gene splicing has the potential of lowering energy costs tremendously. It can eliminate dozens of steps in the process of making all sorts of plastics and chemicals. The transferring of genes into bacteria and then cloning them is itself a low-energy procedure. It cuts down on the use of petroleum as a fuel and as a feedstock. And it can produce the same amount of alcohol or other bulk chemical as the old cracking method at a lower cost. If it couldn't, National Distillers wouldn't be building that new yeast-powered factory.

But the miracle of bioengineering reaches far beyond the chemical industry. The same genetic-engineering procedures applied to yeasts to make alcohol and other chemicals can be used to make insulin and cancer-fighting interferon or even self-fertilizing plants. In fact, by the end of the next decade, it will probably be possible to "order up" a farm animal and have one delivered within a year. It may even be possible to "order up" a plant that produces a combustible substance that can be burned for energy, rivaling petroleum!

•

PATENTING LIFE

In 1980, the Supreme Court ruled that man-made life forms can be patented. The landmark case opened up the entire field to commercial use. Within months, the gene-splicing process patent was granted, and the birth of a new bioengineering era was at hand. A year later, in June 1981, Genentech, one of the new companies created by university scientists to manufacture bioengineered substances, announced that it had produced the first vaccine using gene splicing. It was a vaccine against hoof-and-mouth disease, and it marked the beginning of the practical industry of bioengineering.

Over the past few years, dozens of small bioengineering

companies have sprung up around the United States to exploit the new technology. Genentech was one of the earliest, and it set the pattern. In 1975, just two years after Dr. Charles Boyer of the University of California at Berkeley and Dr. Stanley N. Cohen of Stanford discovered the technique for gene splicing, Boyer met with a venture capitalist to set up the new company, Genentech, to commercialize the budding new technology. From then on, many of the best molecular biologists and biochemists in America moved from the university laboratory to the business world. So many bioengineering companies have been established in California that the San Francisco Bay area, known everywhere as the "Silicon Valley," for its semiconductor firms, is now being called "Siliclone Valley" as well.

Wherever there are top universities with sophisticated biology departments, new companies are springing up. From Stanford, Berkeley and Caltech has come a rush of scientists to set up Cetus, Eugenics and other tiny biotech companies. On the East Coast, the Cambridge area of Boston, home to Route 128 and its myriad computer companies, is now a hotbed of new bioengineering activity. From Harvard and MIT have come Nobel Prize winners searching for the millions of dollars that private enterprise can promise. Some one hundred new companies have been formed to create new drugs, chemicals and foods.

•

NOBEL ENTREPRENEURS

The four leading companies in the bioengineering field are Genentech, Cetus, Biogen and Genex. All of them were set up in recent years by scientists in alliance with venture capitalists. They are in the vanguard of the international race for harnessing the new technology.

The big drug and chemical companies were very slow in understanding the potential of the new technology. But now they are catching on and are spending millions to get a piece of the new high-tech action. They are setting up huge laboratories, "buying" their own Nobel Prize winners to staff them. That will take time, however, and they are impatient to jump on the bandwagon. So the big companies are using their cash to buy bits and pieces of the baby biotech firms. National Distillers owns 11 percent of Cetus; Koppers Company owns 48 percent of Genex; Schering-Plough Corporation, the huge drug company, owns 16 percent of Biogen; Monsanto owns pieces of Genentech, Genex and Biogen.

The "biggies" are also setting up joint ventures with the new companies and are financing specific projects—all with an eye toward training their own scientists in the new techniques and getting an early lead in manufacturing the new products coming out of the lab. For example, Eli Lilly, the world's biggest maker of insulin, is currently building a $40-million plant in Britain to manufacture insulin from newly created bacteria "invented" by Genentech. In exchange for money that Genentech received from Eli Lilly, the bioengineering company granted it exclusive rights to its unique insulin-making bugs. Lilly, of course, is getting a better process for making its insulin, while it keeps its hold on the world insulin market. Its new insulin will go on sale in Britain shortly and will be available in the United States after testing.

•

A CANCER CURE?

The potential for bioengineering that has most captured the attention of the media is in medicine. The prospect of gene splicing providing big quantities of cheap antibiotics, hormones and new wonder drugs is generating visions of ending cancer and other deadly diseases before the decade is out. Right now Genentech is conducting human tests on three products: interferon, insulin and human-growth hormone. Interferon may be the key to combating cancer, as well as influenza, hepatitis, the common cold, and even herpes. Human-growth hormone can be used to fight dwarfism. And insulin, of course, is needed to curb diabetes.

But the Food and Drug Administration requires that new drugs be tested for six to eight years before they may be sold publicly. So, it may be years before biologically engineered medicines are made available to the public.

Before that, the bioengineering revolution will be felt in the chemical and agricultural industries where FDA approval is not needed. Yeast-manufactured ethanol will be on the market before the end of the year. Ethylene glycol, a major ingredient in antifreeze, will soon follow. Cetus will soon sell a new vaccine against scours, a disease that kills 10 percent of all newborn cattle in America every year. And Genentech will be offering its new hoof-and-mouth vaccine overseas by 1984.

But it is down on the farm that an enormous amount of action is now taking place. The same economics that is driving the chemical industry away from petroleum is affecting the agribusiness giants. Nearly all fertilizers, herbicides and insecticides are made from chemicals that, in turn, are made from petroleum. As oil prices skyrocketed during the 1970s, so did these prices. Indeed, the much heralded "Green Revolution" of the 1970s is turning out to be a disaster in Asia and Africa, because the new strains of rice and wheat are chemical-intensive and thus rely on enormous inputs of fertilizers to increase yields. With the soaring price of oil, the prices of those chemicals also shot up, devastating farmers.

Bioengineering promises to reverse that trend by creating new plants that can fix their own nitrogen and make their own fertilizer. In effect, it promises to free agriculture from its chemical chains—and the chains of the big oil and chemical companies.

In fact, so big is the potential that bioengineers are invading agriculture in big numbers. The potential market for agricultural genetics may be $100 billion by the year 2000, compared with $10 billion in medicine. Pfizer is investing millions to "biologically engineer" new strains of soybeans and corn that will be disease- and pest-resistant. Campbell's is looking for that perfect tomato, and Frito-Lay, the potato-chip maker, is trying to design the perfect potato.

•

THE JAPANESE SAKE EDGE

The U.S. lead in bioengineering is formidable. When Germany's Hoechst, the country's largest chemical and drug company, decided to get into gene splicing, it set up a $50-million deal with Harvard and Massachusetts General Hospital. The uproar in Germany was incredible. It was seen as a blot on the honor of the nation. But Hoechst officials insisted that America was in the forefront of the new technology and that's where they wanted to go.

Hoechst's move highlights a big push into biotechnology by the Europeans. France spent $160 million in 1982 alone on the new technology, and the amount will quadruple by 1985. Paris is aiming at 10 percent of the world market by the end of the decade. Rhône Poulenc, one of the country's biggest chemical companies, is working on hybrid cereals that will fertilize themselves. And France's Lafarge Coppée, one of the world's biggest cement makers, is diversifying into bioengineering by buying control of Belgium's Compagnie Coppée de Développement, whose subsidiaries specialize in amino acids. Lafarge is hoping to capitalize on the fermentation expertise of its new companies by mass-producing some of the new products developed by American pioneers.

Britain is doing advanced work of its own in a branch of bioengineering and has set up a company, Celltech, to commercialize the breakthroughs. But so far, there have been few hard results. A London investment group, set up exclusively to put money into new biotech companies, had to look overseas to find promising firms. Biotechnology Investments, put together by none other than N. M. Rothschild, has nearly $50 million in cash to invest. To date, it has put funds into four new U.S. companies. Nothing has gone into British biotech ventures.

Switzerland's Hoffmann–La Roche, the huge pharmaceutical company that gave us that wonder drug of the age of anxiety, Valium, is doing work on gene splicing and is even licensing some of it to the Japanese. And Denmark's Novo, which sells 60 percent of Europe's insulin, is specializing in enzyme production that is important for the commercial fermentation and growth of bacteria. In addition, Sweden's Fortia is selling products that bioengineers use in their work. But despite these efforts, Europe lags behind the United States by many years and will be hard-pressed to catch up soon.

The only real challenger to the American lead in biotechnology is Japan. With a single-minded ferocity, the Japanese have decided that gene splicing should be one of their "targeted" technologies of the future, and they are pursuing it with incredible intensity.

For Japan, bioengineering makes perfect sense. It cuts down on petroleum imports and promises to build an economy based on renewable resources. For an island nation that is virtually resourceless, except for its talented people, this is a wonderful dream. Moreover, many of the products of bioengineering have tremendous value added. A tiny amount costs a great deal—perfect for a country that prospers by trying to import raw materials and convert them into expensive finished goods.

The Japanese frenzy in biotechnology is a belated event. When the revolution hit in 1973 with the Boyer-Cohen gene-splicing technique, Japan completely missed it. The potential for vast changes in manufacturing and in creating new products went totally unnoticed. But after consultations within industry and government, Japan jumped on the bioengineering bandwagon in 1982 and has begun a race to catch up with the United States. The speed with which it is running is astonishing. America had about a five-year lead on Japan back in

1980. This has shrunk to about three years and is closing fast.

The Japanese do not come to the new biotechnology empty-handed. To be commercially viable, the newly created bugs must be grown in tremendous quantities in order to generate big quantities of ethanol, insulin, or whatever they are producing. Fermentation is the key to successful large-scale manufacturing using gene-splicing techniques. And the Japanese have always been leaders in this field.

For centuries, the Japanese have used fermentation to make beer and sake, and they have transferred their procedures to other areas as well. The country, for example, is the world's biggest producer of amino acids, the building blocks of proteins, as well as industrial enzymes, keys to the fermentation process. By combining the new technology of the modification of living organisms with their traditional lead in fermentation, the Japanese hope to repeat their earlier successes in electronics, semiconductors, autos and steel. By adapting a new technology originated abroad to their advanced manufacturing technology, the Japanese fully expect to dominate the market by the end of the decade.

Tokyo is putting together a two-pronged attack. The Ministry of International Trade and Industry, the infamous MITI, is launching a ten-year research program that will cost $110 million. Money will go to fourteen big Japanese companies to support research in three areas: gene-splicing procedures, growing cells in big commercial volumes, and designing new "biofurnaces," or "bioreactors," that will actually contain the fermentation.

This push is from the government. The private companies, for their part, are embarking on massive fact-finding missions to the United States. Just as thousands of Japanese swept through Silicon Valley in the 1960s and 1970s looking for semiconductor and computer technology, so now hundreds are scouring the laboratories of all the major American biotech companies as well as the universities. About two hundred Japanese companies are moving into bioengineering, and nearly all of them are sending people to the United States to gather information. In just one month in 1982, Cetus hosted one hundred Japanese trooping through its labs.

In their race to catch up with America, the Japanese are linking up with U.S. firms through an incredible maze of deals. Green Cross, one of the most active Japanese drug companies, has bought a piece of Collaborative Research Inc., of Boston, making it a partner with Dow Chemical in that company. Green Cross is also involved in joint research with Genex on human serum albumin, used in burn and shock cases, and the company is paying royalties to Stanford University on the Cohen-Boyer gene-splicing patent. A secret group of Japanese institutions bought $4.5 million of Genentech stock in 1982, just to be able to look over its scientists' shoulders. Toray Industries, the giant textile maker, is helping to fund Genentech's research on interferon—in exchange for exclusive rights in Japan. And Mitsubishi Chemical Industries is funding Genentech's research into human serum albumin and will get exclusive rights in Japan as well.

•

THE SPECTER OF FRANKENSTEIN

The bioengineering revolution has been thirty years in the making. Nearly its entire history, so far, has been American, giving the United States an important technological edge against foreign competition.

In 1953, James Watson and Francis Crick deciphered the double helix. They discovered the structure of the DNA molecule, the molecule that bears the genetic code that defines living organisms and makes them do what they do. In essence, they discovered the key to life. Their work showed how DNA carries genetic information on the rungs of its spiral staircase —or "double helix"—structure. Genes, simply, are portions of that staircase.

For the next twenty years, scientists proceeded to map out that double helix, identifying, on the DNA molecule, the genes that produce specific traits. It is the gene, for example, that produces interferon which holds the great promise of fighting cancer.

In 1973, a pair of scientists developed a technique for cutting off various genes from the larger DNA molecule and transferring them into another organism. Boyer at Berkeley and Cohen at Stanford engineered the microscopic procedures of creating new life forms. Another decade would pass before commercialization of that discovery would take place. In the meantime, the scientific community, as well as religious groups, was in an uproar. Man had finally played God, and his actions were threatening the foundation of modern culture.

The uproar in the scientific arena centered on the fact that the host bacteria used to grow the spliced genes was *E. coli*, a common bug found in all humans. The fear was that an altered and deadly *E. coli* would be created and would escape the laboratory to infect the population. In short, a man-made plague was feared. The word *biohazard* was suddenly on everyone's lips, and fears of epidemics swept the country. Newspaper headlines spoke of Frankenstein and of scientists building monstrous killers.

In 1974, the National Academy of Sciences, an honor society of some of the best American scientists, called for a voluntary moratorium on experiments that might produce new, drug-resistant strains of bacteria. This was the first time in modern history that scientists sought to ban scientific research. The National Academy also asked the National Institutes of Health to draw up research guidelines.

By 1976 those guidelines were in place. They called for the use of weakened *E. coli* in experiments—bacteria that couldn't live outside the lab—and they insisted on tight standards for physically closing off all labs doing bioengineering research from the outside. Throughout the country, high-containment laboratories, with double-sealed doors, negative air vents and special scrubbing areas, were built.

There was tremendous pressure on Congress to pass tight regulations on the entire field. Many people called for banning it entirely. In the end, as research continued without any accident, the furor began to fade away. Congress never did implement any legislation. Indeed, the NIH is now easing its earlier guidelines.

But, just as safety regulations are easing, bioengineering is moving into a second, commercial stage. Already there is intense competition among rival companies, and some scientists are beginning to wonder whether cost cutting and speed-ups might not one day lead to leaks of potentially harmful bugs. Moreover, while laboratory techniques have proved safe, commercial biofurnaces that produce vastly larger quantities of biologically altered organisms are new and untested.

As bioengineering companies increase in number and spread throughout the country, local communities are now taking the initiative from the federal government and are raising safety questions once thought to have been answered. A maze of contradictory regulations is being passed in the various towns around Boston, for example, and they are beginning to drive some companies out of the area toward the freer California air. Just as unemployment will come to haunt the new technology of robots and automation, so too will the issue of public safety soon come to be a part of the bioengineering revolution.

•

"C AND C"—COMPUTERS AND COMMUNICATIONS

There was a time when you would have to do the following to send an interoffice memo: get a piece of paper, put it into your typewriter, hammer a bunch of keys, take it out, stick it into an envelope and place it into the "out" basket in the hall. If your typing wasn't very good, you might give it to a secretary for polishing before putting it into interoffice mail. A messenger would pick it up and take it to the mailroom, where it was sorted and carried over to the people receiving the memo. Sending the memo took about a day and involved four or five people and a moderate amount of actual physical labor.

Today, if you work in a typical office that has put in a modern computer system, you do the following things to send a memo: sit down in front of your terminal and type the note —or "keyboard" it, as they now say—onto the TV-type screen in front of you. Put in the names of the people who are to receive it, and hit the "send" button. That's it. If you are a sloppy typist, like most of us, you can make corrections right on the terminal before hitting that button. Sending a memo takes virtually no time, for the message arrives almost instantaneously and involves no one other than yourself. The only labor that goes into it is the typing of the message.

The computer has transformed communication completely in this office. Indeed, it is hard to see where computing and communicating begin and end. The line separating the two is blurred; they merge to form a new form of communication—electronic information. Where once telephone, telegraph and broadcasting separately served to communicate voice, words and pictures, electronic information increasingly combines all three into a single, computerized flow.

Right now, personal computers are pouring into the homes of millions of Americans, providing tremendous new opportunities for writing, calculating or just playing games. But these same little Apples or Ataris can also serve as electronic mail systems if they are hooked up into a larger network. Already electronic bulletin boards are common and soon people will be able to write a letter to their relatives across the country, send it and receive a reply within minutes. Collaborators on books or research reports or even movie scripts in

Los Angeles and New York will be able to work together at the same time.

•

FROM TV TO ECB

Yet this is only the beginning. By the end of the decade, the personal computer and the TV set will blend into each other to create a new Electronic Communications Box (an ECB). This will turn the current TV, which is basically a passive entertainment vehicle, into an electronic terminal on which a viewer will be able to send commands. The TV will become interactive. People will be able to order it to do things, pay bills, put money in the bank, shop for groceries and see an "oldie but goldie" or perhaps a blue movie that isn't on any commercial network schedule. Not only will they be able to get stock-market and commodity quotes, they will be able to trade without going through a broker. Buying or selling gold will be done in the living room. And paying for your losses can take place through the same little computerized box.

The economic logic of the new technology is overwhelming. With the explosion in energy prices and the resulting inflation of the 1970s, it is now cheaper to use electronic communications than it is to physically send people or things through the streets or the air. Companies are already realizing great savings by going electronic. Citicorp, the holding company for Citibank, has a private communications network, as do IBM and Texas Instruments. They own everything from the telephones to the computers. TI estimates that it can send a message to any one of its terminals around the world for less than a nickel. And it can be sure the message gets to the right person. With postal rates up to 20 cents (not counting the labor and paper, which push the cost of most letters to well over a dollar), it makes a lot of economic sense to go electronic.

More than that, with air fares rising, a growing number of

business and professional people are taking the "C and C" rather than the commuter flight. With computers, a system that combines audio, visual and data communications inside a conference room can be set up at a fraction of the cost of sending people across long distances on an airplane. Linked by satellite, with a big screen or several small TV screens, electronic conference centers are springing up all over the country. Ma Bell is advertising them on TV these days. Look for a satellite dish at the Marriott or Holiday Inn the next time you stop for a break. It has a teleconferencing center. By the end of the decade, many of us will have one in our homes as part of our ECBs.

The technological drive to combine "C and C," computers and communications, is wreaking havoc in the closed, controlled world of the communications industry. After decades of being a semigovernment monopoly, protected against competition and market forces in exchange for good service, Ma Bell suddenly finds itself doing battle with the likes of powerful IBM. More than that, newspapers suddenly find their ad revenues vulnerable to electronic newspapers run by dear old "Ma," and the Big Three networks suddenly find themselves squeezed between cable TV and the upcoming direct satellite TV that will beam programs down to a small dish on your roof.

•

CHIPS INVADE MA BELL

When American Telephone and Telegraph Company found itself putting little semiconductor chips into its new Princess phones years ago, it realized that something very important was happening to its traditional business. When its mechanical switchboards were replaced by digital exchanges containing, again, lots of chips, it knew that computers would be a major part of its life from then on.

The government too came to understand this. In a 1980

decision, the Federal Communications Commission (FCC) ruled that AT&T could enter new electronic markets if it agreed to spin off its local subsidiaries and create a new separate subsidiary, a "Baby Bell." Ma Bell agreed, took its fabulous Bell Laboratories and its excellent Western Electric manufacturing arm plus its long-distance trunk lines and stepped forward as a stripped-down contender for the booming new "C and C" markets. Baby Bell was launched in mid-1982, and a whole new communications game was on.

This game will involve many players, but the biggest contender against Ma Bell is none other than IBM, the computer giant. IBM is moving from computing toward communicating at a time when AT&T is moving from communications toward computers. In fact, nothing better illustrates the new competitiveness of the corporate giants than the new headquarters both are building right across from each other in Manhattan. AT&T's headquarters is a massive, monumental structure that oozes power and authority from its size and shape. IBM's skyscraper is slim and functional. The Bell building is thirteen stories higher than IBM's, and it hopes to be looking down on its new rival in more ways than one.

For its part, IBM is moving swiftly to invade the territory of its new foe. It has linked up with a Canadian company to begin work on a new family of computerized telephone exchanges. Mitel, the Canadian firm, has been a successful competitor to AT&T's Western Electric division in producing advanced computerized phone exchanges and has, in fact, grabbed 15 percent of the U.S. market. IBM has even gone so far as to hire MCI Communications Corp., a rival of AT&T in long-distance phone service, to guide its computer salesmen in the new telephone-telecommunications business.

The greatest focus of competition between the two giants will not come in the business world at all but in the millions of homes around America. Both are staking out huge chunks of the exploding home electronic information revolution. The year 1990 will see the marriage of the personal computer and the TV, but no one is waiting for that advanced technology to be perfected. So pressing is the drive toward computerized communication that companies are lining up to stick gadgets on regular television sets now to transform them into new machines. The "wired city" is about to be constructed, with homes across the nation plugged into a single, massive communications grid that offers shopping, entertainment, banking and working services. Either with cable or with a small dish on the roof, houses in America are being plugged into the new electronic information era at an accelerating rate. By the end of the decade, nearly eight million homes will be linked into computerized information services—7 percent of the country's total. By 2000, half will be "wired up."

•

ELECTRONIC PIRATES

While most of the attention in the press has been on the spreading "cable-ization" of the United States, it may very well be that in the end satellite broadcasting will capture the imagination of the nation. Right now, Comsat and other companies are petitioning Washington for permission to send up satellites that would beam programs and information directly into our homes via a small saucer-shaped dish receiver placed on the roof. At only $100 apiece, these antennae would be able to pick up tremendous amounts of electronic communications, from movies to crossword puzzles to lessons in Spanish, without having to go through the expense of laying down cable or even using the phone system.

Already there are individual airwave "pirates" at work, with big antennas pointed at the sky to intercept TV programs from all around the world. Home Box Office, Cable News Network, the *Wall Street Journal* and the Mormon Church all use satellites for their transmissions. A pirate with his own dish can grab from the sky sports, news, movies, opera and pornography. He might also pick up a confidential teleconference involving corporate big shots planning an unfriendly takeover of another company.

Videotex, the common name given to the system of providing texts of information to people over their TVs, also promises to be a multibillion-dollar industry. Retailers, including Sears, Roebuck and Company and J. C. Penney, are testing out electronic catalogues, hoping to return America to the days of ordering everything from clothes to canoes from catalogues. With two-way communication through the "smart" TV, people can simply punch in their orders and their bank account numbers (or their money-market-fund numbers) and have the goods paid for in seconds. Not only would that be convenient for the people who wouldn't have to drive to the store, but the big retailers wouldn't have to go to the expense of building the shops in the first place!

The banks are especially anxious to push videotex, because it would save them tons of paperwork and lots of labor costs. Citicorp has already tested out its Home-base electronic banking service with a hundred customers in an attempt to take the bugs out of its new system. And Chemical Bank is doing the same.

Newspaper and magazine publishers are rushing into the new technology also. Times Mirror Company has set up its own Times Mirror Videotex Services division. CBS has an electronic news magazine being tested in Los Angeles. And Dow Jones, publisher of the *Wall Street Journal* and *Barron's*, expects to open up big new countrywide markets for its business news and analysis. And while book publishers have been very slow in understanding what the new technology might mean for them, what is to prevent them from offering best sellers over TV at a fraction of the cost for hard covers? With videotex, a person can simply order up a specific title at home and read it at his leisure. If he has a printer next to the TV, he could print the whole thing out, or do it chapter by chapter, paying only for what he is viewing at the moment. The potential is tremendous.

Of course, the movie moguls on the West Coast are hoping that the new electronic information systems will open up new opportunities for their products. Cable TV has already whet the appetite of people for selected movies, from classics to "blues," and this could be expanded tremendously to include all kinds of games, educational programs and the arts.

But for all its exciting potential, the possible shift in retailing trends is scaring the hell out of many people. If companies begin offering their goods and services over videotex, they will probably start cutting down on their advertising in newspapers. In addition, AT&T, which has always published the Yellow Pages, is planning to offer electronic Yellow Pages over TV. Because electronics allow the Yellow Pages to be updated continuously, it can make it a convenient place to show the latest movies, sales and perhaps even breaking news stories. This would hit the newspapers extremely hard. So far, the newspapers, through their friends in Washington, have successfully stopped Ma Bell from doing this.

Indeed, newspapers as we know them are certain to be much changed by 1990. With stock and commodity prices available instantaneously over the tube, they may disappear from newspapers. Any immediate, breaking news is more likely to appear on TV hours before it comes out in print. So, the content of newspapers may have to change. More magazinelike, in-depth analysis will be offered to the reader to provide a comprehensive understanding of events. Features will be expanded. Longer stories will appear. And the graphics, the charts, the photos, will probably get much better.

Home videotex or electronic information is not the only change to come about from the merger of "C and C." In mid-1982, Washington received applications from dozens of companies trying to crack the new mobile telephone business. It is called "cellular" radio and takes its name from the fact that it works by dividing up a city or town into "cells," small areas each served by a special low-powered radio transmitter. With a computer switching calls from one cell to another at incredible speeds, it is possible to use mobile phones in cars without any interruption in the conversation. The same technology allows people to walk around with phones and use them whenever they choose to. The only thing needed is a miniaturizing of the bulky telephone itself—a likely event in the years to come. In fact, the growing popularity of the old "beeper" or pager by nondoctors probably will result in a hybrid beeper-telephone gadget by 1985.

•

YOUR PENNIES ARE WORTHLESS NOW

The new "C and C" electronic communications are based on three separate technologies: advanced computers, semiconductor chips and optic fibers. Whereas computers and chips made the information revolution possible, optic fibers are giving it the potential to expand exponentially. In fact, nowhere is the coming-together of computers and communications so evident as in the growth of optic fibers.

Optic fibers are glass cables through which information is transmitted on pulses of laser light. Traditionally, copper cables have carried nearly all telephone information via electric current. But the amount of information generated and transmitted every year has so exploded that copper cables can no longer handle the load. There isn't any room left under the streets of our cities for more heavy copper wiring. In fact, even twenty years ago, AT&T had to turn to microwave systems to relieve its underground copper network of some of the burden. This too has reached its limits.

Glass fibers and light-wave networks will eventually replace all copper wiring. The beauty of optics is that one cable, the diameter of a thumb, composed of 144 tiny, hairlike glass filaments, can carry 50,000 two-way phone calls simultaneously. It would take five copper cables, the diameter of your arm, to do the same thing.

And this is just the beginning. By using lasers instead of

electricity to carry information, optics can create digital replications of the human voice and be used directly with computers. It may soon be possible to simply command your computer to do something without typing in instructions. Remember "Hal," the computer in the movie *2001*?

Optic fibers are so much more efficient than copper cables that everyone who has hoarded pennies all these years, thinking that the price of copper would soar one day, is going to be very disappointed. Optic fibers are going to replace copper within computers and communication equipment, and they are going to replace it under the streets of America. They will carry the data, voice and visual communications of the new electronic information systems going into people's homes and offices. They are also going into all the new weapons systems for which electronics are critical and weight is crucial.

AT&T is already laying a major optic-fiber cable system down the busy Northeast Corridor between Cambridge, Massachusetts, and Moseley, Virginia. A forty-mile link already connects Pittsburgh and Greenburg, Pennsylvania, and another twenty-eight miles in New Jersey will be finished by the end of 1983. By the middle of the decade, an optic-fiber cable will be laid across the Atlantic connecting the United States and Europe. After that, another will be laid in the Pacific to link California and Hawaii.

•

THE FOREIGN ASSAULT

Moving the flood of data along the new electronic-information lines is becoming big business in foreign countries as well as in the United States. In fact, an international competition is opening up, with Europeans and Japanese invading the American market while U.S. companies go overseas.

In optic-fiber technology alone, the United States is beginning to meet intense challenges. While Corning Glass holds nearly all the important early patents in optic fibers, companies everywhere are beginning to jump on the bandwagon. Germany's Siemens, Holland's Philips, and Japan's Fujitsu and NEC are all manufacturing optic-fiber cable.

Once again, Japan in particular is making great strides in new technology. The Nippon Telegraph and Telephone Company, the nation's public-communications monopoly, has been promoting optic fibers for years. NTT uses its $3 billion in annual purchases to promote particular products, and glass cable has been one of its favorites. Japan has a big optic-fibers test going on in the suburbs of Osaka. And technologically, the Japanese are on a par with the United States in the production of the glass fibers.

Japan has been trying to crack the U.S. market for years. In 1982, Fujitsu put in the lowest bid on a contract to supply optic-fiber cable for the last stretch in AT&T's 776-mile Northeast Corridor project. Despite that, however, Fujitsu was turned down by AT&T under heavy pressure from Washington. The argument was national security. The underground communication system is considered part of the national defense, and for that reason several congressmen said that the United States shouldn't become dependent on foreign sources. AT&T turned to its own Western Electric division for the fiber cable. MCI, AT&T's longtime rival, however, disagreed with the choice and proceeded to sign its own contract with Fujitsu for fiber cable. The Japanese had their beachhead, and now the battle is joined.

But optic fibers is just one of the many areas of international competition now swirling around the new electronic information technology. The Japanese, of course, are major competitors for the two other building blocks of the new information system, computers and chips. Yet more than that, Japanese companies are leaders in manufacturing satellite ground stations. NEC in particular has a strong position, having built about 50 percent of all satellite receivers in recent years. In addition, it is a major exporter of computerized telephone exchanges and will compete with both AT&T and IBM.

But it may be in the home electronic-information market that the greatest foreign penetration is taking place. No U.S. company has yet turned out any original technology on videotex. All of it comes from abroad. As the United States moves toward electronic information, American companies are linking up with the foreigners.

IBM is tying up with Britain's Prestel, one of the oldest videotex systems that allows people to call up reams of information on their TV terminals. It has about 190,000 subscribers in Britain.

The French have their own Antiope technology and have ambitious plans to equip 30 million houses by 1992 with cheap terminals that will, in effect, be electronic phone books or "hot" Yellow Pages. Nearly two hundred French companies and government offices have signed up to offer information and services on Antiope, including banks, retail houses and newspapers.

The other major contenders are the Canadians with their Telidon system. In the end, the Canadians may win the videotex market in the United States, for AT&T has announced that it will use Telidon for its own electronic Yellow Pages directory if it gets off the ground, because it is more "user-friendly" than Prestel and has better graphics. With the giant AT&T behind it, Telidon has a good chance of dominating the American market.

CBS and other broadcasters, however, prefer the French Antiope. CBS is using it in a Los Angeles test, while Dow Jones is trying it out in Danbury, Connecticut.

The joining of computers and communications, "C and C," will dramatically change our lives. By the end of the decade, teleconferencing and the ECB will transform how we work and how we play in ways that we can only guess at right now.

But there is a dark side to the new technology as well. In a recent court case, a judge subpoenaed the records of a TV cable company to rule on a case. Suddenly everyone in town who was secretly watching "blue" movies late at night was on a list that could be publicly exposed at any time during a trial.

Now imagine an Electronic Communications Box through which you do your banking, your mail, your buying of booze, your flight arrangements, your hotel bookings, your sending of flowers as well as viewing entertainment. All of these extremely private transactions will now be on a single electronic system, centralized and very accessible. The IRS might want a peek, corporate peddlers of all kinds would like a look, your own boss might like to know what you did outside the office, and your spouse might be curious as well. The new telecommunications technology will pose major new social questions about privacy and security. At the very least, laws will have to be changed. And perhaps some very personal customs.

2

THE TWILIGHT OF OPEC

THE YEAR 1973 HAS A SPECIAL PLACE IN AMERICAN HISTORY. IT saw the U.S. Army retreat from Vietnam, the dollar tear loose from the gold standard, and a little-known Third World clique called the Organization of Petroleum Exporting Countries—OPEC—quadruple the price of oil, sending America and the rest of the world plummeting into recession. After each OPEC price hike, America found its currency further debased, its economy further decayed, its exports more uncompetitive overseas, and its international prestige further eroded.

At the same time, each OPEC price jump sent tens of billions of dollars into the coffers of Arab treasuries. History's greatest wealth tax—the two oil-price rises of 1973–1974 and 1979–1980—drew enormous amounts of capital out of the industrial West, and the booty provided the financial foundation for the renaissance of the Arab world. Thirteen hundred years after the Arabs thrust out of the desert to dominate the Mediterranean, capture Spain and threaten the heartland of Europe itself, Islam was once again poised to burst forth.

The last time Moslem culture broke out of its desert homeland, it dominated the Mediterranean for centuries. Not until the Christian armies of Ferdinand and Isabella defeated the Arabs at Granada in 1492 to push them finally from the European continent did the Islamic thrust recede.

This time, however, the Arab surge did not last hundreds of years. In fact, it lasted less than a decade. By 1982, it was all over. By then it became clear that the Arab renaissance was in fact a quixotic movement, an unsustained spurt supported by an oil bubble that burst in a few short years. In 1982, Kuwait ran its first budget deficit since the 1973 oil embargo; for the first time in twenty years, OPEC lost its rank as the largest producer of oil in the world; the annual OPEC surplus, which had reached $110 billion the year before, disappeared—in fact, OPEC nations borrowed more money from the international banks than they deposited. For oil-producing non-OPEC countries, 1982 was an even worse year. Mexico went virtually bankrupt and had to reschedule $81 billion it owed to such solid institutions as Bank of America, Citibank and Chase, who were unfortunate enough to hold its IOUs. The peso was devalued twice, the banks were nationalized and capital flight became epidemic.

The future was suddenly very clear. The Latins saw it first, before the Arabs, perhaps because the tragic history of Spain is so vivid in their memories. Months before Mexico plunged into economic chaos, a newspaper in Mexico City ran a commentary: "I dreamt that in Mexico it happened as it did to the Spanish empire after the gold. One day it was the same old Spain, the same as before the gold."

•

OPEC TRIGGERS THE HIGH-TECH REVOLUTION

There is no mystery behind OPEC's decline. It is a very simple story of greed. In 1971, the price of oil was $2.10 per barrel. By 1981, after two major price hikes following the Arab-Israeli war in 1973 and the fall of the Shah in 1979, it cost $34 a barrel. That price was simply too high to sustain the world economy as it then existed.

A great deal has been written about how the rise of OPEC transformed the balance of power in the world during the 1970s. The Middle East, always an area of intense Great Power rivalry, came center stage once again, with oil the great prize. The Palestinian question, the existence of Israel, became intertwined with the politics of oil. Washington tilted first toward Iran, then toward Saudi Arabia, in search of some influence in that critical region.

But nothing has been said of a much larger event, an event that will affect the lives of our children and grandchildren in ways not yet imaginable. By raising the price of energy so sharply and so quickly, OPEC transformed the entire base of the world economy. By increasing the price of oil fifteenfold in less than a decade, after nearly a century of stable, cheap energy, OPEC changed the technological foundations of Western society and set in motion vast social and political changes that are only now coming into focus.

Clearly, the world would have gradually moved on in its technological evolution even if OPEC had not existed. But change would have taken decades to occur. By accelerating the pace of energy-cost increases and by raising those costs so sharply, OPEC speeded up the entire process of transformation to a blinding rate. Decades of major economic and social changes are now being compressed into months. The gradual rise and fall of nations, the normal flow of relations within the world, the process of change itself is becoming superheated. All this was an accident, an unintended event. History is full of ironies, of course, and surely this must be one of its choicest. By raising oil prices so quickly and so sharply, OPEC set off the technological and economic changes that buried it —with equal dispatch.

35 MILLION UNEMPLOYED

The Arabs didn't know it at the time but beyond $10 or $15 a barrel, oil turns out to be too expensive to support a heavy-industry economy built on traditional nineteenth-century technologies. Once oil prices started skyrocketing, it took about seven years to begin transforming the world's economic base.

The first reaction to the OPEC price hikes was near-depression. Massive recessions threatened economic and political upheaval. By the end of 1982, after the second massive price runup, over 35 million people were unemployed in the United States and Europe, or nearly 11 percent of the working population. In some places it was much worse. Britain, Belgium and Denmark had one out of eight working people on the dole. Not since the 1930s had so much economic pain been inflicted. Growth practically disappeared. The auto, steel and textile industries came to a screeching halt. The exports of Third World countries in Asia, Latin America and Africa languished on the docks as demand dried up in the West for their goods. Global trade dropped from an annual 10 percent growth rate in the 1960s to a paltry 5 percent by the late 1970s. In 1981, international trade actually declined for the first time in decades and remained near zero for 1982.

With companies shutting their doors, the need for energy shrank, and oil imports declined sharply. But even before that, oil imports started falling because of a major push toward conservation. Per capita energy use in America fell by 20 percent between 1978 and 1981. It dropped another 10 percent in 1982. The impact of the OPEC oil-price hikes on America has been astounding. U.S. oil imports are down sharply since their peak of 1977. At that time, the United States depended on OPEC for a huge 70 percent of its imported oil. By 1982, this was down to less than 40 percent. Nothing illustrates this better than the dramatic change in the oil-to-GNP ratio, the measure of the amount of energy needed to produce economic growth (Gross National Product). In the 1960s, there was a clear 1-to-1 link between energy and growth. You needed a 1 percent rise in oil consumption to fuel a 1 percent increase in economic growth. Today, however, with the switch away from heavy industry and with conservation, it takes only a 0.4 percent jump in oil consumption to provide a 1 percent rise in economic growth. Half as much energy is now needed to support business expansion and new jobs. And that ratio is still declining! It has only just begun.

•

HIGH-TECH SIPPERS

The moment oil imports began declining in the United States, Europe and Japan, politicians started congratulating themselves on the unexpected and dramatic way the West, especially profligate America, cut back so quickly. Who would have thought that Americans, "kings of the road," builders of hermetically sealed glass-box skyscrapers, inventors of the air-conditioned car, would turn to conservation in such a big way?

Actually, they didn't. Of course people took to turning down their thermostats, wearing sweaters and driving less in smaller cars. That helped a lot. But, beyond that conservation, a much more important change was occurring in the economy. What really happened, first in Japan and then in the United States, was far more significant and long-lasting. What happened is the untold story of what OPEC really did to the world by raising oil prices so drastically. The switch from cheap to expensive energy triggered off a revolution that is only now beginning, a revolution that is taking the world to a new technological plateau, a new economic base and, inevitably, a new balance of power among the nations of the world.

The most important change in demand for imported oil is coming from the shrinking of those heavy industries that depended on it for so long. Not only is the West learning to use less oil in making steel, but it has begun to use a lot less steel. The number of autos made each year has fallen tremendously over the past six years, and those cars that are coming off the assembly lines are tiny compared to the gas-guzzling behemoths of the 1950s and 1960s. In 1970, 37 percent of all new-car sales in the United States were big "standard" autos. Subcompact autos took just 2 percent of the market. By 1982, "standard" cars had shrunk to 10 percent of all new sales, while subcompact autos took a fat 17 percent of the market. In addition, imports grew from 15 percent to 27 percent during that decade, and most of those were small cars. The very nature of the automobile has changed, and with it all the steel, aluminum, rubber and plastic that go into it.

The high price of oil decimated the automobile, chemical, heavy-machinery and textile industries. And as they decline, so do their enormous demands for energy. Built on cheap oil, they prospered for nearly a century on it. When oil became expensive, they began to die.

The new industries of the twenty-first century—computers, biotechnology, electronics—use a fraction of the energy that the old industries consumed. Automated factories with robot-run assembly lines need only a small percentage of the energy to operate compared to the old, people-run Detroit plants. As the world moves into the new industries of the future, the demand for energy and for imported oil will continue to fall. It is a massive, long-term trend that will reverse itself only if oil returns to something approaching $10 a barrel. More likely, it will sell for $25 to $35 a barrel. And prices might spurt higher in the years ahead, if only briefly. But higher oil prices would only accelerate the basic switch to energy-sipping high-technology industries that, in turn, will reduce consumption even further. OPEC cannot win.

•

WASHINGTON'S OBSOLETE FOREIGN POLICY

Just as Washington and the media have turned a blind eye to OPEC's unintended role in triggering off an historic technological revolution, so too are they neglecting the foreign-policy implications of OPEC's actions. Every passing year cuts America's and the West's dependence on the Middle East. Every passing year moves the region out of center stage for U.S. decision-making. Washington doesn't realize this yet. It is still trying to buy off the Saudis with AWAC planes and arms. But the switch from heavy industry to high technology is changing the balance of power in the world, and one of the biggest losers is OPEC.

How this is occurring is a story of many parts. The fundamental cause is the transformation of the industrial base of the world. But there are other factors working as well. Just when demand for OPEC oil is falling, the supply of oil from non-OPEC sources is soaring. It takes only about 50 cents to get a barrel of oil out of the vast underground reservoir of the Arabian desert. It takes about $10 to do the same thing in the raging waters of the North Sea or the frigid ocean off Alaska's North Slope. Once the price of oil passed this $10 level it made offshore oil production in high-risk areas profitable. New supplies suddenly appeared not only from the North Sea and Alaska, but from Mexico, West Africa and even Australia.

Just as important, once Washington started decontrolling prices for domestic oil and gas, the resulting high prices sent drillers to the hills. In 1981, nearly 80,000 wells were drilled, an all-time high. And while it didn't produce a huge amount of new energy, it did stem the decline of U.S. oil reserves and slow down imports.

With demand for its own oil falling while supplies of non-OPEC oil are rising, OPEC is quickly losing control of its one asset—the price of the world's energy. In 1982, while the official price was set at $34 a barrel, the market began pushing it lower and lower. By March, the price of the same barrel of oil sold by Saudi Arabia for $34 was going for $26 in the "spot" market in Amsterdam. The worst price hawks of bygone years, Libya, Iran and Mexico, started breaking all the rules by offering tremendous discounts to consuming nations. Cut-rate oil began flooding the markets. In an effort to shore up the price, OPEC cut back production. Desperate measures were taken, and by the time it was all over, the spot price had edged back up to $32 a barrel. The price paid was high, but in the end, OPEC was no longer the largest producer of oil in the world. In fact, OPEC had to cut its production to levels not seen since 1969, to stop the price from falling to $25. By May 1982, OPEC was producing at a rate of 20.3 million barrels a day, while non-OPEC sources were pouring 21.6 million barrels a day into the market. The sharpest drops were in Venezuela and Kuwait, which saw virtually half their production chopped. Saudi Arabia, the largest producer, took the biggest cut, from 10.5 million barrels a day to 6 million. The glut was ruinous. In order to temporarily support the price, OPEC had to sacrifice its dominance in world oil production. By the beginning of 1983, oil prices were falling once again as countries ranging from Libya to the Soviet Union offered quiet discounts that dropped the cost to $28 to $30 per barrel.

No one really knows just where the price of oil will go from here. But the odds are that it will not go up. Wars and revolutions might push the spot price over $34 in the years ahead, perhaps to the $40- or even $50-a-barrel range, but the upward surge will be temporary and short. An expansion in global economic growth will increase demand for oil somewhat, but that too will not send prices higher in any permanent way. For the economies of Japan and the United States are shaking down into high-tech sippers of expensive energy, and that will continue to cut demand for imported petroleum for decades to come. Higher oil prices will lead only to faster changes away from heavy industry toward high tech—and less energy consumption.

And while that is taking place, there is another big surprise in store for consuming nations. The huge increase in new oil supplies from non-OPEC sources that is flooding the market today, was attracted out of the ground by the price hike of 1973—the very first OPEC shock! The second OPEC oil shock has yet to hit. In a year's time, the second price hike of 1979 will be bringing oil out of the ground from an entirely new set of countries. China in particular is now considered one of the great petroleum plays of the decade. The entire South China Sea may contain as much oil as the Arabian desert. New strikes off Yucatán show that Mexico may also have as much oil in reserves as Saudi Arabia—and plenty of economic and political reasons to want to export as much as possible. In addition, there are the waters of Southeast Asia near Thailand, Malaysia and Burma. Geologists only know there is plenty of oil there. They don't know how much. The Falkland Islands, so bitterly fought over by the British and the Argentines, may also contain a huge basin of petroleum. The fields off West Africa near Angola and Gabon hold huge quantities of oil, as do the frigid Arctic and Antarctic regions around the poles. And finally, there is the vast new discovery off the coast of California that may rival the North Slope.

The decline in the demand for imported petroleum will also be aided as industry switches from costly oil to cheaper coal. Once oil passed the $13-a-barrel mark in 1979, it became too expensive for fueling boilers or running ships that burn the gooey, low-grade petroleum. Together, these two items make up one half the world's oil consumption. This change in itself is triggering off a mammoth change in energy usage as furnaces are refurbished to take coal rather than oil. In Japan the entire cement industry has already switched from oil to coal. In America, the switch to coal and domestic gas now saves nearly 800,000 barrels of oil a day. And in France, which has never had much of an allergy to nuclear energy, nearly 70 percent of its electricity needs will soon be generated by atomic power plants.

•

OPEC POVERTY

Something else is happening that will bring enormous amounts of new oil to market, further undermining OPEC's central position in world politics. Nothing terrified Mexico or Nigeria or Libya more in early 1982 than the sudden drop in oil prices. When these countries tried to maintain the higher $34 official price level, the big oil companies and the dozens of independent oil buyers simply walked away. Britain offered petroleum of exactly the same high quality as Nigeria for eight dollars a barrel less. And so did many others. With customers leaving, production fell and revenues dried up.

The cash squeeze came at a terrible time for nearly all the oil-producing countries. In the 1970s, with the promise of never-ending riches from petroleum exports, they began embarking on gargantuan development projects costing hundreds of billions of dollars. The politicians of Mexico, Venezuela, Indonesia, Algeria, Libya—the most populous oil-producing nations—promised their people that they would industrialize, create jobs and end poverty within years, not decades. The poor and the middle class watched the sheiks, the bureaucrats and the elite squander their petrodollar patrimony on Rolls-Royces, private jets, mansions, diamonds, gold, trips abroad.

They watched in patience only because they were promised that soon they too would share in the unbelievable wealth. It became politically necessary for the leaders of the oil-producing nations to order up the industrial infrastructure of a modern country. And they did—on the assumption that oil prices would continue to rise for the rest of the decade, if not for the rest of the century. They knew nothing about technological change, conservation, non-OPEC oil or alternative fuels. So they bought and bought. From Europe, Japan and the United States came factories, airports, dams, cars, airplanes. Rice, wheat and other staples were imported in vast quantities and sold at low, subsidized prices to the restive and growing urban populations. Entire cities were built in the Saudi desert. Mammoth petroleum complexes arose from the dunes. The oil producers grew at fantastic rates—three, four, five times as fast as the West. Just as the industrial countries were once totally dependent on OPEC for energy, so OPEC and its fellow travelers soon became totally hooked on the West for industrial imports. They couldn't stop buying. It would have been political suicide.

But then came the bills. The incredible bills running into the hundreds of billions every year. For a while, there was enough money coming in to pay for the flood of imports. Then, the bottom dropped out in late 1981 and early 1982 as prices began to soften. Just when some of the biggest bills were presented for some of the largest steel mills and petrochemical plants ever built, revenues began to plummet. Politicians were suddenly rattled to their bones in places as far away as Algiers and as near as Mexico City. Saudi Arabia was forced to offer a cool $1 billion to keep Nigeria afloat and prevent it from cutting prices to sell more oil. Libya stopped paying its bills to the Italians, bills which came to over $1 billion. Venezuela had such a shortfall of revenue that it had to curtail its huge development plans. At the same time, the political futures of President Herrera Campins and Oil Minister Humberto Calderon Berti were thrown into doubt.

Mexico was the worst hit in this crisis. With a big and fast-growing population, it has vast development plans, and the entire program has stopped dead. Falling oil prices forced Mexico to devalue its peso not once but twice in the space of six months. The second time, pandemonium broke out. A massive flight of capital started as the middle class and the rich rushed to put their cash into dollars and get it out of the country as soon as possible. Billions crossed the border before the government declared a dollar moratorium and froze $12 billion in local accounts. By that time the peso was trading at over 100 to the dollar compared to 25 just a year before.

Where once the currency was worth about 4 cents, now it is less than a penny.

The Mexicans had to go hat in hand to Washington and the international banks for help. The United States advanced the desperate Mexicans $2 billion to cover imports of petroleum for the Strategic Reserve and for grain imports. But the Mexicans were also forced to go to the International Monetary Fund for loans, and to institute an austerity program that can only mean more unemployment, higher prices and a further cut in middle-class living standards in the years ahead. And yet there is only one solution—export even more oil to the United States, even if prices continue to fall.

Mexico is not the only oil producer in this bind. This demand for billions in cash to pay for costly development plans will remain a constant pressure for higher oil production in the decade ahead. Nation after nation is bent on importing the industrial accouterments of "modern" civilization, as well as buying off a politically restive population. Britain is counting on North Sea oil to pay for the rebuilding of its ancient and shattered industrial base. It will also need at least $5 billion to replace the damaged fleet after the Falklands fighting. Iran and Iraq will need oil revenue to build their economies after a disastrous war. Nigeria and Indonesia are both desperate for greater revenues to feed their booming populations. Algeria has only about ten years' worth of oil and gas left and is racing to build up an industrial base before it disappears.

•

SHEIK YAMANI'S POLITICAL NIGHTMARE

Sheik Ahmed Zaki Yamani, Saudi Arabian Oil Minister and the most powerful individual in OPEC, knows that his cartel is fading in political importance in the powerful capitals of the world. He was not happy about the sharp runup in oil prices that followed the fall of the Shah, and during the months afterward he made sure that his country produced flat out to prevent them from moving any higher. Had it not been for Yamani and Saudi Arabia, the official price would almost certainly have gone to $40 a barrel. It had shot up to $41 a barrel on the spot market by mid-1980 and was heading even higher before the Saudis opened their taps, producing 11 million barrels a day instead of their regular 8 to 9 million. This immense supply on the markets drove the price back down to the $34, but even this worried Yamani.

Yamani lives with the fear that OPEC has already priced itself out of existence. At $34 a barrel, he believes, it makes economic sense for the industrial countries to switch to coal, gas and nuclear power. He knows that this change will soon make Saudi Arabia and the Middle East much less important to the United States, Europe and Japan—and that will make the House of Saud, his benefactors, that much more insecure and unstable. In early May 1981, Yamani warned that "the West is cutting its dependence on OPEC, and this definitely threatens the security of the region."

Yamani is not a man given to hysterics. When traveling abroad, he takes his own squad of British former SAS bodyguards, the secretive professional soldiers that were used so well in the Falklands. When he enters a room for a news conference, these guards clear a path for him. If he is in traditional dress, Yamani sweeps in, sits down and then consciously takes a few moments to fix his robes. Once he is comfortable, Yamani invariably looks up with some surprise at the assembled mob of TV cameras and print journalists as if to say, "What, all this for me?" Despite the chaos of screaming and shouting that is commonplace at these press conferences, Yamani handles questions with a quiet, calm dignity. He never raises his voice. Like a lot of powerful men, he speaks very softly, forcing everyone else to quiet down. When he is clearly emphasizing a point he will use the word "definitely." He will say "We will definitely increase production," or "Oil prices are definitely going up." In the anteroom to his office in the Petromin Building in Riyadh, a continuous stream of male flunkies flows through the people waiting for an audience with him. Nonalcoholic liquids are constantly being offered to the oil executives nervously sitting there. According to Americans who have gone through the experience, the powerful oil types constantly eye each other to figure out who the other guys are, what they may be doing there, and how they might manipulate one another.

Of course, Yamani is absolutely right in worrying about the West's declining dependence on Middle Eastern oil. Without oil, Washington couldn't care less about most of the Arabian Peninsula. Without oil, the PLO would lose its financing, its clout and its power. Indeed, the Arabs' silence greeting the Israeli invasion of Lebanon in 1982 was a measure of their decline in power. No mention was made of an oil embargo. Nothing was said about pulling billions out of Western banks. Nothing but deadly silence.

•

THE SAMSON SYNDROME

Few in the West will regret the retreat of OPEC as a world power. At one time, at its zenith in 1980, it threatened to dominate not only the world's energy supply, but its financial system as well. Amassing hundreds of billions of surplus petrodollars—cash left over even after spending fortunes on development and weapons—the OPEC nations were on the verge of taking over the international supply of capital as well as oil. By the end of the 1970s, new Arab banks began to lead the likes of Citibank and Chase in the United States, as well as the powerful Deutsche Bank and Dresdner Bank of Germany. Without the Arab banks and their control of the world's petrodollars, it was nearly impossible to do business, to keep the financial flows moving, to keep trade moving.

But that is now history. OPEC's share of the oil market is falling and its petrodollar surplus is simply gone. With that, the political importance of the Middle East will begin to fade and once Washington wakes up to these changes, it will stop being a central focus of American foreign policy. The world is moving into a post-OPEC era of high technology that operates on much less energy. The faster it moves toward this twenty-first-century society, the faster OPEC will drift off the front pages of *The New York Times* and sink into the pages of history.

As a legacy, OPEC is leaving behind a technological revolution that is just beginning to alter the balance of power around the world. Some nations are rising to the new challenges while others are mired in the ways of the past. Some countries are gaining new power, while others are losing it. Samsonlike, the Arabs are pulling down the international political system built after World War II. We are now in the process of creating a new one.

3

THE DECLINE OF GERMANY AND THE BREAKUP OF EUROPE

•

OF ALL THE NATIONS IN THE WORLD THAT MIGHT BE EXPECTED to move easily into the high-tech era, Germany is certainly one of the first to come to mind. In so many ways, the words *German* and *technology* are interchangeable not only in America but in Hamburg, Munich and Bonn as well. Where else is the well-made machine so worshiped? Where else is the *Meister*, the skilled craftsman, so heroic? Where else is precision engineering perceived as a high art form?

There are two stars in the German movie *Das Boot* ("The Boat"), released in the United States in 1982—the commander and the submarine itself. One of the most popular movies in Germany that year, it highlighted the German belief that superior men using superior technology can defeat any enemy, achieve any goal.

The movie had a second theme as well. It openly celebrated German nationalism. It was, at the same time, anti-Nazi and pro-German. For decades after the war, German nationalism was in the "closet," an unmentionable emotion that people on both sides of the Atlantic preferred to ignore. Indeed, most

Germans refrained from mentioning it. But nationalism is a growing theme in Germany today, and once again it is intertwined with the idea of technology. This time, however, it is a declining technology that is triggering off a surge of nationalism in the country.

•

THE KISSINGER CONNECTION

The current wave of nationalism now sweeping Germany has its roots in the early 1970s, in the policies of détente that Henry Kissinger championed. Indeed, it may well be one of history's greatest ironies that it was Henry Kissinger who opened a Teutonic Pandora's box that may eventually unhook West Germany from its late-twentieth-century Western moorings. For, as a scholar, the German refugee was a student of Klemens Metternich and his attempts to unite war-torn, mid-nineteenth-century Europe by creating a delicate balance of power. Yet it was under Kissinger, the international political practitioner, that the delicate postwar balance of power of the Atlantic Alliance began to unravel. For Kissinger's détente became Willy Brandt's *Ostpolitik*—his opening to the East. And while Washington quickly scuttled détente as a foreign policy, Germany's infatuation with the East grew. The idea of reunification—the dream of one united German nation spanning East and West—has dominated Germany for centuries, and it is now being brought back to life. Dormant since the end of the war, Pan-Germanism is undergoing a resurrection.

Yet it is not solely politics that is spinning West Germany out of the orbit of the West. Kissinger has been criticized for his failure to see the vital role of economics in global politics, but no one could have foreseen the oil shocks of 1973 and 1979 and the technological revolution that they would ignite. For, while Kissinger and Brandt set the political stage for the reemergence of German nationalism, it would take Germany's falling behind in the race for the technological heights of the 1980s to trigger a shift away from NATO, the Common Market and the entire Atlantic Alliance.

•

THE FADING ECONOMIC MIRACLE

No one can truly understand why millions of Germans have demonstrated against the stationing of new U.S. cruise and Pershing missiles in their country—missiles requested by Chancellor Schmidt in 1978 to match a Soviet buildup—without knowing about the growing technological and economic decline of Germany. No one can truly understand Bonn's attempts to play the "broker" between Washington and Moscow, rather than the loyal ally, without knowing that West Germany counts its trade with Communist East Germany as part of its own internal economy. No one can understand Germany's stubborn refusal to give up financing and building the Siberian gas pipeline to Europe, a project that will earn Moscow tens of billions of dollars, without knowing that the country's steel and heavy-machinery industries are in deep trouble. And no one can comprehend the fascination with fringe political groups among Germany's youth without knowing that German unemployment is at a twenty-nine-year high.

For the one thing West Germany had after World War II was its great "Economic Miracle." Despite the humiliation of losing the war and the shame of murdering millions of innocents, Germany was able to point the way to the new postwar world economy. Germany's role in that global society was extremely limited and strictly economic. But at least it was important to the West. The country's economic dynamism pulled all of Europe behind it. Germany led economically and was proud of it.

Now the Economic Miracle is over. The Germans, cast adrift on the world scene without a vision, without a goal, are returning to old romantic notions of a *Volk*. Increasingly, people talk about a Germany not simply of businessmen but of strong leaders taking the people beyond the consumerism and individualism of Western life. More and more Germans dream of uncoupling Germany from the Atlantic Alliance, moving closer to the East and, finally, by standing between the two big power blocs, uniting the hundred million Germans now split between East and West.

This political drift is not something that will take decades to effect. It is picking up momentum at a fantastic clip, and 1983 will be a crucial year in the political life of Germany and the Atlantic Alliance. Germany must then decide whether to proceed with a plan to accept the new nuclear-tipped missiles. In 1978 NATO agreed that if the SALT talks did not produce a major reduction in Soviet missile strength in Europe, then the United States would augment its forces by stationing cruise and Pershing missiles in several European countries. Germany is to have most of them, along with Britain, Italy and Belgium. But if the West Germans now reject this proposal, NATO will be hurt, perhaps terminally.

How the German Economic Miracle is failing in the early 1980s and the immense changes it portends for the international balance of power is one of the great stories of our time. Between 1955, when France, Britain and the United States officially ended the Occupation, and 1980, Germany was one of the economic marvels of the world. It had one of the highest growth rates and one of the lowest inflation rates in the West. Millions of Turks, Italians and Greeks had to be imported to make up for labor shortages. Not only did they sweep the streets, but they manned the factories that manufactured VWs.

Germany's reputation as a maker of excellent consumer and industrial goods soared. People in America, Europe and Asia rushed to buy Leica and Rollei cameras, Grundig hi-fi equipment, BMWs, and billions of dollars' worth of heavy machinery and chemicals. The best scissors, the best lenses, the best machine tools came from Germany. Exports boomed, gold and money flooded into the country and the Deutsche Mark became one of the three most important currencies held by central banks and the rich alike.

•

NINETEENTH-CENTURY TECHNOLOGY

Paradoxically, Germany's phenomenal success after the war was due in large part to the fact that the technological base of its economy had not changed for a hundred years. Heavy machinery, steel and chemicals made up the core of Germany's economy during the decades after 1945—the very same industries that formed the heart of the German industrial revolution in the middle 1800s. Germany's economy remained part of the nineteenth-century technological revolution.

Perhaps more than that of any other industrial power, Germany's economy was built on heavy industry and cheap energy. Oil prices after the war were as low as they were in 1920, and even though Germany's factories were destroyed by Allied bombers, the people had the advanced skills that were needed to run a modern economy. When the Korean War broke out, demand for the country's traditional goods began to skyrocket. The plants were rebuilt with even more modern machinery, the people went back to work, and the same products that made Germany famous and powerful before 1945 began to pour forth from its factories—heavy turbines for generating electricity, precision-made tools, steel, electric consumer goods, VW "bugs," trucks, and chemicals of all kinds from a huge petrochemical industry.

Germany's economic success outpaced all of Europe's. Its people were soon the richest on the Continent, with per capita income soaring above that of the United States by the end of the 1970s. It became the locomotive for the European Common Market, set up in 1957, and was soon the third-largest economy in the industrialized world after those of America and Japan.

Germany reached its economic zenith in the late 1970s, when the U.S. dollar began to plummet out of control as inflation ripped apart the American economy. A decade and a half of inflationary spending to finance the Vietnam War and build the Great Society had weakened the United States to the point where the OPEC oil shocks sent it reeling. German finance ministers took to publicly lecturing Americans at the annual meetings of the International Monetary Fund (IMF) on how their country should properly run its economy. Economic success gave the Germans renewed pride, and the clouds of World War II began to dissipate. By the end of the decade, German government officials were no longer apologizing for World War II or the Holocaust. As one high Bonn official put it at the time, "We are past our Auschwitz diplomacy."

This was exactly what Konrad Adenauer and Ludwig Erhard intended back in the 1950s, when the two set out to anchor Germany firmly in the West. Adenauer, the first Chancellor of Germany after the war, and Erhard, his right-hand economist, were convinced that their country's future lay in the Atlantic Alliance within an integrated Western Europe. Adenauer believed that the only way to dilute Germany's corrosive and often deadly nationalism was to bury it within a larger entity—Europe. He fought to get Germany into NATO and tried to set up a unified European army only to be stopped by Charles de Gaulle. Erhard, the architect of the German Economic Miracle, pushed hard for Germany to enter the Common Market. Even then, however, not more than a few years after the war, Adenauer and Erhard had to fight tremendous battles to implement their strategy of anchoring West Germany to the West. Their efforts were seen as a betrayal by Germans who wanted reunification with East Germany to be the keynote foreign policy for Bonn. They demanded loose ties with the West and much closer relations with the Soviet Union as the way to join the two Germanys together again. Only by distancing itself from the West, they argued, could West Germany hope to persuade Moscow to give up its hold on East Germany.

But Adenauer and Erhard prevailed, and the Economic Miracle became the most important event for Germany after the war. For the next twenty-five years, Germany left behind its traditional concern with its political "place in Europe" and turned to business. Germany tended the store in the Common Market, providing billions to tide over the French or the Italians from time to time, in exchange for free access for German exports. It carped at the United States during Vietnam, made noises about de Gaulle but, in the end, became fully integrated into the West. It was even persuaded to rebuild its army to help the West hold the Soviet Bear at bay.

Germany's economic prosperity allowed much of the population to ignore the fact that Germany, nearly a century after Bismarck, was still not a united nation. The building of the Berlin Wall bluntly reminded them of that division; yet, at the same time, the West's total lack of resolve in tearing the wall down also suggested there was no great enthusiasm abroad for reunification. Most Americans and Europeans see the division of Germany into East and West as a permanent fixture of global politics, as a just result of the war that Germany began and lost. Although no government official would publicly admit it today, the division of Germany is also quietly seen as a way of possibly preventing another war in the future. When the Soviets whisper, "You take care of your Germans and we will take care of our Germans," people in Washington, Paris, London and elsewhere in Europe still breathe a sigh of relief.

•

THE TECHNOLOGY GAP

Yet this is all now coming undone. The technological base that underpinned Germany's Economic Miracle is quietly becoming obsolete. Like a speeding car that shoots off a pier and hesitates that one moment before plummeting into the sea, West Germany today is a nation confidently moving through the twentieth century blindly unaware of the economic catastrophe that has already befallen it. Few in Bonn—much less Washington or Paris—realize that the millions marching for unilateral disarmament and neutralism or the hundreds of thousands shouting anti-American slogans are making political statements that have an economic underpinning.

At the heart of the shift in German politics away from the West is an economic decay that is only now beginning to surface. Of all the major countries in the Western Alliance, no country will fall so far and so hard in the coming post-OPEC era as Germany. For West Germany is fast losing the high-tech race to Japan, the United States and perhaps even France. It may soon find itself a second-rate economic power, the new "sick man of Europe."

So far, the politicians in Bonn, the businessmen in Düsseldorf, the union leaders in Munich, and the people in general have convinced themselves that the country's high unemployment, low growth rate, and bloated budget deficits are caused simply by yet another cyclical recession that will pass. They do admit that the problems are a bit more severe during this economic downturn than in previous recessions, but they promise everything will turn around in the months ahead. They are dead wrong.

The Germans may not know this yet, but the entire industrial base of their country is eroding. The nation that built the most advanced chemical-, electrical-, automotive- and mechanical-engineering industries in the world over the past century is unable to see that its past success was based on cheap energy—which no longer exists. Germany today is a nation that cannot make the change from mechanical engineering to bioengineering. It cannot make the leap from precision-engineering the machines of yesterday with their thousands of moving parts and motors to the throwaway electronic devices of today and tomorrow. It cannot make the jump from petroleum-based chemicals to biologically produced pharmaceuticals.

Germany continues to make the best nineteenth-century products on earth—heavy turbines, wonderful cars, and precision tools. But it cannot compete when it comes to high technology—robots, telecommunications, "bug" factories, computers, semiconductors, consumer electronics. Its attempts at manufacturing twenty-first-century products are feeble and its moves to sell them on world markets are blithely smashed by both Japanese and American competitors. IBM has 60 percent of the German domestic computer market, and it would have much more if the German government did not favor domestic producers such as Siemens with local contracts.

In fact, nothing better illustrates the fall of Germany from the technological heights than its sad relationship with the Japanese. Siemens, the biggest electrical giant in Germany, has been forced to turn to Fujitsu for its big mainframe computers. Siemens buys Japanese computers and laser printers and sells them in Germany under the Siemens label. But it was Siemens that set up Fujitsu nearly a century ago. Once the pupil, now the teacher. "Fujitsu is superior to Siemens now," says Takanamori Mizuni, former senior economist for the Fuji Bank in New York. "Five years ago, Siemens was superior."

The Japanese are not the only ones superior to Siemens. In mid-1982, Italy decided to modernize its entire phone system, a multibillion-dollar undertaking. Instead of turning to Siemens, which rebuilt the phone system after the war, the Italians went to an American company, General Telephone and Electronics, with the contract. The other companies in the running were L. M. Ericsson of Sweden, CIT-Alcatel of France and the American IT&T. Siemens wasn't even in the telecommunications ball game.

Even in the country's strong industrial products, the domestic market is being lost to foreigners. Japanese machine tools, now computerized, are replacing German models. Toyotas and Hondas have captured 10 percent of the local car market nearly overnight and would take 20 or 30 percent if the Japanese were not practicing self-restraint. Just a few years ago, German industrialists were proudly telling their American friends that Japanese autos were too cheap and tacky for German consumers and couldn't compete against superior German design. Today, German auto makers are falling over themselves to buy foreign spot-welding robots to reduce the cost of their cars and to improve quality.

What this translates into is a long-term structural decline for Germany in the post-OPEC era. There is only one solution to this problem, a solution that Japan has already turned to and America is now struggling to accept—breeding new industries based on energy-efficient technologies in the hope that they can spawn more jobs than are being lost as the older, "dinosaur" heavy industries decline. But Germany is failing at that. Politicians explain away the postwar record unemployment with soothing words of economic cycles and promises of better times ahead, but they will prove to be wrong. Jobs lost today in steel and autos and chemicals will not be revived tomorrow.

•

HOW GERMANY LOST IT

How Germany lost its leading edge in technology may well prove to be one of the most interesting—and important—tales of our time. It is a story of many parts—of cultural conditioning, historical imperatives, arrogance, and specific government policies.

The basic truth is that Germany is finding it nearly impossible to make the critical switch from mechanical to electronic technology, one of the crucial changes taking place as we move into the high-tech 1980s. For Germany, the switch is all-important because it is so dependent on mechanical engineering. Yet, with an economy that is only 25 percent smaller than Japan's, Germany uses less than half of the microelectronics of its Pacific rival. Even compared with America, German consumption of chips is tiny. For many reasons, the Germans cannot apply the new microelectronics to their old industries. And as the international manufacturing base switches from machines to electronics, the Germans are falling further and further behind.

Germany came late to the Industrial Revolution, as it did to nationhood. When its economy finally took off in the nineteenth century, it was under the economic engine of the motorized machine. In fact, many of the key innovations of the machine age were made by German inventors. None other than Ernst Siemens, founder of Siemens, was responsible for the modern electrical motor, and his brother William made the modern steel arc furnace possible. The same genius for machines maintained the country's prosperity for a hundred years.

By the beginning of this decade, mechanical engineering in Germany employed more workers—one million—than any other industry, and it exported about $30 billion worth of goods and services annually. Power generation and electrical products were second, motor vehicles third and chemicals fourth, as employers and exporters. While this once was a great advantage when oil was cheap, it is an albatross when the cost of energy is so high.

One of the underlying reasons for Germany's inability to move forward may be that the German tendency toward perfection and order that worked so well in a mechanical era is actually a liability in this period of electronics. When machines were built to last decades, the German drive to engineer and reengineer thousands of parts until they all meshed perfectly was commercially laudable. A sense of order not only fit a more general attitude toward society, it worked wonders in designing complex machines and huge factories.

But in the fast-moving world of electronics, those traits are becoming archaic. While 20-ton electric power generators can take years to build and last decades, the life cycle of the computer can be measured in two or three years. Memory chips went from 2k to 8k to 16k to 64k to 256k in the space of a decade. Each microchip had a more complex architecture and was more powerful than its predecessor.

Speed is crucial in electronics, and the Germans are used to moving very slowly and carefully. This is true of German executives as well as workers and scientists. The corporate culture in Germany has more in common with a government bureaucracy than with a young American software company. A reluctance to take risks is epidemic throughout the business and financial groups of Germany. The slow-moving markets of heavy mechanical and electrical industries that didn't change for decades bred a generation of ponderous German "execucrats" who have no taste for the fast-moving pace of the high-tech era.

It is, therefore, no surprise that every time Siemens brings out a new memory chip after years of research, it finds that its American and Japanese competitors have gone on to bigger and better things. A perfectly fine-tuned 8k made-in-Germany semiconductor chip brought out by Siemens may bring joy to the hearts of the electronics engineers who designed it, but it is of no use to German industry if it has already been surpassed by a 16k chip made in Osaka or Silicon Valley. A perfectly made mechanical typewriter that outlasts any model put out by the competition may bring joy to AEG-Telefunken or Triumph-Adler, fading powerhouses in office equipment, but they are now being made obsolete by the electronic typewriters made by Olivetti in Italy, Brother in Japan, or IBM.

Just as important, the value of perfection can work wonders in the machine age, but is poisonous in twenty-first-century society. In microelectronics, *imperfection* actually has to be built in, in order to make things work. Redundancy is inserted into microchips so that when some circuits burn out or fail, others are already in place to pick up the streaming electric current. Any attempt to build the perfect chip produces delays that can put it behind the next generation coming off the assembly lines.

•

HITLER AND LOSING THE LEADING EDGE

The cultural baggage of another age that is weighing down on West Germany's economy is made even heavier by the legacy of Adolf Hitler and the Nazis. It is now clear that in many areas, German research and development have not kept pace with those of America and Japan. Electronics has suffered a great deal, but a major area of backwardness is in genetic engineering—one of the most promising industries of the future. Here Germany is suffering from the legacy of Hitler and the short-sightedness of its leaders after the war. Hitler gutted the university system of Jews and anti-Fascists during the 1930s, and while such famous scientists as Albert Einstein made their way to America, thousands of less-well-known people too left—or were killed. The biochemistry departments in particular were destroyed by the Nazis. How ironic that in its search for racial purity, Nazi Germany, forty years later, killed off a new industry built on genetic impurity, which makes living "factories" by taking nuclei out of one type of cell and implanting them in others!

Those biochemistry departments were never really reconstituted. It didn't seem to matter much at first. After the war, the chemical industry, which had been one of the foundations of the first German Economic Miracle in the late nineteenth century, was rebuilt. Germany quickly became the world's biggest exporter of chemicals. Some of the biggest chemical companies in the West are still Bayer, BASF and Hoechst.

Unfortunately for Germany, the chemical industry is unique. Not only does it use oil or gas for energy, like all other types of industries, it also relies on oil and gas for its raw materials. Plastics and fertilizers, Saran Wrap and Baggies are all petroleum-based. The chemical industry is, therefore, twice as vulnerable as any other industry to increases in oil prices. And when OPEC raised prices for both energy and petroleum feedstock fifteenfold over the past decade, it gutted the industry.

Chemical companies in the United States ranging from DuPont to Dow quickly saw the light and moved to spend tens of billions of dollars to change their basic operations. They are trying to move away from manufacturing bulk chemicals—such as naphtha or polyvinyl chlorides, which use huge amounts of oil and gas—to making very fine, specialized chemicals that command very high prices. More than that, they are trying to edge in on the big pharmaceutical companies by going into "life sciences"—drugs. For example, with oil prices so high, these chemical companies might make a penny per pound on bulk chemicals, but they could get $1,000 per ounce for interferon. Everywhere around the world, American and Japanese chemical companies are selling off their refineries and buying into tiny bioengineering companies. Even such food companies as Ajinomoto, which gave us the food additive (and headache-giver) MSG, are going into pharmaceuticals.

The Germans are only now waking up to this trend. But their efforts are strongly hampered by the legacy of Hitler. In fact, the Germans are not only far behind the Americans and the Japanese in genetic engineering, they are behind the British, the French and the Swiss. Hoechst's deal with Massachusetts General Hospital to set up a program in molecular biology reflects the backwardness of German research. In return for $50 million in cold cash, Hoechst gets first claim on all patents coming out of the research. But more importantly, it also gets to train its own scientists in bioengineering at Harvard.

West German scientists, of course, were furious that the

chemical company did not set up its genetic engineering research facilities in any of the big universities or the Max Planck institutes. Hoechst, in the past, has been one of the nation's largest private sources of university funds for research, and the deal with Harvard and Massachusetts General was seen as a national betrayal. And indeed it was. Professor Hansgeorg Gareis, head of Hoechst's pharmaceuticals division, told his critics that Germany was simply not at the leading edge of genetic engineering and was not about to get even close in the years ahead. He went on to say that German universities had become too bureaucratic and inflexible, and were unable to move quickly into new technologies. The fastest route for Hoechst to get the knowledge and skills in bioengineering was to move to the United States, and it did just that. And as if to rub a bit more salt into German sensibilities, he said that Hoechst was opening a small genetics laboratory in Japan as well. German academia was livid.

•

HITLER AND VENTURE CAPITALISTS

The Nazis not only seriously weakened Germany's universities but also destroyed a whole generation of risk-taking investment bankers. Before the war, there was a thriving venture-capital business with bankers, many of them Jewish, providing capital to growing German corporations. There is nothing of this left in Germany, and the banks have become stodgy caretakers of industrial behemoths.

A symptom of this financial disease is the total absence of a thriving stock market. To be sure, there are several stock markets in Germany, and dozens of issues are traded every day. But it is nearly impossible for a new company to raise capital by selling stock to investors. It is simply not done. A scientist or engineer with an original idea cannot translate it into a business, cannot try to make himself into a millionaire. For that reason more than any other, it is incredibly rare for new companies to develop in Germany. There are no Genentechs or Apple Computers in Munich or Düsseldorf. There are few, if any, German entrepreneurs willing to take new inventions and parlay them into their own companies. People and money managers with lots of cash who are looking for long-term equity growth turn to America for action. Germany is a venture-capital desert.

Worse than the anemic new-issues market is Germany's crusty and ingrown banking system. The injection of massive amounts of capital in young, growing companies was critical to Germany's early industrialization, just as it is in America's current move to revitalize its economy. Corporations like Siemens, AEG, Krupp, and Daimler-Benz would never have succeeded in the mid-nineteenth century without money from banks. The banks at that time were young and growing themselves. The big three of German banking—Deutsche Bank, Dresdner Bank and Commerzbank—all have their roots in that era of booming growth, new nineteenth-century technology and brash German entrepreneurs. When Ernst Werner Siemens, the founder of Siemens, needed money to expand his telegraph or turbine business, he walked into the new Deutsche Bank, which had been founded in 1870, and got it. And it was no accident that within decades a Siemens was president of Deutsche Bank.

But that was during Germany's first Economic Miracle. There is no comparable financial sector in Germany today. In fact, since World War II, German banks have become the main stockholders in German companies. The commingling of business and finance worked wonders when the country was rebuilding after the war. Capital was efficiently allocated to the old industries. This period ended during the late sixties, however, and the centralized system is now strangling any efforts at building a post-OPEC economy based on new technologies. Unlike their grandparents, German bankers are no longer willing to take risks. This generation of bankers does not understand the potential for new technologies. They are comfortable with the past of their fathers and their grandfathers and are willing to put capital into steel, chemicals, heavy machinery—all nineteenth-century technologies. The new world of the twenty-first century is passing them by, and they in turn are causing Germany to be left behind by the new twenty-first century. As the Japanese say, they have lost the "animal spirit."

•

THE GREENING OF GERMANY

It may be hard for the generation that rebuilt Germany and fostered the Economic Miracle to change the attitudes and policies that were once so successful. So it is natural for the country to turn for the future to the postwar generation that grew up in the 1960s and 1970s. But Germany is not finding its young people to be adequate guides to the twenty-first century. Indeed, the generation that should have the fresh ideas, enthusiasm and abilities to lead Germany in making the traumatic switch from nineteenth- to twenty-first-century technologies is not interested in technology at all.

Germany today is a country built on mechanical and electrical engineering that cannot find enough young people to fill its engineering schools. It is a business society, with a growing share of its young people voting against capitalism. It is a modern nation wherein a large segment of its people are increasingly irritated with rationalism, with science, with innovation. It is a democracy increasingly attacked by millions who view its institutions as "Western" or foreign and catering to a sordid individualism. They want to reject that for a purer vision of the German *Volk*, and greater authoritarianism. There is even a whiff of violence in the air, perceived as a cleansing agent for the impurities of Western capitalism, and it is not confined solely to the likes of the Baader-Meinhof gang.

Political romanticism is nothing new to Germany. As Gordon Craig points out in *The Germans*, it began in the late eighteenth century as a reaction against the rationalism and secularism of the Enlightenment. For all of the *philosophes*' emphasis on modernity, rationalism, cosmopolitanism, science and progress, the Romantics insisted on history, instinct, fantasy, pessimism, death, the cult of the individual, and the imagery of the dark and forbidding woods. With industrialization coming so late in German history, nearly two hundred years after that in Britain and France, the resulting social upheaval led many to flee to the fantasy world of Hansel and Gretel and the operas of Wagner.

This Romanticism died out in Germany before 1830, but throughout the rest of the country's history it would reappear—when the society was adrift, when a sense of powerlessness over life prevailed, when a longing for a mythical past or future became fashionable, when no single national goal united the people—elements present today. The Weimar Republic was afflicted with a population infected with cultural pessimism and an antipathy for the modern present. The Federal Republic is beginning to experience them as well.

Right now, with unemployment at its highest in decades, there are tens of thousands of skilled jobs going unfilled because people are not studying engineering or the sciences. America has shortages of engineers, but that stems from schools not producing enough of them, not empty seats. And Japan, of course, with half the volume of America's GNP, graduates twice as many engineers. Thousands of jobs go begging in Germany today for lack of qualified people. Companies are scrounging the campuses, but are constantly coming up against a contempt for "progress." Leading corporations are so afraid of the prevailing atmosphere that they are launching massive propaganda campaigns to lure young people back into engineering schools. Siemens has commissioned a survey of public attitudes in Germany toward technology. It has become so desperate that during a recent Hanover Fair, one of the biggest industrial events for machinery and equipment in Europe, German industrialists put on a show, called "Youth and Technology," that used rock bands to make the world of engineering more appealing.

But few in Germany believe that music will stop the growing contempt for technology. If anything, that hostility is growing and is being channeled through new "Green" political parties sprouting up in Germany. As the name implies, the Green parties got their start promoting ecological and environmental issues. They were in the forefront of the antinuclear movement during the 1970s. But they have broadened their constituency to express a much deeper discontent with the way Germany is heading. They are against the stationing of U.S. nuclear missiles in Germany. They are against the materialism of postwar Germany, the same materialism that gave the nation its national goal after the war. They are very anti-American and increasingly critical of the Common Market and NATO.

In local elections in 1982, they won enough votes to put significant numbers of representatives in local governments. So attractive are they becoming that many young people in the established parties are leaving for the "Greens." This is not the generation that can plot Germany's difficult voyage to the twenty-first century. They are looking backward, not forward.

•

BLOATED BUREAUCRACIES

If the young in Germany tend to look backward toward a simpler, more pastoral existence, those now in power in Bonn tend merely to hold onto the status quo. Economic policies that worked so well in the past have now turned sour, and politicians do not have the courage to change them. Indeed, there are few persons in Germany with the vision to outline the policies needed to take Germany from here to there.

With the creation of the Common Market, the movement

le and capital become freer in Europe than at in history. The entire Continent took off eco- country benefited as much as Germany. But rowth came to a stop with the OPEC shocks, ntry made a good recovery after the 1973 as been devastated by the second in 1979–

ars, Germany built one of the biggest wel- n history. Unemployment insurance and far more generous than in the United ople laid off were entitled to nearly their rs. Big payments were made to families And industry was just as pampered. The billions on subsidizing exports of goods tab picked up by the taxpayer. The gov- afford the transfers to the people, be- the nation's economy was expanding rapidly, and revenues were pouring into the treasury.

But with the soaring price of energy, the economy stalled. Like every other non-oil-producing nation in the world, Germany was hit with what amounted to an enormous wealth tax imposed by OPEC. Billions of marks began flowing out of the country, and Germany, which had been so proud of its trade surplus, suddenly found itself going into the red. Gasoline prices shot up, of course, draining money out of consumer pockets. Capital spending by businesses fell sharply, economic growth plummeted, and unemployment rose to 2.5 million by 1983—10 percent of the work force.

Suddenly, the old energy-intensive, heavy-industry base that had projected Germany onto the world scene was no longer adequate. It couldn't generate enough new jobs or new wealth for the country. But even now, four years after the second oil shock, this fact has yet to sink in among the politicians, the unions and the businessmen running the country. Instead of cutting back on the benefits pouring out of state coffers, instead of redirecting the economy away from high-energy-use industries, the politicians of Germany are simply treading water, hoping that a global recovery will somehow produce a rising sea to lift the German boat.

Of course, the labor unions are not exactly encouraging the government to cut back. They are, in fact, pressuring Bonn to spend more and more for jobs and growth. And businessmen, once proud free-marketers, are increasingly turning to Bonn for help. The government has had to step in to save the once mighty AEG-Telefunken electronics giant by guaranteeing hundreds of millions of dollars in loans. The unions wanted the government to simply buy the company, to preserve jobs. Even the renowned steel industry, once Europe's most efficient and profitable, is beginning to turn to the state for aid.

Germany—along with most of Europe, to be sure—has met the OPEC oil shocks not with cutbacks and new industrial strategies for high-tech industries, but with debt. The government is expanding costly social programs to help mask the rising unemployment, and they are putting tremendous strains on Bonn. In order to keep the hundreds of billions of dollars' worth of benefits flowing to the people at a time when revenues are falling, Bonn has resorted to borrowing. In Germany, government debt has risen 500 percent in the past decade, far more than in the United States. Government spending now makes up 46 percent of Germany's national income, and while that looks low compared to 60 percent for Belgium and 65 percent for Sweden and France, it is a lot higher than the 30 percent for the United States and Japan. Indeed, it is so high that German interest rates went soaring in 1982, and thus killed off any attempt at economic recovery. And while Chancellor Helmut Schmidt—before he was voted out of office—blamed the United States and its tight-money policy for Germany's own killer rates, it was the country's own bloated budget deficit that was at the root of the problem. If ever there was an economic environment made to discourage entrepreneurial activity, it is now Germany. If ever there was a nation poised to stumble as the world moves into the post-OPEC era, it is Germany.

•

THE POLISH CRISIS FORCES GERMANY TO CHOOSE THE EAST

The technology gap opening up between Germany on the one side and Japan and the United States on the other can have only one effect—to turn West Germany to the East. As German goods become less attractive and less competitive in Europe and America, German corporations will increasingly look to the less sophisticated markets of the Soviet Union, Eastern Europe and the Third World. The scenario is already clear. With France, Italy, Britain and the smaller European countries importing their high-tech industrial goods from the United States and Japan, German exports will suffer and the nation will increasingly lose its preeminent position of economic locomotive for the Common Market and engine for growth in the Western Alliance. Moscow will then beckon, and for a political price—perhaps becoming "neutral"—the Germans will receive huge contracts for their aging heavy industries. The hidden agenda, of course, will be the reunification of the two Germanys and the destruction of NATO.

While political pundits worry that the siren call of the Soviets may draw West Germany out of the Western orbit in decades to come, people closer to the scene in Europe fear that the break with the West is already under way and may be completed by the end of the decade. Indeed, they point to the fact that ties between West Germany and the East are already deep, and even shrill demands from Washington are not deterring the Germans from a decision to expand their economic and political ties with the East. The Soviet invasion of Afghanistan and the Moscow-inspired military takeover in Poland are not turning West Germany away from *Ostpolitik* and détente.

Nothing illustrates this as clearly as the fight over the Siberian pipeline to Western Europe. The Soviets are now building a $15-billion gas pipeline to Germany, France and Italy that will supply Western Europe with a large percentage of its gas needs in the 1990s. For Germany, it will supply up to 30 percent of its gas supplies. For Russia, it will provide nearly $10 billion a year in hard currency for decades—an incredible amount of cash to an economy that is in terrible shape.

The United States has bitterly fought this "Deal of the Century," as Soviet propaganda called it—but to no avail. Washington wants to punish the Soviets for their heavy-handed role in crushing Solidarity and the imposition of a military junta in Poland. The Germans have refused. More than that, the German banks offered, with government prodding and support, to finance the enormously expensive pipeline at extremely low interest rates. Of course, the Germans were not alone in this. The French and Italians all plumped for the pipeline, and all of them provided cheap financing for the Russians. But Germany was the key.

Despite threats from Washington, despite whispered words of withdrawing U.S. troops from Europe and a resurgent neo-isolationism in America if they went through with the pipeline deal, the Germans would not back down. Germany simply cannot do without the business and the jobs. Already in deep recession, Germany has to turn to the East for business. Entire corporations face bankruptcy without the pipeline. The steel industry in particular, the bedrock of heavy industry since the nineteenth century, is in severe trouble. Mannessmann, based in the Ruhr, is especially desperate—and so are the labor unions associated with it. Mannessmann is scheduled to sell hundreds of millions of dollars' worth of pipe for that project, and with Europe and the United States in recession, with steel demand falling everywhere, the only market is in the Soviet Union. Other German companies face the same choice. AEG, on the verge of bankruptcy, has a huge contract for gas compressors for the pipeline. Without the contract, it would go under.

The message in the Siberian pipeline deal is very clear. The Soviet Union offered West Germany a lucrative market for its heavy industrial products. Moscow did not import computers, semiconductors or robots from Germany, it took steel pipe and turbines. Germany, for its part, could not sell those products anywhere else in the world, so it provided extremely cheap financing for the Soviets to allow the deal to go through. The "Deal of the Century" may be the first of many to follow as Germany falls behind in the race for the technological heights of the 1980s and slides away from the West.

•

HISTORY REPEATS ITSELF

Indeed, the Siberian pipeline deal may symbolize a shift back to old traditional trading patterns for Germany—patterns that were supposed to have been reversed after World War II. From the beginning of German industrialization in the middle 1800s, Russia and the East have been crucial markets. Alfred Krupp exported his earliest steel cannon to the tsar, as well as Britain, Spain, Austria and Egypt, while his own king dithered about the virtues of the old brass guns. Ernst Werner Siemens exported telegraph equipment to Russia in the 1850s and might have gone under at that time had not the Eastern market offered profits for his young company. One of the first foreign business offices set up was by Ernst's brother, William, in St. Petersburg, now Leningrad. That was in the mid-nineteenth century.

The ties between Germany and Eastern Europe deepened as the nineteenth century wore on. Nearly the entire bourgeoisie of Poland, Hungary, Bulgaria, Czechoslovakia, Yugoslavia and much of European Russia was composed of either German or German-Jewish immigrants. To this day there are still millions of Germans living in Russia, a legacy not only of the war but of the prewar period.

All this ambiguity about Germany's place in Europe was supposed to end in 1945. The Allies demanded, and Adenauer and Erhard agreed, that West Germany be permanently tied into a union with the Western democracies. And for thirty-five years, it seemed as though the days of Germany being *das Land der Mittel* ("the country in the middle") between East and West were over. Indeed, it seemed that the "German problem"—that centuries-old problem of just where Germany fit within the European body politic—had been solved.

Yet while Western Europe went about its business of recovering from the war and building its prosperous welfare societies of the 1960s, West Germany quietly went about undermining the intention of the Allies. While Adenauer and Erhard solidly locked West Germany into the West, they also allowed steps to be taken to pursue Germany's traditional political objective, a single, united nation. For openers, the Constitution of the Federal Republic proclaims right at the top that reunification of the two Germanys is the main goal of West German foreign policy. When it was passed, in the fifties, the Allies didn't object.

The Western Europeans, for their part, agreed to something else that was far more important. In effect, they agreed to let East Germany join the Common Market through the back door. Few Americans realize that East Germany has access to the Common Market for its exports, but it is an economic—and political—fact of life. Decades before West Germany began to fall behind, technologically, and years before the OPEC oil shocks, West Germany persuaded Europe to count its heavy trade with East Germany not as imports from a foreign nation but as internal trade within a single country. Since 1957, East Germany has had a back door into all the markets of Western Europe. It has sent goods to West Germany only to have them reexported to France, Italy and other countries as "made in Germany." "We made a terrible mistake at the Rome Treaty by allowing the Germans to enter together," according to Jean-François Deniau, former cabinet minister for foreign trade under Giscard d'Estaing. "We were supposed to be tying Germany to the West, but by allowing the East in, we did not completely succeed."

This *Interhandelsblatt*, or "intercountry trade," is financed by a huge interest-free loan that West Germany gives to East Germany every year. But it is all very much of a secret. West Germans do not publish statistics on their trade with their Eastern brothers. They insist that the trade is small compared to the over-all trade of their country, but they refuse to provide the numbers to back it up. In fact, since the flowering of détente and *Ostpolitik* in the early 1970s under Chancellor Willy Brandt, trade between West Germany and the Soviet Union and its Eastern European satellites has soared. Between 1970 and 1976, trade tripled, without including the *Interhandelsblatt*. Bonn's figures show that West Germany is dependent on the East for 8 percent of its over-all trade. But State Department officials believe the real figure is a lot closer to 20 percent.

Moreover, the dependency on the East is focused precisely on those West German industries that are now facing technological trouble. One third of West German exports to the Soviet Union are in machinery, and there are hundreds of small and medium-size companies, not to mention the Mannessmanns and AEGs, that face bankruptcy without the Eastern markets. As West Germany falls behind Japan and America, it will have to turn further to the East for trade.

Not only does Bonn offer an interest-free loan every year to East Germany to finance trade between the two countries, but the people of West Germany themselves provide enormous sums of money. One of the major benefits of détente for all Germans on both sides of the Iron Curtain is the ability of West Germans to travel east to visit with their relatives. Every year, two million Germans cross the border, bringing with them enough Deutsche Marks to make West German money the second currency of East Germany. People in East Germany with access to marks are a class apart from their Communist brothers. They can buy special consumer goods in stores set aside for purchases with foreign currency. A two-tiered society is now developing in East Germany, and it is based on possession of West German money. Of course, the East Germans raise the ante by "taxing" travelers for their visits to their relatives. And another large sum of money is raised every year by the "sale" of people. The Communists allow several thousand old people and political prisoners to leave the East permanently each year if Bonn pays a blood price for them. Between 1974 and 1978, some 14,000 prisoners were "bought" for $400 million. All this cash keeps the East German economy afloat while tying the two Germanys closer and closer together—the major policy goal of West Germany since the war.

In fact, this trade between the two Germanys and Bonn's insistence that the East be included in the Common Market reflect how widespread is the desire for reunification. It is not just the Left, the Greens and the young people who are pulling away from the United States, NATO and the Common Market but average middle-class Germans. People with relatives in the East, unions dependent on exports, and corporations desperate for markets for their goods—all want *Ostpolitik* and eventual reunification. When the conservative Helmut Kohl defeated the Social Democrat Helmut Schmidt in late 1982, he immediately declared he was in favor of *Ostpolitik* and the Siberian pipeline. "We must not forget this: it is not just the hippies, but most Germans, who want close ties with the East," says Deniau.

As West Germany falters in the transition from heavy industry to high technology, as it falls further and further behind other nations in the move toward the twenty-first century, it will pull away from the West. Only a dramatic change in policy can reverse this political shift and prevent the destruction of the Common Market, NATO and the Atlantic Alliance.

4

THE DISINTEGRATION OF THE SOVIET EMPIRE

•

THE TECHNOLOGY REVOLUTION UNLEASHED BY OPEC IS AFfecting not only the West but the East as well. In fact, just as the capitalist nations of the Common Market are pulling away from one another as they struggle to deal with high oil prices, so too are the Communist countries beginning to whirl out of Moscow's control. Indeed, the Soviet empire is disintegrating at a faster pace than the Atlantic Alliance, and the entire map of Europe may soon be redrawn for the first time since World War II.

•

IMAGINE

Imagine a place where a man called Boris the Gypsy is arrested for the illegal possession of a million dollars' worth of diamonds. Boris implicates Galina, the daughter of the ruler of that country. Galina was married to a circus performer but her current husband, Yuri, is second in command of the national police. Boris is hauled into jail by officers of another police agency that rivals Yuri's. People everywhere whisper about the "meaning" of it all.

Imagine a place where the ruler is an ancient tyrant. Deaf, fat, sickly, he refuses to give up his immense power. Men buzz around him, waiting for death to remove his decaying body, so they can make their play for power. A woman, a mystic from the hills of a faraway province, visits the old man to "lay on hands." After each visit, he rallies, keeping his human vultures at bay.

Imagine a place where unemployment is outlawed and everyone works. Yet people drink so much they die on the job. Women drink to the point where their children are born dead and deformed. The government officially deplores the drunkenness yet profits from its people's alcoholism. Taxes on liquor provide a tenth of the state's entire revenues.

Imagine a place where all health care is absolutely free. No one has to pay anything to see a doctor or get into a hospital. But people have to wait weeks for an X ray and months for an operation. To get into a modern, specialized facility takes an expensive bribe.

Imagine a place were the shelves of all the food stores are nearly bare. Only a few scrawny chickens, a couple of foreign sausages, one or two cabbages can be found. Yet the people buy plenty of food—from the black market, a massive underground economy.

This place is Moscow, but not the Moscow of Tsar Nicholas, of Rasputin, of the late nineteenth century. It is the Moscow of the 1980s, of the Union of Soviet Socialist Republics, of the nation with the world's second-largest GNP. It is the Soviet Union of missiles and satellites, of fighter planes and helicopters. It is modern-day Russia, ruled by Leonid I. Brezhnev when he lived and now by Yuri Andropov, head of the KGB for fifteen years.

•

VODKA COMMUNISM

Where once, just after the 1917 Revolution, people dreamed of building a new "Socialist Man" of superior values and skills, they now skulk about their factories and their homes guzzling vodka and cheap bathtub booze. Where once rulers promised their people the highest standard of living in the world and Nikita Khrushchev boasted of surpassing America, "burying it" economically by 1980, they now grumble about worker laziness, inadequate meat and shoddy goods. And where once Russians believed they were creating a moral society, in which different ethnic and religious groups would be bound together by ideology and pride in the future, they now talk the language of racism and militarism.

There is an ugliness, a meanness spreading through Russia these days that sounds the death knell for that society. Its ideology is bankrupt; its dreams are failed; its people prefer the anesthesia of alcohol to the reality of their lives; its soldiers fight colonial wars in Asia and guide Polish Quislings in the destruction of democracy in Eastern Europe. The Revolutionary promises of social change and economic growth, intended to mold a vast empire of Russians, Ukrainians, Moslems and Uzbeks, no longer work, and strong forces are pulling that empire and its Eastern European satrapies apart.

The Kremlin today feels itself under siege by a hostile world. The binding ideology of Communism is being replaced by the siege emotions of Russian nationalism, xenophobia and anti-Semitism. The people, engulfed in corruption all around them, are embracing the "romance" of Stalin. Just as many West Germans increasingly long for the simpler days of a strong leader and clear, old-fashioned values, so too do many Russians look back to the Stalin dictatorship. So bad is life in the Soviet Union today that millions long for a man who killed as many Soviet people as Hitler did. "At least he was strong," Moscovites say. "At least prices fell," they repeat. Some are so disgusted with everyday life that they go beyond longing for Stalin. On April 20, 1982, a group of young people actually held a profascist rally in Pushkin Square in the middle of Moscow to mark the birthday of Adolf Hitler.

No one can understand these strange events without realizing that the Soviet Union, of all the major industrial countries of the world, is the furthest behind in the technology race. While the United States is struggling to catch up to Japan to build the industries of the post-OPEC future, the Soviet Union is still trying to catch up to Europe to build the industries of the past. While the United States and Japan attempt to harness the new technologies of robotics, biotechnology and telecommunications, the Soviet Union continues to build goods based on nineteenth-century technologies of steel, cement and heavy machinery.

No one can understand why Moscow desperately wants the billions in new revenues from the Siberian gas pipeline to Western Europe without knowing about the need to import huge amounts of Western money to stem the country's economic decline. No one can truly understand why the Kremlin allowed Solidarity to flourish for so long without sending in its tanks without knowing about the financial crisis the country is facing. No one can understand the massive Russian buying of Western factories and the KGB's massive campaign of technology espionage without knowing about the dramatic fall in domestic productivity. And no one can comprehend the workers' incredible longing for the ruthless dictator Stalin without knowing about the failure of the present leadership to stop the chronic corruption of Soviet life and to provide food and consumer goods on a par with the West.

For the one thing that the Soviet Union had for twenty years after the war was the prospect that it would one day overtake the United States and prove the superiority of communism over capitalism. And for a long time during those years, the Soviet Union did indeed grow faster economically than the United States—twice as fast in the 1960s. But that is all over now, and the Russians can point to only one success, arms. And even that is proving to be an evanescent mirage fading just as it becomes reality. The Soviet Union has reached military parity with the United States—for the moment. By the end of the decade, America may very well again be superior, propelled by the technologies of twenty-first-century society that the Soviets are finding impossible to create themselves and will find increasingly difficult to import or steal. The high-tech military glitter of the Soviet Union is a superficial veneer dependent on Western technology. At best it is the current state-of-the-art technology that the Soviets can buy off the shelf. At worst, it is several years behind. It was no accident that the Israelis, in their June 1982 invasion of Lebanon, completely destroyed Syria's Soviet arms through their more advanced technology. By combining superior American F-15s and F-16s and their own home-grown sophisticated electronic countermeasures (ECMs) against the Syrians, the Israelis were able to destroy the Soviet SAM missiles on the ground with ease, while knocking down nearly ninety MIG-23s and MIG-25s without a single loss. The Kremlin rushed a top-level mission to the Mideast to find out what happened, and it learned that advanced Western electronic warfare had just made a good part of the Soviet air force totally obsolete.

No one is more sensitive to the impact of technology than the technology-obsessed Japanese. Naohiro Amaya, a silver-haired special adviser to MITI, talked with me over tea in mid-1982 in New York about Russia and winners and losers in the race for technology. The Soviet Union and Eastern Europe are cases of "total system failure," said Amaya. "The Russians can produce good SS-20s, but how long can they continue to do so? I am quite skeptical."

Without the dream of overtaking the West, centrifugal forces are pulling the Soviet Union apart, sending the Russians spinning back to their insular past. Internally, the leaders of the Soviet Union increasingly look at themselves not as

Soviets but as ethnic Russians. As economic growth stalls, each group in the Soviet empire is struggling for a bigger piece of the stagnating pie. The military takes ever more resources from the civilian sector. The Moslems, Ukrainians, Balts, and other groups breathe down the necks of the Russians, who are increasingly worried as the demographic tide turns against them. They will soon be a minority in the Soviet Union that they have dominated for centuries. The growth rate for the Great Russians is running at 6.5 percent compared to 33 percent for the southern Moslem republics of Tajikistan and Uzbekistan. While demographics pulls the country one way, another pressure is tearing at it elsewhere. A new class system is beginning to dominate Soviet life. Workers see 17.5 million party members leading a privileged life of cars and clothes and *dachas* and separate stores stocked with foreign goods. They openly complain about a new "feudal" class arising as this group's children get special placement in the nation's best schools.

The disintegration of the Soviet Union is not something that will occur centuries from now. It is accelerating, and a climax is sure to occur by the end of the century. It may be that the Russians can use their military to physically subjugate all the other peoples of the empire, including those of the Eastern bloc. But in the past it took high economic growth as well as strong military force to facilitate Soviet control. It was necessary to offer the Hungarians, the Czechs and the East Germans the promise of a better economic tomorrow, when Russian tanks crushed their budding attempts at freedom. And over the past decade, Moscow has had to put out as much as $30 billion in subsidies to take care of its far-flung empire, while spending tens of billions on imported food to satisfy its own people.

As the Soviets fall further and further behind technologically, they will no longer be able to do this. Already Moscow faces a growing guns-or-butter debate that will only get worse as Washington increases American military spending. That means that the fifteen separate republics of the Union of Soviet Socialist Republics and the dozen or so foreign satellites of Eastern Europe may one day soon try to go their independent ways. And the rulers in the Kremlin may have to decide soon whether to allow them their freedom or use the mailed fist to maintain the empire.

•

THE ECONOMY THAT STALIN BUILT

Joseph Stalin built the modern Soviet economy. He wanted a modern army to protect the homeland from ever being invaded again from the West by a Germany or by Asians from the East. He also wanted an army to project the Communist revolution abroad. To do this, Stalin built an economy totally dominated by heavy industry to support a huge military machine. Today the Soviet economy *is* a military-industrial complex. It does not merely *have* one as does the United States.

Stalin built an incredibly cumbersome management system for the Soviet economy. Party bureaucrats at every level control economic production and distribution. Planning is centralized from the top down, goals are set, orders flow from the top down. Rigidity is the key characteristic of this immense bureaucracy. Under Stalin a massive dose of terror was also used to enforce control. When Khrushchev took over, most of the *gulags* were dismantled. But the centralized economic and political planning apparatus remained.

That bureaucracy has proved to be hugely successful in remaking the Soviet Union from a peasant society into an industrial nation. With the party in control, the Soviets were able to push through a forced-draft industrialization of the country that was the envy of much of the world. Despite the huge cost in lives, by the 1950s and 1960s Soviet economic growth was expanding at twice the U.S. rate. In the sixties alone, it roared ahead at nearly 6 percent every year, while America crawled along at 3 percent. Despite the fact that the military always received the major share of government funds, the civilian sector of the economy increased dramatically as well during the first two decades after World War II. Not a year went by at that time when consumers were not promised a better life. And got it.

These were the years when Soviet production of iron and steel, cement and coal rushed past that of the United States and Europe. By 1980, the Soviet Union was number one in the world in these essential products. In terms of actual output, it was in the top ranks of the economic powers. The centralized Communist system of economic growth appeared to work.

•

THE RECEDING TIDE OF SOVIET POWER

The Soviet system reached its zenith during the 1970s. Just as America began its decade-long decline in power, mired abroad in Vietnam and eroded domestically by inflation and debasement of the dollar, the Soviets reached a new plateau. Industrially, they came abreast of Europe, and militarily they may have even pulled ahead of America. While the West was caught in economic stagflation, the Soviet economy prospered. Soviet power was extended, through Cuban or East German surrogates, throughout Africa. Soviet-backed North Vietnamese and Vietcong troops defeated American-backed forces, producing a traumatic humiliation for the United States. Détente brought Western Europe much closer to Moscow, and fat contracts offered by the Kremlin to the corporate giants of Germany, France, Britain and Italy allowed it to help pry the Atlantic Alliance apart.

This tide of Soviet power is now receding. The same technological forces sweeping Europe, the United States and Japan are tearing through the Soviet economy. The same forces making the industrial base of modern Germany obsolete are eating away at the economic viability of Russian steel factories. Just when supremacy over the West seemed at hand, just when the dream of dominating Europe and surpassing the bastion of capitalism, the United States, appeared at the horizon, a revolution in technology is snatching it away.

No one in Moscow is much aware of what is taking place. The bureaucrats put the blame for their nation's problems—the low growth rate, the need to import food, the warehouses full of goods that no one will buy—on external, foreign factors. The blame for bad harvests can be put on God or the elements. Blame for the failure to meet planned targets can be put on the lack of Western loans. But the truth of the matter is that the aging patriarchs now in the Kremlin will go down in history as the last of the mighty Communist rulers.

The powerful economy that made the Soviet Union second only to the United States is quickly becoming obsolete. Like Germany, so long its model, the Soviet Union is a nation built on heavy industry. All this was based on cheap energy, energy that no longer exists. Like Germany, the Soviet Union today is a nation that is not making the switch from mechanical engineering to bioengineering, from chemicals to pharmaceuticals, from massive machines to throwaway electronic computers. And, like Germany, it is falling in power.

Indeed, the Soviets are still trying to catch up with Germany and the West in advanced nineteenth-century industries. Their Lada car, exported to Belgium and Italy, is a Soviet-built Fiat, twenty years out of date. Their supersonic passenger plane is a copy of the Concorde. In fact, it hasn't flown much since crashing at a Paris air show years ago. And if it did, each flight would be a drain on Moscow's treasury.

As much as Germany pioneered in the technologies of the nineteenth century and built its heavy industrial base on those innovations, so did Russia borrow and buy from Germany to build its own economy. Germany was the model for Russia under the tsars, the model for the Soviet Union under Stalin and remains the model for the Communists to this day. Siemens built the first telegraph lines in Russia and the first heavy electrical turbines. Krupp sold its first steel cannon to the tsar, replacing the old brass guns. Unfortunately, the Kremlin doesn't realize that Germany's supremacy is now history, and a new technological revolution is sweeping the world. For the aging men of Moscow, there is no new vision of the future, only a tired old bureaucratic inertia, repeating the past.

•

THE FAÇADE OF SOVIET TECHNOLOGY

Yet the Soviets are able to project an image of their country as a modern, advanced nation. It is a mask, a high-tech façade of military might, of jet planes, missiles, satellites and submarines, and it offers the world only one side of the Soviet enigma. Behind that screen lies an economy poised for a crash that will shake the strongest Kremlin walls. So sharp will be the fall that it might well result in the passing of the Soviet Union as a military superpower. Indeed, it might mean the passing of the Soviet bloc and the emergence of a collection of separate internal republics and independent Eastern European countries. How this may occur is another complex tale. As in Germany, we must look to history and culture for the beginning of the explanation and then to government policies built up over the past six decades for the rest.

The most important point about the Soviet Union in the 1980s is that the country is the least prepared of all industrial nations for the switch to a twenty-first-century society. The Soviet Union is the most backward of all countries in harnessing the new locomotive technologies of the post-OPEC era. Indeed, it is the most underdeveloped of all developed countries. By any measure, the Soviets are years behind Europe and perhaps decades behind Japan.

The Soviet Union, with an economy much larger than Japan's, uses only a tiny percentage of microelectronics in its products, and nearly all go into its military. The Soviets have one of the lowest per capita computer ratios of any industrial country. They have only recently heard of bioengineering, and their telecommunications systems are ancient. The Soviet Union is basically a technological dwarf, and its military prowess hides that fact. Unlike the Germans, the Russians were never great industrial innovators. The Industrial Revolution was alien to the empire of the tsars. Russian inventors, unlike the British or the Germans, did not play any major part in generating the technologies that formed the basis of either the earliest industrial revolution based on the steam engine and textiles in the seventeenth century or the second wave in the late nineteenth century based on electro-mechanical innovations, heavy machinery and steel. Technology from the very beginning was not something to be created from within, but something "Western," "foreign," to be imported from the outside.

Moreover, individual creativity has never been one of the key human values in Russia as it has been in the United States, Britain or France. Ideas, inventions for their own sake, have never been rewarded. Only when harnessed for the state did they have any value.

If anything, Russian culture is authoritarian. The Communists have built on centuries-old values. Risk avoidance is the game to be played, not risk taking. Risk avoidance was the most important skill a peasant could have a century ago, and it is the most important skill a Communist bureaucrat can have today. It is no accident that the NATO high command directs its armies to attack the control centers of opposing Soviet and Eastern-bloc forces. For the Russian generals control their armies down to the smallest units, leaving no flexibility or freedom to their field officers.

What this means for the Soviet economy is an elaborate, ponderous, incredibly complex system of programs and five-year plans that attempt to set targets for hundreds of thousands of factories, tens of millions of workers and billions of items and services. Without a pricing system or markets, each economic decision must be made by party bureaucrats who control every layer of the economy.

Decision making is achingly slow. Soviet planning isn't anything like the "scientific," rational process it is supposed to be. Instead, it is an exercise in old-fashioned logrolling that might make Lyndon Johnson smile. For example, the current five-year plan composed by Gosplan, the central planning agency, was put together by Nikolai K. Baibakov in his gray headquarters just across from the Kremlin. It was published on December 3, 1981, and was made into law several months later, when the Supreme Soviet parliament voted it through. Of course, the rubber-stamp legislature has never vetoed such a plan.

Heads of various production ministries and bureaus have spent years putting pressure on Baibakov to influence the shape of this Gosplan. Their major tactic is to set the lowest possible production quotas and receive the greatest possible amount of supplies. Each faction tries to promote its own interests. The Moslems from Central Asia, for example, fought long and hard for massive water projects and got them. The military, of course, gets the highest priority in everything it requests.

Ironically, the new five-year plan was dead the minute it was published. Every five-year Soviet plan is a running program. All the goals and quotas that show up on pretty charts are really nothing more than wishful thinking. They are continually changing as the years pass. Factory managers are constantly on the phone with their ministries getting their quotas revised downward because of late deliveries, lack of parts, worker absenteeism. The huge Fiat factory, for example, at Togliatti City, named after the onetime head of the Italian Communist Party, took more than a decade to build. By the time the mammoth complex was completed, it was years behind anything in the West.

The economy built by the bureaucrats can produce massive quantities of goods. What it cannot do is make anything of quality. The command management system can set goals for specific quantities of steel or cement, and the economy will in fact crank out those quotas. But the Soviets have not been able to quantify such things as "newness" or "color attraction" to consumers. Without a pricing system or markets, they never know whether the millions of shoes being manufactured are what people really want. They have to guess, and very often they guess wrong.

But as long as the quotas are met, the production managers will get their Black Sea vacations. It doesn't matter that the Soviet economy is the most wasteful in the world, with energy consumption 40 percent higher than that of Europe or even that of the profligate United States. It doesn't matter that the steel actually produced is the wrong thickness, that the clothes are ugly, that the cement is thin. Soviet managers are known to have shipped the wrong-width steel plating for nuclear power plants—and the plates were actually used in order not to fall further behind schedule!

The Soviets might be able to live with these values in an era of big machines and massive projects. In an electronic age, they are crippling. The Russian way of waiting for orders from above, of having a heavy bureaucracy make all economic decisions, of delay and procrastination, of risk avoidance are all anathema to the new era of high technology. When it took fifteen years to build the biggest dam in the world, the Russian system worked after a fashion. But the life cycle of a chip is measured in short two-year frames. Computers change often. Even as people in the United States rush to buy Apple IIs, the more powerful Apple II-E personal computer is coming on the market.

As electronics replace machines, as biology replaces chemistry, as robotics customizes the assembly line, ending long runs of standard products, speed and flexibility are the crucial skills of the twenty-first-century society. Change is imperative and can't wait years for dozens of committees to discuss possibilities and make decisions. Individual innovation is vital for the generation of new ideas and technologies. The slow-moving dinosaur that is the heavy-industry core of the Soviet economy cannot come close to adapting itself to these new values. Its workers don't even dream of having these skills, certainly not through their alcoholic haze.

•

THE LYSENKO LEGACY

In addition, the Soviet Communists have some very special burdens to labor under, when it comes to the new technology of bioengineering. Not that anyone in the Kremlin really knows much about bioengineering. In 1982, the scientific and political rulers decided that they should do something about developing a capability in this new area. The reasoning was very simple. All of a sudden everyone in the West was talking about it. That was enough for the commissars.

Unfortunately, of all the industrial nations in the world, the Soviet Union is perhaps the least prepared to deal with bioengineering. Just as Hitler did away with a generation of biochemists in the 1930s in so drastic a way that it still haunts West Germany, so too did Stalin purge Russia of its best biologists in the 1930s. All in the name of Communism.

Between 1927 and 1929, disaster struck the winter-wheat crop in the Soviet Union. Stalin's campaigns of forced industrialization and collectivization decimated agriculture and the nation faced famine. At that time Trofim Denisovich Lysenko, a trained horticulturist, offered a way of increasing productivity on the farms at an incredible pace. He promised fantastic results in just one season's time. Lysenko turned his back on traditional genetics and said that the slow methods of selective breeding to increase crop production were wrong. Chromosomes, genes, plant hormones—none of that even existed; what did count was acquired characteristics. Basically, Lysenko argued that the environment could produce changes in plants and the changes, in turn, could be passed on to the next generation. He went on to "prove" that by wetting down and cooling off the seeds of winter wheat and planting them in the spring, the crop's yield could be dramatically increased.

Lysenko was a nobody at this time. The big gun in Soviet plant biology was Nikolai Vavilov, director of the V. I. Lenin All-Union Academy of Agricultural Sciences. But Lysenko's antigenetic ideas tickled Stalin's fancy. After all, the Communists were trying to build a new "socialist man" in a generation's time, and Lysenko's concept of "environment making the organism" fit right in with the prevailing ideology. Genetics was soon perceived as bourgeois and contrary to the ideals of Communism and the needs of Soviet agriculture. A series of public debates took place in 1934 between the Lysenkoists and the scientists. Stalin backed Lysenko, and biology became politicized. Vavilov was arrested and sentenced to death. He died in prison in 1943 as did a number of other geneticists. Lysenko became the director of the Institute of Genetics of the USSR Academy of Sciences in 1940 and stayed until 1965. He virtually dominated all of Soviet biology for twenty-four years.

In the end, of course, it turned out that Lysenko's ideas were ridiculous. His statistical "proof" was phony. In the early 1960s the Soviet Union once again found itself with a terrible crop shortage on its hands. Collectivization and bad weather had once again produced the threat of a severe food shortage. Khrushchev turned to Lysenkoism for help and found none. That Lysenkoism conformed to Communist ideology meant nothing at this point. A major agricultural crisis occurred, and Khrushchev fell in 1964. Lysenko was right behind him. He was dismissed from all administrative posts in 1965.

By that time, however, Soviet biology was in a state of total atrophy. Politics, not science, had dominated the field for three decades and it never really recovered. Two whole generations of geneticists trained in modern science were gone from the Soviet Union, and the country was about as prepared for bioengineering as Zaire.

•

COPYCAT SOVIET TECHNOLOGY

In late 1981, fishermen off the coast of North Carolina picked up a Soviet buoy. It appeared to be a standard oceanographic device designed to measure the currents in that part of the sea. Inside, however, there was something more. The device turned out to be a sophisticated listening machine aimed at gathering information on the U.S. Navy. Defense scientists took the buoy apart, found a microchip circuit board and pulled one of the chips off. They then inserted a chip made in the United States. It worked perfectly. The Soviet chips were exact duplicates of the American chips. The Soviets probably bought the circuit board during the seventies, broke down the components and rebuilt them. "Reverse-engineering" is a major part of Soviet research.

More importantly, however, the buoy incident highlights an underlying strategy that is basic to Soviet technology. The Soviets have never stopped copying the West in their efforts to modernize their country. The habits and values born centuries ago remain. Today, the Soviets still look to the West for their technology, and as a consequence, their machines more often than not look exactly like Western prototypes. There is no greater compliment for an American or European manufacturer than to have an exact copy of his product made by the Soviets.

Copying has a long tradition in the Soviet Union, longer even than in that copycat of Asia, Taiwan. Soviet cars, of course, have traditionally been modeled after Fiats. But the Soviets are also carrying this "me-tooism" into high technology. They are so fond of the Unimation welding robot that they have begun making exact replicas of it—calling it the K-690. Of course, it is totally illegal to do this without paying licensing fees, but the Soviets are famous for this as well. The Soviets are also in awe of IBM's computers, so much so that the entire group of Ryad computers they developed with the

Eastern Europeans, in common use throughout the Communist bloc, is closely patterned after the IBM 360 and 370 series. And the same goes for minicomputers. In the 1970s, the Soviet Union and the Eastern European countries imported more than 3,000 minicomputers from the United States and Europe. None was being made domestically at that time. Now, however, the minis are being copied and manufactured domestically.

To be sure, the Soviet Union today does have a decent high-technology base from which a good deal of the sophisticated military work gets done. But most of it was purchased or stolen or copied from the West. With Soviet cosmonauts circling the globe, it seems quite preposterous, but it nonetheless remains true. Without the impetus to innovate, without the flexibility to change rapidly, the Soviets are chronically dependent on the West for technology and will remain so until the society radically changes.

So pervasive is Western technology in the Soviet military and civilian economies that only a few examples suffice to illustrate Moscow's copycat technology strategy. All these examples also illustrate the fallacy of the arguments used by hungry American, European and Japanese corporations who say that selling high-tech goods to the civilian side of the Soviet economy provides jobs and profits for their own countries without enhancing the Bear's armed power. For it is quite clear that all technology in the Soviet Union is "dual-use" and has a military component. Indeed, the military factor comes first.

In the late 1960s and early 1970s, Western companies sold one and a half billion dollars' worth of machinery to build the huge Kama River truck factory. American corporations, such as the Pullman Company, were heavy participants. Unimation sold twenty of its welding robots, and dozens of others from the Japanese found their way to the Kama River assembly lines. The Western companies were assured that the trucks would be for civilian use. The American companies, in particular, used this reasoning to persuade Washington to allow them to sell the goods. About ten years later, Moscow sent an army into Afghanistan. Most of the 80,000 Soviet troops arrived on trucks—trucks built at the Kama River factory complex with Western automotive technology.

The same strategy is being used in microelectronics. Throughout the sixties and seventies, Russian ICBMs were enormously powerful, but not very accurate. For accuracy you need electronics and computers. During those years, the Soviets began buying dozens of different types of machines and materials from many countries around the world. They bought things called "epitaxial growth furnaces" and "crystal pullers." They bought "mask aligners" and "probe testers." Most of the purchases were made in Europe through dummy Soviet companies set up specifically to tap American technology. Motorola, one of the top three U.S. chip makers today, was a specific target of the Soviets during the 1970s. They bought components through its Belgian subsidiary—a fact that Lionel Olmer, Commerce Undersecretary for International Trade, and a leading opponent of technology transfer to the Soviets, doesn't forget. He worked for Motorola during that time and closed down the foreign offices selling to the Soviets.

None of the purchases individually meant much. But when assembled, they gave the Soviet Union complete factories for the making of chips and microprocessors, small computers-on-a-chip. No one knows for sure how many factories the Soviets have built to produce these electronic devices, but one U.S. intelligence source believes the Soviets had bought enough machines and materials from the West to build at least three—two for production and one to cannibalize for parts. This, of course, is tiny compared to the dozens of chip-making plants in the United States and Japan. But it is enough to satisfy the military.

Even so, the two Soviet factories could not reproduce American chips in an exact fashion. When Control Data Corporation obtained from a Hungarian source one of the Russian-made microprocessors that go into the Communist-bloc Ryad computers, it found some slight changes. The Soviet microprocessor was basically an imitation of the 8080A chip made by Intel, the U.S. company that invented the first microprocessor in the world. Whole sections of the Russian chip were copied from the Intel model, but the Soviets were unable to duplicate some of the more advanced production techniques, especially the miniaturization processes. The Soviet chip was examined by U.S. engineers in 1980. It was date-marked 1977, and the Intel microprocessor it duplicated first came out in 1974. The Soviet chip was 27 percent larger than the original Intel chip and 58 percent larger than the 1980 Intel version of that chip. Even with Western machines and materials, the Soviets were not able to completely copy the most sophisticated American semiconductor technology.

However, that didn't really matter when it came to the military. Soviet efforts at duplicating Western electronics were sufficient to change their "dumb" weapons into "smart" ones. The great "MIRVing" of the giant Soviet ICBMs that began in 1979–1980, following the United States by several years, was based on the chips and microprocessors manufactured at these factories. Without them, the Soviets would not have been able to increase the accuracy of their missiles, the United States would have been far ahead in the arms race with its old generation of weapons, and we would not now be faced with a $1.6-trillion bill by the Reagan Administration for modernizing the nation's arsenal.

The Soviets recently announced that they are ready to go into high-volume production of some of these computer chips. That means that after satisfying the military needs of the nation, the technology will now be diffused downward into the civilian sector. Unfortunately, it is too late. What they are now prepared to do is produce chips that are basically ten years old. The chips that Moscow is now prepared to offer to the civilian economy are called LSI (large-scale integration) chips. Invented in the United States in the early 1970s, they found their way into the new electronic watches beginning in 1973. They are all over the high-tech marketplace now, in tiny calculators, in radios, in microwave ovens. In fact, they are about to become obsolete. So fast is change in the chip business that a whole new generation is right around the corner —the VLSI (very large-scale integration) chip. These chips are far faster and more powerful than the old LSIs, which the Soviets are only now getting ready to mass-produce.

This is a classic example of how difficult it is for technology to get diffused throughout the Soviet economy. Even though the technology is copied from the West, it still must go to the military first. Only after the military's needs are satisfied is the technology made available to the broad economy. And by that time it is obsolete. Technology diffusion is one of the major problems of the Soviet economy and cannot be solved under the present bureaucratic system.

Paradoxically, the Soviet generals know this and are already moving quickly to gain access to the advanced Western VLSI technology. They realize that their scientists and engineers cannot make the innovations that are necessary to create such high-speed integrated circuits, and they are now launching a massive campaign to get the equipment needed to build VLSI chips from America and Japan. Both countries are in the forefront of VLSI research. Moscow is coordinating efforts to gain access to foreign university, corporate and military laboratories working on the microelectronic technology. Corporations in the United States and Japan are also major targets of Soviet action. VLSI chips should begin making their way into U.S. missiles and airplanes in the next two years, perhaps revolutionizing tactics and strategies and bringing superiority back to America for the first time in over a decade—if the Soviets don't get them as well.

While Moscow expends tremendous energy to tap Western technology directly, it is also turning to its Eastern European satellites for help. East Germany, Czechoslovakia and Hungary have always been far more innovative than the Soviet Union. We all know that Rubik's cube came from the mind of a Hungarian mathematician, yet few Americans realize that the Czechs invented soft-lens contacts along with their famous machine guns. After the war, Moscow turned to these countries for help in rebuilding its heavy industry. It drained them of factories and skilled people. East Germany, in particular, was called upon to provide "reparations" in the form of the superb heavy equipment it was famous for.

Now the Soviets are using East Germany to tap the high technology of Japan. In a quiet agreement signed in the middle of 1981, a sixty-member East German delegation went to Tokyo and initialed a $3-billion trade deal. East German Communist Party chief Erich Hoenecker followed shortly after to sign. The heart of the agreement is the purchase of advanced electronic equipment from some of the biggest Japanese corporations. Toshiba and other Japanese companies will be building entire factories in East Germany, providing it with some of the most up-to-date electronics technology available. That technology, of course, will soon be heading east to Moscow.

The Soviets are also looking to Finland as a bridge to Western technology. While not nearly as tied to Moscow as the Eastern European nations, Finland's orbit of freedom is severely restricted. No premier can be elected in Finland without the Kremlin's OK. From the Finns, the Soviets are trying to arrange a massive transfer of robotics technology. The Kremlin leaders are planning to have 50,000 robots installed by the end of the decade.

This could prove to be a bonanza for the world's robot makers. To take advantage of this prospect, Unimation Inc. has just cut a deal with the biggest privately owned company in Finland, Nokia, to build a robot factory that would supply much of Scandinavia and all of Russia with the Soviets' favorite robot, the Unimate. Unimation also has a license tie-up with Japan's Kawasaki Heavy Industries, which has been building the Unimates for years. In fact, about ninety of the robots have found their way to the Soviet Union already. But with Nokia, the Soviets may be able to import hundreds every year. Right now, Washington does not prohibit robots from being exported to the Communist bloc, but with Washington trying to tighten up technology transfers, it is only a matter of time. With the Finns and the Japanese supplying the machines, Moscow will be able to circumvent any prohibition placed on Unimation by Washington.

•

THE THREE SOVIET ECONOMIES

The current technology revolution is already tearing the Soviet economy apart. There are really three economies existing in the Soviet Union—the military, the civilian and the black, or underground, economy. Sometimes they intermingle synergistically, but most often they act as parasites on one another.

Most State Department and CIA estimates put the portion of the Soviet economy churning out goods for the military at about 12 to 15 percent of the country's gross national product. That compares to about 5 to 6 percent for the United States. The Rand Corporation, however, puts the figure much higher; it believes the military absorbs nearly 40 percent of all industrial output. This military sector of the Soviet economy works very well compared with the rest of the country. It has first call on all supplies in the country, first call on skilled workers and engineers, first call on transportation. High-quality items are produced on schedule. Planes pour out of the Ulanovsk aircraft factory, submarines slide out of their drydocks at the Severnodvinsk shipyard, and tanks move down the assembly lines at plants throughout the nation.

According to intelligence sources in Washington, the manufacturing capacity of the Soviet military sector increased by some 80 percent during the 1960s and 1970s. At the same time, of course, American capacity shrank tremendously after the Vietnam War debacle. New Soviet factories specifically designed to build more tanks and armored personnel carriers, a new B-1 type of bomber and other long-range military aircraft, strategic ICBMs and dozens of smaller missiles and new high-performance jet planes are still being built. Shipyards are being expanded to build new submarines and a new generation of aircraft carriers.

The surge in military spending is taking place when the entire economy is slowing down dramatically. It is doubtful that the Soviet Union will have more than 1 to 2 percent economic growth for the rest of the 1980s—compared to 6 percent a decade ago. Already the civilian economy is feeling the rival claims of the military sector, and it will get a lot worse. In fact, 1981 marked the first time since the Communists took over that the government was not able to live up to its promise of increasing the people's standard of living. It was a fateful year, and its significance was not lost on the men inhabiting the Kremlin. It partly explains their desperate need to import enormous amounts of grain from the United States, Argentina and Canada. It explains why leaders who know they must import billions of dollars' worth of Western technology every year are willing to part with precious foreign exchange to buy something that will be quickly consumed with no lasting effect on the economy. It is basically ransom money—with the Kremlin leaders paying the masses of the Soviet Union in bread and meat.

•

CIVILIAN ECONOMY: GUNS OVER BUTTER

Despite huge expenditures for that meat and bread, the standard of living in the Soviet Union is now declining. Since the late 1970s, while housing, clothing and other consumer items have increased in terms of quantity and availability, supplies of food, which eats up half to three quarters of the household budget, have actually fallen by about 10 percent. Meat rationing in provincial cities is now common, and milk and butter often disappear for weeks on end. In fact, at "insider" meetings held secretly for party members, Kremlin leaders are now passing the word that things will be getting worse, not better, in the years ahead. Moscow is now officially predicting sharply lower growth of 3 percent for the current Eleventh Five-Year Plan (1981–1985). That probably means 1 to 2 percent real growth, given the history of past forecasts. And the blame is being put at the feet of the Americans, who are increasing their military spending dramatically, provoking an economic war with the Soviet Union.

But Moscow will be hard put convincing its people that foreigners are the sole cause of its economic malaise. The factories are full of alienated workers who spend more time drinking and loafing than assembling manufactured goods. Moscow likes to blame the terrible losses of the Second World War for a lack of manpower, but the truth is that with 135 million people in the work force, sufficient labor exists to do all the work if productivity were at Western levels. Increasingly, people hate working for the state. They much prefer working in the growing underground economy, where they can get paid in valuable goods not found in the stores. A huge percentage of the work force actually works "off the books" in the Soviet Union. In fact, the Soviets have semilegitimized it through the *shabashnaya rabote* ("work on the sabbath" system), in which groups of Soviet workers band together and hire themselves out as construction crews. The crew gets 1,000 to 1,200 rubles a month—about three times the average worker's salary—and works eighteen hours a day for seven days a week until the job is done. The *shabashniks* usually moonlight from their regular jobs and get that salary as well as the unofficial pay from the project manager. That manager, however, gets people who are willing to work.

For those people who don't hire themselves out for construction, there is another activity they can indulge in—drinking. Three billion liters (800 million gallons) of hard liquor are produced by the state annually in the Soviet Union. The underground economy offers another three billion liters of cheap Samogon vodka. So pervasive is drinking in the Soviet Union that some United States estimates put the number of deaths related to alcohol at 15.9 per 100,000 of population in 1976. This figure is completely outside the range of similar statistics for the West. In America, the comparative figure for that year was 0.18 per 100,000.

Compared to the agricultural sector of the Soviet economy, even the industrial sector works like a dream. The country is now in the middle of the fourth bad harvest in five years. Moscow has bought more than 40 million metric tons of grain in recent months—a record. At closed meetings in early 1982, party members admitted that production would hit only 160 million tons for that year, an enormous 70 million tons below target. In fact, so needy are the Soviets that they are once again the best foreign customers for America's grain exports. And if current projections are correct, they will remain so for the rest of the century. At the 26th Congress on May 24, 1981, Brezhnev announced his long-awaited Special Food Program, the work of thirty-nine planning agencies over a year and a half. The new plan will spend an incredible $230 billion on agriculture during this decade, increasing its share of all investment in the nation from 27 to 33 percent, a mammoth sum given the present strains on the economy. Despite the additional money, however, nothing was done to solve agriculture's two biggest problems: distant Communist Party managers telling collective farmers what to grow and the state subsidizing of inefficient collectives. Brezhnev merely created a new layer of bureaucracy, the Agro-industrial Commissions, to carry out his orders. In the first half of 1982, Soviet grain imports were running at their highest level in history—190,000 tons a day.

•

UNDERGROUND ECONOMY

It is impossible to calculate how big any underground economy is for any society. Many people in the IRS believe that as much as 10 percent of the American GNP is "off the books," with people exchanging services and goods for cash or even barter. Italy's may reach 15 percent. But the Soviet Union's "black" economy is probably the biggest in the industrial world. Some estimates go as high as 20 percent of the $1.06 trillion net national product.

The Soviet underground economy is very different from the American or Italian. People are not trying to hide from taxes in Russia. They are trying to obtain goods and services unavailable in the official civilian economy. The most important are services. For example, while medical care is free in Russia, the wait to get into a hospital is often weeks and the quality of the treatment is mediocre. To get into a prestigious cancer research hospital where the care is relatively good, that person has to offer, as a "gift," goods available only at a hard-currency store that is open to foreigners. Without the gift, there is no way to get into the hospital.

Housing is another problem in the Soviet Union. While great strides have been made in recent years in building huge new blocks of housing around Moscow, moving into them is normally a shocking experience. Instead of a finished apartment, families find pipes that lead nowhere, unpainted walls, floors that are crooked, doors that won't close and toilets that won't flush. At the same time construction crews are always found around newly opened apartment buildings. They are into an interior finishing scam. For several hundred rubles, they offer the family "help" with the pipes, floors, etcetera. All the work that should have been done on state time is now done off the books for cash.

If it is goods rather than services that people want, they go to the *Tolkuchka*s, the semilegal outdoor markets found on the rims of all major Soviet cities. There buyers and sellers hang out, bargaining in whispers over Italian shoes, tasty sausages, books and the most sought-after consumer item in all of the Soviet Union—a used car. Under the gaze of Interior Ministry's agents, who keep the trading and selling down to a certain level, people clinch their deals orally and move off to meet later at a designated rendezvous point. Of course, meat and moonshine are sold everywhere in the cities, not just at the outdoor markets.

The civilian sector of industry could not survive without the underground economy. The inflexibility of the party would strangle all economic activity if factory managers did not cheat. In Kursk, for example, a calculator factory also quietly turns out spare auto parts. Factories regularly build up unofficial inventories of items to trade with other factories. A whole network of middlemen has grown up in the country, many of whom are paid in dollars and diamonds. Without the invisible, underground economy, people would not be able to get their consumer goods, and managers would not be able to get their parts. For that reason Moscow tolerates it. But it is corruption, and the Soviet people know it.

•

THE OPEC MIRAGE

For a time, in the 1970s, the decline of the Soviet economy was hidden, paradoxically by OPEC. Moscow quite unexpectedly found itself benefiting from the actions of a few Arabs who pulled off one of the greatest wealth heists of all history—pushing the price of oil up from $2.10 to $34 a barrel in seven years. While most Americans know about the fabulous oil flowing out of the Middle East, few realize that the Soviet Union is the largest producer of oil in the world—bigger than even Saudi Arabia. It is also the second-largest exporter of that liquid energy.

As oil prices soared, so did Moscow's revenues. As inflation was triggered off in the West by the rising energy prices, Moscow also saw its traditional exports of gold, diamonds and furs jump in value. After South Africa, the Soviet Union is the biggest producer of gold and diamonds, and when gold exploded from $34 an ounce to $875 in 1980, while diamonds tripled in price, money poured into the Kremlin's coffers. In the 1970s, OPEC did as much to make the Communists rich as it did to make the sheiks wealthy.

As cash flowed in, so did massive Western bank loans. By 1980, some $80 billion of credit had been extended to the Eastern bloc, with the Soviets taking some $12 billion and the Eastern Europeans taking the rest. Poland, of course, wound up with a massive $20 billion IOU to the likes of Manufacturers Hanover Bank, Chase, Germany's Dresdner Bank and dozens of others. After all, these "prudent" bankers argued, Poland has lots of coal for export and Moscow promises to act as an umbrella over all its satellite loans, guaranteeing them. What is the risk?

The oil, gold and diamond riches plus the Western credits allowed the Soviet Union, Hungary, Poland, Rumania and Czechoslovakia to import huge amounts of Western technology. A virtual flood of chemical plants, textile factories, steel mills, even automobile factories, was sent east from Germany, Italy, France, Britain and Japan.

But while the higher prices of oil brought huge amounts of cash and loans to the Communist bloc, it also began undermining the very same industrial base they were trying to build. As in the West, the OPEC price hikes forced a massive shift from cheap to expensive energy throughout the world economy. That made even the most modern steel complexes that were shipped to the East obsolete before they were uncrated. In addition, most of the hundreds of factories sold to the East were supposed to be paid for by reexport of their manufactured products. But when the OPEC oil shocks hit the Western economies, the expected market for those goods evaporated. The new, modern industrial base in the East, built on the riches of oil and the credits of Western bankers, was suddenly transformed into an ancient relic of the past to take its place along with the steel factories of Germany's Ruhr valley and even the glistening new plants in America's South.

Until 1980, the cash flow into the Soviet Union hid the corrosion of the country's industrial heartland. Moscow passed big subsidies on to its satellites by selling them oil at a 40 percent discount. The impact of rising energy prices was delayed for years. Then the bottom fell out. In 1982, energy prices began sagging. Gold prices plummeted. Diamond prices dropped sharply. OPEC began to fade as a powerful cartel. It became clear that oil prices would stay in the $25-to-$34-a-barrel range for the rest of the decade as demand fell and supplies surged. This high energy-price level was enough to make the old heavy industries based on cheap energy obsolete and bring on the new technological revolution of robotics, bioengineering and telecommunications. But it was not enough to shield the Soviet economy anymore. Without constantly rising revenues from exports of oil, the economy began to run itself into the ground.

By 1981, growth had declined to a mere 1.5 percent. The Polish crisis, another bad harvest, the never-ending need to import Western technology, and the sudden conversion of liberal bankers to a "born again" conservatism led to a dramatic financial squeeze on Moscow. For the first time since World War II, the Soviets began dumping huge amounts of oil, gold, diamonds—everything they could sell. Quite suddenly, the props of oil and precious metals were removed and the Soviet and Eastern European economies were hit as the true impact of the fifteenfold jump in oil prices raged through their heavy industries—industries that were built on cheap energy.

Just at this time, Soviet oil production began to peak out at twelve million barrels a day. Estimates from the CIA now show a steady deterioration of Soviet production, especially from the shallow fields in Europe. From now on, gas will begin replacing oil as the major energy source for the Soviets, gas that comes from far-away Siberia, expensive gas that must be exported to Western Europe in order to generate hard currency for technology imports.

The OPEC price hikes took more time to wash through the Soviet heavy-industry economy than through Europe, the United States and Japan. But now they are drilling directly through the massive, centralized economy as quickly, and as devastatingly, as a laser beam through butter. The oil-price hikes will leave the Soviet economy in ruins, light-years behind the Japanese and the Americans, decades behind the Western Europeans. The strain is already loosening the bonds that tie the multiethnic Soviet system together, and it is increasing tensions between the captive Eastern European nations and Moscow. As the Soviets fall further behind the West, as their military parity begins to shrink once again in the face of new electronic warfare weapons, the Kremlin's leaders will be forced to choose between decentralization of the empire or armed might. Centrifugal forces, unleashed by the same technological revolution that is sweeping the West, are threatening to redraw the red map of Communism as well.

5

DEINDUSTRIALIZATION OF THE THIRD WORLD

•

FOR THE PAST FORTY YEARS, THE COUNTRIES OF LATIN AMERica, Asia and Africa have been struggling to dig themselves out of the deep pit of poverty. The tactics have varied from country to country, some emphasizing the free-market approach, while others went in for more centralized, socialist policies. Aided and abetted by the "development set" professionals in the World Bank, the IMF or the United Nations, they have all, despite their different political colorations, attempted to use one basic strategy—industrialization.

Countries as diverse as Zaire and Pakistan, Ghana and the Philippines all agreed that the way to modernize, the way to join the club of advanced Western nations, the way to become just as powerful as their former colonial rulers, was to build big steel plants, huge dams, massive aluminum complexes, vast car-assembly lines. If they were lucky and, like Venezuela or Indonesia, had oil, they threw up gargantuan petrochemical "crackers" to refine their crude.

Just as important, the Third World opened up its borders to the multinational corporations in hopes of building an industrial base. Assembly lines were set up everywhere, employing millions to put together industrial products that were then exported back to the West.

Tens of billions of dollars flowed out of Europe, America and Japan to finance these industrial projects. To be sure, a huge amount of money was wasted, with billions going into arms. And dictators such as Idi Amin spent more of their time killing off rivals and a good chunk of the population than on raising standards of living. Yet, these madmen were the exception. By the end of the 1970s, the dominant image of most of the Third World was a huge, smoking steel factory rising out of the rice paddies of some peasant country, towering, like a modern colossus, over the people kneeling in the mud below.

These factories were the hope of the future. And the future became mortgaged to them. By 1982 the Third World had borrowed enormous sums totaling $600 billion to pay for these industrial behemoths. Governments taxed their people to pay for them, sacrificed to buy them, bribed to get them. Whole villages were wiped out to make way for dams, tribes were decimated to clear land for mines—all in the hope that these factories would take the poor into the promised land of modernity and wealth.*

•

"CONCORDES" OF THE THIRD WORLD

But like so many promises, this one is turning sour. The technological revolution now sweeping the West in the post-

* It wasn't only the Perus or Thailands or Nigerias that pinned their hopes on heavy industrialization. The very same strategy used in Asia, Latin America and Africa over the past decades was also applied in Alabama, Mississippi, Tennessee and Arkansas. The American Southeast underwent the same deluge of heavy-industry building as countries in the Third World. Huge steel factories, auto-parts plants and assembly lines were built. And the same hopes for wealth and modernity expressed in Bangkok or Lima were voiced in Birmingham and Atlanta.

OPEC era is about to hit the Third World as well. Nations that have spent the past forty years struggling to move away from their agricultural roots into the industrial era will suddenly find that the world has already moved on. After going into hock to the international banks, after exacting huge taxes from their people to import sophisticated plants and equipment, developing countries will soon be left with the most modern factories in the world that produce goods that no one wants.

The gigantic multibillion-dollar steel complexes of India and Pakistan are about to become monuments to obsolescence. It is perhaps one of the cruelest ironies of late-twentieth-century life that the Arabs, seeking to redress what they saw as centuries of humiliation inflicted by the West, rammed through gigantic oil-price hikes directed at the United States, Europe and Japan. Yet some of the hardest-hit victims turned out to be their Third World brothers. OPEC raised the international debts of these countries by incredible amounts during the 1970s, as they scurried to borrow money to pay for higher oil-import bills. And in the end, it made all their efforts at building modern industrial societies futile. As the developing countries struggled to get right up to the edge of the Industrial Age, they discovered that it was already being superseded by the Age of Silicon.

Already mass layoffs are spreading like a plague throughout the Third World. As Japan and the United States move to automate their factories by installing robots and other advanced machinery, they are increasing the efficiency of their domestic operations tremendously. In fact, so productive are their new assembly lines that now, in a growing number of cases, it costs the same to produce at home as abroad.

For decades American and Japanese corporations went to Asia and Latin America in search of cheap labor. First automobiles, then textiles, and finally electronics facilities were shipped abroad to take advantage of low wages. The multinationals created millions of jobs in their assembly plants, most of them semiskilled. The widespread unemployment so prevalent in these countries was, to a major degree, sopped up by these foreign operations.

Paradoxically, electronics has turned out to be an extremely labor-intensive industry. In Malaysia alone, 100,000 people work in the electronics industry, assembling semiconductor chips and other high-tech products. Twenty-four factories make electronics assembly the second-largest employer in the entire country. In the Philippines, 20,000 people work in the industry, and electronics exports are the biggest earner of foreign exchange after traditional commodities such as sugar and coconut. In Mexico, the across-the-border manufacturing zone employs close to a half million people who work in plants putting together items that are then sent back to the United States or elsewhere.

In fact, nearly all of the goods produced in the overseas factories are made not for the local market but for export. Nearly all of these factories operate twenty-four hours a day, six days a week, with three shifts of workers.

By the early 1980s, this began to change. Japan started closing down dozens of overseas plants assembling its semiconductors and electronic products. Hitachi, Fujitsu and other companies began to bring production home to new, robot-run factories. U.S. companies, just catching up to the Japanese automation thrust, are right behind. Signetics Corporation is cutting its 2,300-person work force in South Korea in half by 1986, when it will complete an automation program at home. Motorola and Fairchild Camera and Instrument, leaders in the semiconductor field, are already moving some of their production lines back to the United States, where computer-assisted assembly of the chips has lowered costs so much that American factories are now as competitive as Asian assembly plants.

Right now, to prevent huge political repercussions, American and Japanese companies are gradually cutting back their overseas production. Production managers of three-shift factories are laying off an entire shift, while keeping two and running at only two-thirds capacity. In Thailand and Mexico, unpaid "holidays" are becoming very common. But clearly, the crunch is just ahead. The moment the new generation of assembly robots is introduced—by mid-1985—the factories overseas will simply be closed down. Designed specifically for assembling electronics parts, these new robots are already on the scene. The Japanese are producing them. IBM is licensing hundreds from Sankyo Seiki and will sell them under its own brand name by the end of the year. Two other Japanese companies, Dainichi Kiko and Pentel, also manufacture these small assembly robots and sell to the U.S. market. As soon as these robots are put in place in domestic factories, there will be even less reason to try to tap the cheap-labor markets of Asia and Latin America. Production will be drawn back home, and a massive wave of deindustrialization will sweep through the Third World. The *superlumpenproletariat* that will emerge in the United States, Europe and elsewhere as robots and automation spread will be swelled by millions of newly unemployed in the Third World. And that includes the hundreds of thousands of people in America's own Southeast.

At the same time, developing countries will soon find that the billions they have poured into steel, petrochemical and aluminum plants to modernize their economies and make the leap into the industrial league have been wasted. The Third World has been busily creating societies built on nineteenth-century technology, the heavy industry that is no longer feasible in an era of expensive energy. Already the huge steel complexes in Venezuela and India are able to operate only by heavy government subsidies. They could never compete in a free market. These symbols of postcolonial independence and industrialization that so many developing countries built in the past two decades are nothing more now than white elephants—the Concordes of the Third World.

•

HONG KONG ATARIS

Not all the developing countries will find themselves ruined by the technological changes of the twenty-first century. Those countries able to adapt and plug into the post-OPEC economic era will do extremely well. They are certain to join the ranks of the winners. Already underway in several Third World countries is a major economic change that augurs well for their future.

In Asia and elsewhere around the world, a major split is developing between those countries with governments that passively accept the economic ravaging of their societies and those that do not. Malaysia, the Philippines, Thailand, Indonesia—all await the closing of electronics, automobile and other assembly operations with trepidation and not much else. They passively accepted the benefits of multinational corporate investment in the 1970s in terms of jobs and taxes, and they are passively awaiting their departure.

These governments did little to control the multinational giants when they entered their countries. And the multinationals, in turn, simply set up shop to exploit the cheap—often female—labor available. Given the chance, multinational corporations can easily act as marauding international predators. Without constraints, they will often prowl the world in search of low-paid workers able to assemble their products. When they invest in developing countries run by politicians who have no guiding plan for their nation, no vision of the future, no idea which technologies and which industries are needed to get there, multinationals will go for the cheapest setup possible. In countries where politicians have such a vision and where governments actively pressure high-tech multinationals to share technology and upgrade their operations, the corporations play a very different game, with much more of the benefit accruing to the local people.

In Asia, the "Four Tigers" of Hong Kong, Taiwan, South

Korea and Singapore believe that the future is in their own hands. It is no accident that Atari home video games are now being assembled in Hong Kong. It is even no accident that pirated imitations of Apple computers are being put together in Taiwan. Just a few years ago, Taiwan was infamous for its counterfeiting of jeans, records and books. Now, the great copycat of the East has moved on to high technology. The Four Tigers of Asia are moving aggressively to shift to a post-OPEC economic strategy. Over the past few years, they have shifted their industrial base from simple assembly of electronics components to more sophisticated products like radios, watches and TVs. Now they are upgrading once again to an even higher level of technology, moving into computers, software, and computer games. Factories in these countries are not being hit at all by the deindustrialization sweeping the Third World. If anything, employment is increasing. Soon, they will be invading America and Japan with their own computer hardware.

The most critical element in the developing countries' future is their learning that brain power is now the most important resource of any nation. Cheap labor and traditional raw materials, the two commodities that have sustained Third World economies for the past three hundred years, will no longer have the value they once had during the old heavy-industry epoch. With manufacturing about to become as cheap at home as abroad, with new materials replacing the old, developing countries that do not adapt to the new high technology will devolve into more poverty and chaos.

It is already easy to read the tea leaves for many developing countries. One look at their system of education can tell you what the future holds. If, as in India and the Philippines, an enormous university system turns out lawyers and accountants and liberal-arts majors to compete for civil-service jobs in an already bloated bureaucracy, then the prospects are poor. If, on the other hand, countries train their young people in engineering, mathematics and the sciences either at home or abroad, the chances are that they will succeed in this new post-OPEC era. It is no accident that Taiwan is building a new science-based industrial park at Hsinchu, that it employs one thousand scientists at its new Electronics Research and Service Organization and that Taiwan, with twenty thousand students, makes up the second-largest contingent of foreign students in the United States.

In fact, South and East Asian men and women constitute the biggest category of foreign students in America after a fast-shrinking population of Iranians, and most of them major in engineering, business administration, computer science and mathematics. Three hundred thousand foreigners went to study in the United States in 1981, and by the end of the decade that figure will soar to 900,000. Moreover, foreign students tend toward practical business and applied technology in their studies in America. Foreigners in general make up half the Ph.D. candidates in engineering in the United States today, as well as half the first-year doctoral candidates at the Wharton School of Business. And whereas in the 1960s and 1970s most of them remained in the United States after graduation, more and more are now returning home.

•

CHINA'S RUSH INTO THE PAST

One of the fastest-growing foreign populations in the United States is the mainland Chinese. Measured by that standard alone, China would be expected to join the ranks of the fast-growing Pacific Basin countries in the race toward the high-tech future. Indeed, China has already launched several satellites on top of its home-grown missiles and appears to have the accouterments of an advanced technological base.

In fact, however, China has little chance of catching Taiwan or Korea in the near future. India, for all its problems, is a much better bet. China's inability to stick with a single, consistent economic policy has hampered its economic growth from the beginning of the Communist takeover in 1949. Dramatic swings to the Left and the Right have left the Middle Kingdom with an entire generation of lost scientists and engineers. The Cultural Revolution aborted the education of millions of people, and an entire new generation must first be trained before any technological "great leap forward" can take place.

Just as important, Peking's current policy of opening to the West to import foreign technology and goods probably will not last for more than a few more years. Already students are being called home from their overseas study because of a rising xenophobia, a fear of Western capitalist "pollution." New students are not being sent abroad.

In addition, economic policy keeps changing. Grand schemes to build 110 giant projects to propel China forward were announced after Mao's death, but they have nearly all been abolished. Contracts signed with foreign companies were broken, although efforts were made to compensate those companies in some manner. Now the emphasis is on small, light industry. Perhaps that too will change. There is no clear vision of the future in China and no cadre of skilled people to guide the country in its efforts. In the end, this will prove to be the most important handicap to the Middle Kingdom.

•

ASIAN SILICON VALLEYS

For the students of the Four Tigers, going back home increasingly means returning to a society that values the skills and training received in the United States. In 1980, for example, the Taiwan government set up a ten-year electronics-industry development program that will provide money to develop new "made in Taiwan" high-tech products. The government is doubling its research and development expenditures between

1980 and 1984, and by the end of the decade the amount could total $325 million, 3 percent of total production value in the country.

It is also emphasizing quality in its products. Taiwan today is at the same stage as Japan back in the 1950s. At that time, Japanese goods were considered cheap and tacky in America and around the world. They fell apart much as made-in-Taiwan umbrellas collapse today. In electronics, that can be the kiss of death. Quality is more important than even price in many electronic components, and Taiwan must change the way it works before it will be able to break into the twenty-first century.

Still, much progress is already being made. Private enterprise is getting very interested in high technology because it realizes that future profits can lie only in that area. The giant Tatung Company, which now makes TVs and other consumer electronics, is entering the field of semiconductors and computers. Tatung and other Taiwanese companies are setting up engineering laboratories in the United States to develop new products, and it is going to bring out its own minicomputer by 1984. Tatung is setting up its scientific facilities in the United States not only to tap skilled native talent, but also to hire Taiwanese engineers who have remained in America after their schooling.

The chase after highly skilled engineers and scientists is a global one; there are simply not enough to go around in this period of rapid technology change. Ironically, while foreign companies are flooding into the United States to get at its pool of skilled people, U.S. corporations are going overseas for talent. That includes the developing countries as well. While Tatung invades America, U.S. high-tech companies are going to Taiwan to hire needed engineers. Texas Instruments, Motorola and Wang Laboratories (founded in Massachusetts by An Wang, called "the doctor" by his employees, a mainland Chinese who got his Ph.D. in physics from Harvard and went on to produce the first commercial word processor in the world) have all set up shop on the island. Even Matsushita Electric is there, making use of the local talent.

More than ever, local talent around the world is moving out on its own to set up domestic companies capable of taking on the high-tech heavies of America and Japan. Small electronics companies are blossoming all over Taiwan, with names like Multitech International or MicroTek International. Multitech was founded in 1976 by several engineers. It has designed a "Dragon" Chinese-language computer that is selling well in Taiwan and could boom in China in years to come. The company plans to start producing English-language terminals soon and enter the exploding U.S. market.

Singapore, as always, is moving faster and further than any other developing country in making the shift from nineteenth-century to twenty-first-century technology. It had the foresight back in 1979 to see where the global economy was moving and put in motion a New Economic Policy aimed at getting the island totally out of labor-intensive, low-wage businesses into high-tech industries. Interestingly enough, Singapore's main policy weapon in this strategy was to raise wages sharply, by 20 percent a year for three years, to price its labor supply totally out of the market for assembling cheap electronic components or textiles. For a time, Singapore appeared to have stumbled badly. Inflation rose from 4 percent in 1979 to 10 percent two years later. Productivity dropped sharply. Factories closed. But by 1982, investment in new industries was soaring, and a growing number of people were working on computers and complex aerospace parts. A National Computer Board was set up in 1981 to develop the city-state's exports of computer software. It is headed by Philip Yeo, who is also permanent secretary at the Ministry of Defense. A wholesale shift in the economy is underway as Singapore tears itself away from the old global economy based on heavy industry and joins the new international economy based on high technology.

Another country that looks like a sure winner is Israel. Sitting somewhere on the spectrum between developing and developed, perhaps right next to Singapore, Israel has a future that clearly lies in high technology. The country's Weizmann Institute produces first-rate scientists and engineers. Israel is a leader in biotechnology and electronics, especially military electronics. This will expand as the country takes advantage of its recent triumph over the Syrians in taking out their Soviet-made SAM missiles through electronic warfare. Demand for these electronic systems is soaring, and the Israelis now have a major edge. In addition, such companies as Elscint are big names in the United States with their CAT scanners, and new firms such as Interpharm are in the race to produce the first commercial products using the new biotechnology.

Just as important, U.S. companies are pouring into Israel to tap its mental resources and the available government subsidies and research grants. Intel, Motorola, Control Data and National Semiconductor all have research facilities there. National Semiconductor is using fifty Israeli engineers to develop its new 32-bit microprocessor. The large number of scientists and engineers, the burgeoning number of local and foreign companies, the close ties between government and business, and even the climate, make Israel something of a Silicon Valley in the Negev.

•

BRAZIL TRIES THE FRENCH GAMBIT

Another way some developing countries may escape from sinking into the pit of deindustrial despair is to try the French formula—trading market access to a closed economy for access to technology. This option is open only to those big Third World countries where a large consumer base already exists, a consumer base that can provide the profits necessary to entice the multinationals to part with their technology. A

Zaire, a Colombia, even a Nigeria probably would not be able to use this gambit.

To play this game it is essential for Third World countries to be able to close off their economies to the multinationals. Many cannot, because they are too dependent on industrial markets for their goods or because their government is so corrupt that any effort to deny access fails. Both these types of countries have "porous" economies, out of control of the leaders.

But the French formula could work for others. Already Brazil and Korea have found the power to force major concessions from foreign corporations in exchange for access to their medium-size markets. Brazil in particular is in a good position, because it is building one of the Third World's largest military-industrial complexes and that market for electronics, aerospace and other high-technology goods is especially appealing. Moreover, Brazil is spending billions to upgrade its telecommunications grid. Like France, Brazil can therefore offer to hungry foreign corporations two major electronics markets—the military and the PTT (post office, telephone and telegraph authority). Both are very big, multibillion-dollar markets, and both are government controlled, allowing Brazil to offer specific market segments and guaranteed profits to foreign multinationals—if they play the game by trading technology.

So anxious are foreign companies to get into the market that in mid-1982, several agreed to launch Brazil's first telecommunications satellite and accept local merchandise—not hard currency—as payment for the contracts. The contracts were signed even before the negotiators came up with a list of Brazilian goods that were to be exported. A consortium of Hughes Aircraft and Spars of Canada are going to build the drum-shaped satellite along with a spare, while the French-led Arianspace is going to launch it from Cheyenne, Guyana, aboard an Ariane rocket. The Spars-Hughes group got the contract because it offered the lowest bid. Moreover, by teaming up with the Canadians, Hughes was able to tap into the cheap subsidized credit that Ottawa offers on its exports—a lot better than what the United States offers. The French, for their part, were able to undercut NASA's shuttle by $3 million. As part of the package, an exchange is going to be arranged by the Western companies and Embratel, the Brazilian telecommunications company. Embratel already makes one of the world's best-selling twenty-seat commuter airplanes that many small U.S. airlines have bought, and it may trade these planes for the satellites.

Mexico too is making progress in pressuring foreign companies to part with their technology. But its future is far more clouded than Brazil's, despite its petrodollars. Fueled by the oil boom, Mexico has a large middle class with lots of money to spend. Yet it does not have any ambitions for building a modern military, its communications facilities are primitive by today's standards, with no plan to upgrade them, and its income is leveling off as oil prices soften. Moreover, Mexico has yet to show that it has a strong political bureaucracy with enough vision of the future to take the nation forward. A flood of petrodollars floated Mexico through a decade of incredible corruption and mismanagement. So much money was available, however, that high economic growth was possible even though billions were being siphoned off and sent abroad by the elite. But with the country forced to the brink of bankruptcy in 1982, the easy days are over. The next two or three years will reveal whether Mexico has the political will to break into the twenty-first century.

For the moment, U.S. computer companies, among others, believe there is a big enough market to warrant their trading some technology for access. There are 16,000 computers installed in Mexico, and the amount has been growing by about 20 percent every year. In April 1982, Mexico City decided to tighten quotas on computer imports as a way of pressuring American companies to increase their use of local producers. Before the door slams completely shut, dozens of U.S. computer manufacturers are rushing south to set up factories. IBM, with nearly half the Mexican computer market, has submitted plans for production. And Hewlett-Packard was allowed 100 percent ownership rights for its new plant in Guadalajara in exchange for promises to buy a large portion of Mexican-made electronic components.

But this may prove to be a major problem. There aren't any local companies in Mexico making integrated circuits or other electronic components. For the moment, Hewlett-Packard and others will have to buy simple items such as sheet metal and plastics for the casings. In the end, though, U.S. multinationals may have to tutor Mexicans in their own production before they can buy significant amounts of high-tech products from them.

Another problem is that there are very few private Mexican companies available as partners for U.S. corporations. The decline of the oil price and the devaluation of the peso has gutted the only strong private conglomerate south of the border, the Monterrey-based Alfa Group. It had to request a moratorium on a whopping $2 billion in foreign debt in May 1982, most of it owed to American banks. There are only a handful of other private companies in the country. However, Mexico City is still insisting that foreign manufacturers of personal computers take on local partners—even if they don't exist.

•

THE COMING NORTH-SOUTH TECH WARS

There are some kinds of technology that Third World countries will not be able to buy at any price, and it is not the super-most-advanced stuff either. When Third World nations threaten to use imported technology to kill off major industries in the West, they will suddenly find themselves locked out of the laboratory. Furious threats, quotas, tariffs—none of them will end the high-tech embargo.

In the end, it will be up to the people of the Third World, and no one else, to make the last great leap into the twenty-first century. Japan, the United States and Europe will only bring them to the brink. They will not suicidally create competition for their corporations and threaten their own people's jobs by exporting all their technology. Brazilian, Taiwanese, Korean and Singaporean engineers and scientists will have to take the final step into the future, because a high-tech embargo of the most advanced technology will prevent them from doing it any other way.

This is no nightmare of the distant future. It is happening today in South Korea, and it is already creating tremendous economic problems and political tensions.

No one is more aware of the potential of a technology embargo by the advanced nations than Byung-Chull Lee, the chairman of the board of the Samsung Group of industries in South Korea. Mr. Lee is one of the great industrial pioneers of our time. Along with such men as Chung Ju Yung, chairman of the $10-billion Hyundai Group, he is a living Asian reminder of the men of America's past, Cornelius Vanderbilt, John D. Rockefeller, Andrew Mellon—the robber barons who built America in the late nineteenth and early twentieth centuries. In this country, we are already down to the third and fourth generations of the founding fathers of our economy. Their corporate dynasties for the most part are run by managers, bland men in gray, who are caretakers of the industrial empires built by men of vision and force. In South Korea, the originals are still alive, their sons are still in the wings, and their grandsons are still in school.

Lee is one of these men. He is ancient now, nearly eighty. His small body is well into the shrinking stage of old age. He no longer has the square, muscular bulk of Korean men. His skin is pulled taut around his face, his teeth are machine-made and he sucks in air through the side of his mouth in big gulps, as if he were connected to some oxygen source that was on the verge of being taken away.

But there is a fierceness about Lee, an inner toughness that emanates from the man. The people around him, the translator, the adviser, tower over Lee physically but orbit him, keeping a prescribed distance. His direct look into a man's eyes, his set face, his determined patience and, above all, his flashes of fury tell much of how he came to build one of the great industrial empires of Asia. Samsung is one of four gigantic Korean *zaibatsu*, or conglomerates, that dominate the entire economy much as the Japanese *zaibatsu* control Japan. The company alone accounts for 8 percent of the nation's entire GNP. Samsung is heavily into steel, textiles, TVs and other consumer electronics. It is also one of Korea's largest shipbuilders.

About a decade ago, the government in Seoul decided to make shipbuilding a major South Korean industry and Samsung linked up with the Japanese to build several enormous drydocks. At the time, Japan was the largest shipbuilder in the world and the most advanced. The Japanese wanted the huge profits from the Korean business, and they signed the deal. By the late 1970s, Korea was one of the three biggest makers of supertankers, container ships and other vessels in the world. But the country's low wages and high quality began to threaten Japan, which saw its own orders shrinking. Samsung was one of the Korean companies taking away business.

The Japanese counterattacked by automating their shipyards. They started putting in computer-controlled manufacturing processes. They invented robots that did much of the welding. By 1982 they were back in business. Japan could once again build cheaper ships than Korea.

To remain competitive, the Koreans needed the new Japanese shipbuilding technology. Samsung and others went to Tokyo to buy it. And, for the first time, they were refused. No amount of money offered was enough. Money was no longer the point. The Japanese simply said no.

On the winter morning that I met Mr. Lee for breakfast in

his hotel suite, this information was very much on my mind. The technology embargo had not made any of the newspapers or magazines. It is something that people don't talk about publicly in the business world. I had heard about it from a Japanese government official who was bemoaning the fact that Japan was in so much difficulty because of the growing competition from the Third World, especially from Taiwan, Hong Kong, Singapore and South Korea. His comment was by way of saying that "you Americans are asking too much of us. Look at all our troubles." His attitude was all too familiar, even his use of the term "in difficulty" to describe Japan was all too common. But his comment on withholding technology stuck in my mind. It was an opening shot in a much greater economic conflict. Perhaps the greatest fight of the next two decades.

I remembered the Japanese remark at the breakfast with Mr. Lee. The table before us held tea and coffee cups, some rolls and a huge bottle of Chivas Regal, an Asian symbol of wealth and well-being. Mr. Lee was dressed in a conservative blue, pencil-striped suit that fit him perfectly. He was no imitator of the Japanese businessmen of the 1960s with their ill-fitting black suits and too-wide ties. Lee looked as good as any Wall Street investment banker.

Lee, the son of a wealthy landowner, was born during the time when Korea was a colony of Japan. He received a traditional Confucian education in Korea and went to the prestigious Waseda University in Japan. Only a handful of other Koreans were allowed into Japan at that time, and Tokyo hoped they would make loyal colonial servants.

We talked politics for some time, first of Washington and Reagan, then of Seoul and General Chun. He liked Reagan, of course, and defended the General, who had recently come to power in Seoul following the murder of President Park Chung Hee. After each of my remarks, Lee's translator would talk to him in Korean. He would then reply, and then the translator would speak to me in English. That pattern of conversation went on for a short time. Then I said: "I have heard that the Japanese are cutting off Korea from technology, especially in shipbuilding, because they are afraid of the competition. Is that true?" This time Lee did not wait for the translator to finish my comment. After the first pause in the translator's speech, he exploded in a furious diatribe. "It is more than just rumor. The Japanese are unfairly stopping the export of technology to us. We are turning to the Europeans and Americans for technology. We have an agreement with a European company for technology. We are looking for an American company." Lee's hand chopped the air as he spoke, slicing the Japanese with each breath. The man could barely contain himself in his seat. And in the end, as a final, vicious cut, he said: "The Japanese have a very superficial economy. They must import everything they export. If Japan is excluded from the world trading nations, they will go from number one to number ten!"

Lee is trying to move the Samsung Group into the future through high technology, and the Japanese action threatens to stop him—and Korea—cold. Millions are being poured into semiconductors and advanced electronics at Samsung, and its founder hopes to place the company in the ranks of world-class high-technology corporations before he dies. He wants Samsung to be among the General Electrics and the Hitachis of the world. He has the vision needed to guide his creation and his country to the future, but the Japanese high-tech embargo threatens to undercut the entire strategy.

Indeed, any high-tech embargo could easily crush Korea's ability to successfully make it into the twenty-first century. Seoul has an ambitious five-year research and development plan that is expected to move the country into semiconductors, personal computers, telecommunications, computer-controlled machine tools and optic fibers. The government is putting heavy emphasis on local design and engineering for the future. But the next decade is crucial. Linking up with foreign companies to gain access to technology is absolutely required for the immediate years ahead. Samsung is already in the lead in many of these fields. It has an agreement with Corning Glass for optic fibers and a Samsung–Corning Glass company already exists. Yet, the high-tech products on which Korea is betting its future are the very same products that Japan and the United States are hoping will carry them into the twenty-first century. Convincing them to part with their technology will be one of the hardest tasks of any Korean government. And any decision to limit Korea's technology access will prevent the nation from ever digging out of its "Third World" status.

•

THE LAW OF THE SEA

The same simple issue of technology transfer and the obsolescence of products is behind the incredibly complex negotiation surrounding the now infamous Law of the Sea Treaty. Countries that have built their entire future on the export of certain commodities fear that in the years ahead industrial demand for them will plummet, sending prices falling and their own economies reeling. Some of these commodities will simply cease being needed as the world's economic base shifts into its twenty-first-century high-tech mode. The American, Japanese and European corporations that once relied on many of these items are making new products that just don't use them. Copper, of course, is the best example. Whereas copper was critical for wiring everything from traditional telephone lines to new computers, optic fibers are now much more efficient and cheaper. And optic fibers, like semiconductor chips, are basically made out of sand! The economies of Chile and Zambia, however, are based on copper exports. Another example: when American cars were enormous gas-guzzling giants weighing many tons, it took several tons of iron, a huge amount of coal and thousands of barrels of oil to make one. Now that autos are barely half their old size, only about half the raw materials are needed to make them. By the end of the decade, cheap, lightweight ceramic engines will be running most of our machines on the road. And like optic fibers, ceramics are really refined sands and clays, the stuff pots are made of. What will the major exporters of the commodities needed by nineteenth-century industries do then? Who remembers the Spice Islands and their pepper exports to Portugal, the West Indies and their sugar exports to France and Britain, indeed the American South and its cotton exports to Britain?

This past is not a distant memory for the Third World leaders. Many of them remember how the rise and fall of earlier commodity prices devastated their nations. Brazil's incredibly poor Northeast was a prosperous region decades ago, when it exported huge amounts of sugar to Europe. Egypt remembers the days when it was one of the great cotton exporters of the world.

This is why the Third World is trying so desperately to pass the Law of the Sea legislation—they are frantic that new deep-sea mining technology will soon open up huge new underwater mineral fields that will flood the market and send prices for their own exports plummeting. They are afraid that the little control they now have over certain raw materials valued by the industrialized nations will slip away to the technologically superior multinationals of America, Japan and Europe.

The potential riches of the sea are indeed stupendous—trillions of dollars' worth of copper, cobalt, manganese, zinc, nickel and other minerals clumped together in potato-shaped nodules, thousands of feet beneath the Pacific. Many of them are strategic minerals that the United States now must import from often hostile nations—minerals that will have an even greater importance as America changes its industrial base in the years ahead.

For nearly a decade now, negotiation has been dragging on in the United Nations over how the oceans' riches should be divided up. Talks have produced an incredibly complex treaty that covers everything from rights of passage for naval ships through narrow straits to offshore energy and fishing rights. And it specifically deals with underwater mineral rights—who shall control them, who shall price them and who shall mine them.

The final draft of the Law of the Sea Treaty calls for the creation of an OPEC-like cartel called the International Seabed Authority (ISA), run by the UN, to oversee all the exploration and mining of the sea. Controlled by the Third World, which would have a majority vote on the ISA, it would fix production and therefore prices. The goal, of course, would be to prevent prices from falling below present levels and to raise them as much as possible by curbing mineral supplies. The treaty would force U.S. companies, the most technologically advanced in deep-sea mining, to sell their technology to the UN cartel in exchange for permission to mine the seabed sites.

The strategy of the South is not unlike the French gambit—close off a rich market to foreign multinationals and then trade access for technology. The French, of course, are trading their rich domestic markets in military electronics and telecommunications for foreign technology. But in this case, Third World countries are trying to exchange a potentially rich resource base, the seabed, for technology. In addition, they are trying to limit exploitation of that resource base to protect their own mineral industries.

The first step in this strategy is to somehow control the resource base, the seabed. In a way, the Third World nations are trying to use legal means to define the new underwater frontier as "theirs." Nothing like it has ever taken place. In the past, frontiers belonged to the people who discovered them and exploited them. With the oceans, the Third World is trying to prevent that. To accomplish their goal, developing countries are trying to gain acceptance of the principle that the seabed minerals belong to the "common heritage of mankind," and the UN is the guardian of that patrimony. Profits from deep-sea mining, under the Law of the Sea Treaty, are supposed to be divided among all countries, not just the individual consortiums that have the technology to exploit the fields.

The Third World's strategy on seabed minerals has much in common with its efforts to create a new information order to control information flow. The same players and the same dynamics are at work. The transfer of advanced telecommunications technology in exchange for access to domestic data flow is the principle behind that effort. The United Nations, once again, is the arena for the push by the Third World. And the United States is, again, opposed to regulating the freedom of private interests.

On April 30, 1982, the Law of the Sea Treaty finally came up for a vote, and the United States rejected it, along with three other countries—Turkey, Venezuela and Israel. But 130 members of the UN voted for it. Sixteen others, including Britain, West Germany and the Soviet Union, abstained. France and Japan, both with ambitions for a big stake in deep-sea mining, voted yes.

•

SEABED SOCIALISM

Washington, of course, violently opposes the notion that the unexplored reaches of the deep sea belong to "mankind." The frontier has always played a major role in American life, both as a concept and as an economic reality. And a frontier, according to most Americans, belongs to no one until it is discovered. It then belongs to the explorers and the developers. If the principle of Seabed Socialism is allowed to prevail, then the next step could be Space Socialism, with the UN running all space exploration.

This frontier mentality is particularly strong in the White House, where rugged individualism and the free-market spirit hold ideological sway. To Ronald Reagan, a frontier belongs to the person who can take it and use it—not some artificial grouping of Third World countries at the United Nations.

Paradoxically, U.S. corporations have less of a problem with the Third World's particular principle of international sovereignty over the oceans' minerals. The four big seabed-mining consortiums do not mind sharing the profits with the UN. What they do object to, however, is the control over production that the ISA will have, a control that will quickly determine prices for the minerals, and their own profits. As long as the Third World controls the ISA, production ceilings will be kept very low for the underwater nodules in order to keep a tight rein on the supply and demand for their above-ground minerals. The private corporations know they cannot ask the banks to come up with the $5 to $10 billion in financing they need to launch commercial seabed mining under these conditions. The banks would never agree if some other body controls production. The promise of paying back the loans could never be covered.

Standard Oil of Indiana, which belongs to the Ocean Minerals Company group, along with Lockheed Aircraft (the sea is making some very strange corporate bedfellows), blasted the treaty as "so seriously flawed, the company opposes its signing and ratification in its present form." Ocean Mining Associates, led by U.S. Steel and the Sun Company, said it would fight it. And the Kennecott-led and Inco-led consortiums aren't too happy about it either.

Even though the treaty has now been signed by 130 countries, it must still be ratified by all the member governments, and that will take at least two or three more years. The United States can change its mind at any time and join, but it won't. What Washington will probably do is sign something else. One idea is an RSA, or Reciprocity States Agreement, that the United States would sign with other industrial powers, leaving the developing countries to their original treaty. An RSA would provide some harmony among the various national legal codes and prevent too much overlapping of mining sites; in other words, it would limit claim jumping. Germany, Britain and maybe even the Soviets would probably sign an RSA with the United States, if only to cover themselves with Washington and the technologically advanced multinationals. France might eventually sign as well.

The U.S. underwater-mining groups will begin operations by the middle of the decade. By the early 1990s, perhaps half of our most important minerals will come from beneath the sea. Without the technology, the Third World will be helpless to stop the multinationals, short of war. Only by military means will they be able to stop the American ships from going into international waters for the nodules. The inevitable result will be a sharp decline in the prices of many minerals, from cobalt to nickel. Copper, already being displaced by optic fibers, will be particularly hit, and the millions of people now saving pennies will have nothing to show for their speculation except drawers full of heavy metal.

For the Third World, the impact will be far more devastating. Their treasuries will be empty. The high-tech revolution sweeping the West will undermine their entire economies. The commodities on which they now depend will drop in value. New materials will replace many of them. Others will simply not be needed in the world of electronics and computers. And still other raw materials will be swamped by supplies from deep under the sea. Prices are going to fall on many commodity exports and practically disappear on others as demand vanishes.

The only Third World countries that will be able to make it in the twenty-first century are those capable of forcing technology transfers out of the West. Perhaps a half dozen, at the most, will succeed. Certainly not China, nor Nigeria, nor Egypt; probably not Mexico, nor India, nor the Philippines, although they have a chance; and maybe, just maybe, Brazil, South Korea, Taiwan, Hong Kong, Israel and Singapore.

The transformation of the world economy from heavy industry to high technology will change the balance of power not only among Western and Communist nations, but within the Third World as well.

6

ELECTRONIC MERCANTILISM

•

THE BAR AT THE HOTEL PIERRE IN NEW YORK IS A FAVORITE watering hole for wealthy Europeans or Europeans on the corporate dole. The British prefer the Waldorf or the Barclay. The Latins go for the splashier Helmsley Palace or the glitzier Park Lane. But the Continentals—the Germans, French, Italians and Swiss—love the Pierre. Go there any night in the week and you will find them at work or at play.

Dr. Hans T., an old acquaintance from the days when I covered the gold markets and international finance, always stays at the Pierre. He is Swiss, from the French-speaking canton surrounding Lucerne. He is a big man, with a cherubic face, perhaps a little overweight but not enough to keep him from the pleasures of eating and drinking that he so enjoys.

One December night in 1979, before the snow covering the trees in Central Park across from the hotel began to turn New York slushy brown, we sat and talked. Hans' back was to the bar and I faced him as we drank. In addition to the growing heaviness in his Swiss-English accent that came with the alcohol, Hans was constantly turning around to eye the bar, where there were two particularly beautiful and elegant women. Unfortunately for our conversation, two women in skin-tight evening gowns, one wearing white, the other black, were drinking—and attracting the attention of about a dozen sleek, silver-haired men in $800 suits. The woman wearing white was black and the woman wearing black was blond. For five hours, Hans spoke to me, craning his neck every ten minutes or so to look over his right shoulder at the bar.

At two in the morning we finished lamenting what the year had brought—the second OPEC oil shock, the zooming price of gold and the plummeting dollar. It had been a good evening, funny and enjoyable, but I had expressed my pessimism about the state of this country more than once. As we left, Hans leaned over to me, rubbing his neck, and he said, "Don't worry about America so much. The United States is the OPEC of information."

At the time, the statement sounded like a non sequitur. Years later, it is now apparent that Dr. Hans was a lot more lucid at the Pierre than my memory of him. If Hans has invested his clients' money with an eye to his insight, he is making them quite rich. For what Hans predicted that snowy night was that technology would soon become the most important commodity in the world and that nations would attempt to cartelize it, limit it, and bargain with it as they once did with gold and silver. High technology is triggering a wave of protectionism around the world that resembles nothing so much as the mercantilism of the eighteenth century, when France, England, and all the other great powers of that day passed laws closing off their domestic markets to foreigners in a race to amass the most bullion. Indeed, it is now clear that one of the great ironies of the 1980s is that the new high technology in many ways is leading us back to the past, not the future. Instead of opening up new trading lanes, doing away with tariffs and quotas, the race for high-tech proficiency is leading governments to close off their borders, to clamp down on the free flow of goods and capital. One of the great international "crimes" of the decade is the breakdown of world trade. And while officials in Washington, Tokyo, Paris and London hate to admit it, it is the struggle for supremacy in high technology that is at the root of this return to what is basically a premodern, archaic form of commerce. We are entering the era of high-tech tribalism and we are speeding forward to the past.

•

DATA WARS

Nothing illustrates this better than the global battle over telecommunications. A burgeoning new international telecommunications grid is spreading over the world. It is quickly extending its electronic tentacles into every nation, every city, every household from Los Angeles to New York, São Paulo to Osaka, Paris to Stockholm. Possession of data is becoming the most important strategic factor anywhere. The international economic, political and military status of a nation is increasingly determined by its access to worldwide information and the possession of computer hardware that collects and processes it. The semiconductor chip is replacing the oil barrel as the symbol of economic growth, military might and political influence.

Where once, during the Great Age of Mercantilism, nations lusted after gold, they now view information as "golden." Three hundred years ago, politicians enforced mercantilist policies designed to attract as much yellow metal as possible while blocking any from leaving their borders. Today we see the world rushing headlong into a new era of electronic mercantilism where government "data police" monitor all transborder information flows, and politicians attempt to build up their countries' telecommunications muscle.

Just as the railroads of the nineteenth century tied together entire continents, providing huge new markets for the burgeoning heavy industry of that period, so too the telecommunications revolution is knitting together a vast global market for the new high-tech products of the twenty-first century. In addition, information itself is quickly becoming one of the most valued products of our time. Telecommunications will be one of the four or five major growth industries of the next decade. Success in it will largely determine the pecking order of the balance of power in the post-OPEC era.

For the moment, the United States dominates this new global information order. No other country in the world possesses the computing power, data banks and satellites to generate and process information on any comparable scale. No other country has the international spread of multinational corporations and military facilities to tap into burgeoning overseas electronic files on foreign markets, products, consumer tastes, rival companies and even government bureaucracies, suck them dry electronically and bring the data back home—in microseconds. No other country has the ability to process the enormous amounts of information now at hand and interpret them in meaningful and profitable ways. In short, no other nation has electronic power to control data and benefit from its use as has the United States.

America's ability to dominate the information era has become vital to its economic health. Without data, the entire service sector, the fastest-growing sector of the economy over the past decade, would die. As the United States—indeed the world economy—moves away from heavy industry under the impact of high energy prices, information-based "clean" industries are booming. Communications, banking, retailing, insurance, accounting, engineering, health, tourism, travel—industries that together now employ two out of every three Americans—would all grind to a halt.

With the internationalization of markets, only up-to-the-minute information can provide the competitive edge to win contracts and profits. And while U.S. manufacturing has been declining under the impact of the twin OPEC oil shocks, service industries are booming. U.S. banks, for example, are more powerful than their European, Japanese and Arab rivals. They are masters at using SWIFT, an incredibly sophisticated computer network linking 800 banks in seventeen cities around the world. American banks clearly influence the ebb and flow of trillions of "stateless" dollars, Deutsche Marks and yen that wash across national borders every day, beyond the control of any single government.

As the factory of the future comes into place, with computer-designed and computer-controlled assembly lines, information processing is becoming critical to the manufacturing industries as well. With telecommunications, white-collar managers sitting atop the General Motors headquarters building will soon be able to monitor not only the assembly lines of Detroit, but plants in Spain, Mexico, Germany and Britain. Telecommunications equipment will allow top management to control all levels of production not only here, but in countries around the world. In a few short years, it will be possible to electronically check the activities of every man, woman or robot working on a line or in an office at every minute of the working day in any nation. The technology already exists for this. Just take a peek at the ads in the business press by IBM and MCAUTO, a division of McDonnell Douglas Aircraft that pioneered in computer-aided design and manufacturing (CAD-CAM) equipment. The potential for productivity gains will be stupendous as people get the power to alter entire product lines to meet quickly changing market demands. They will also be able to speed up or slow down assembly lines in hundreds of factories in dozens of countries to squeeze out the most profits. Data flow will permit enormous savings and generate huge profits. But it will also allow the accumulation of enormous power—power that both individuals and governments are jealously guarding. And unions are just beginning to wake up to the new technology—and oppose it as best they can.

•

DATA COPS

Even now, the information revolution is generating a new series of social and political problems for the twenty-first century. In fact, we are currently in the early stages of what future historians will call the "data wars of the 1980s." Barriers to the transborder flow of data are going up everywhere. Every month some government "arranges" to curb the passing of information from computers inside its borders to computers across the line. Information policy is becoming one of the most critical international issues of our time. The freedom to transmit data across borders is replacing the old issue of open borders for goods and investments that so dominated international arenas in the fifties, sixties and seventies. Indeed, information freedom, the right to keep the lines open, is now one of the key debates in the United Nations.

Already governments are deeply involved in controlling the flow of data. The United States is the only nation that still maintains an "open borders" information policy, but that is quickly changing. Europe, led by France, and the developing countries, led by Brazil, are increasingly "info-protectionist." Data cops are beginning to run around spying out where information is coming from and where it is going to. Government boards are being set up to monitor information flow within countries and across borders. Laws are being passed forcing all computerized data banks to register with a data-protection agency. And in some places centralized data-control agencies are being set up. All computerized information that flows in and out of a country may well soon pass through a single, huge, government-controlled computer apparatus that is constantly monitored. Information will then be vulnerable to being copied, altered or even stopped by government authorities. Even now, many U.S. multinationals are hesitant about using certain computer facilities in particular countries for fear that government agencies listening in will pass the information on to their own competing corporate rivals.

•

WE ARE WIRED

Individual privacy was the original reason for government involvement in information policy back in the middle 1970s. This concern is still a very real one. The more our lives go "on line" and the more we use computers to work, to play, to order things, to pay for things, the more we leave electronic "tracks." These electronic tracks are far more visible and far more accessible than the messy trails we used to leave in the old paper-receipt days. It is becoming much easier to create a profile on an individual's life once that life is tracked on computers. It is becoming easier to check our movements, our income, our desires, as we move "on line" with videotex and interactive TV. Indeed, privacy and privacy codes will become one of the most important social issues of the 1980s. Some of the heaviest policy battles between Republicans and Democrats will soon be fought out over the new meaning of privacy.

Europe is much further along than the United States in making computer privacy a significant political issue. In 1973, Sweden became one of the first countries to begin licensing all automated personal files. A privacy inspection board, the Data Inspektionen, was set up and has passed judgment on nearly 30,000 cases involving disputes over privacy infringements. In 1975, the Data Inspektionen said that Siemens, the German electronics giant, would not be allowed to transfer personnel files from its Swedish branch to Munich headquarters. Siemens wanted to use its big computers in Munich to process the files. The Swedes said the files had data on nationality, family, job qualifications and education that the Germans shouldn't have and stopped it. Earlier, the Data Inspektionen prohibited a Swedish health department from sending to Britain computerized tapes on citizens that were going to be used to make 80,000 plastic cards. Again, it stopped the export of data about local inhabitants overseas.

In Norway, all computerized data banks, including public-opinion polls and credit registrations, must now be licensed by the government. They cannot be sent abroad without explicit approval by the government. In Germany, a complicated computer-privacy act that gives many local governments the power to oversee data protection will probably require 20,000 data "cops" in the years ahead.

Brazil has the most nationalistic transborder data policies of any of the developing countries. The government already refuses to allow transborder data links in cases where intra-Brazilian alternatives exist or where foreigners control the data banks. A Special Information Secretariat decides on information policy for the country. The fact that it reports directly to the National Security Council says a lot about what the debate over information policy is really about. In the next few years, Brazil will complete a telecommunications network that will allow all data transmission to be centralized in the hands of Embratel, the government telecommunications monopoly. An American or foreign multinational would then have to apply to Embratel for a data hookup and tell the government what the data will be, how it will be processed and where it will go. The Information Secretariat will monitor all transmissions and will be able to cut off any company if it doesn't like what is being sent.

•

PRIVACY POLICY

The social implications of the drive for computer privacy codes are enormous. In the name of privacy and the preservation of democracy, governments are centralizing even further the collection of information on individuals. In the name of privacy, government data directorates are being formed to oversee info flow both inside countries and across borders. In the name of privacy, data police are being formed to make sure that data banks are registered with the government, information is restricted and multinationals kept in their place. In the drive for individual protection, it may well be that privacy is lost.

What seems at first paradoxical—privacy lost in the name of privacy gained—becomes much clearer when we look below the surface arguments for data control. For the drive for privacy among nations around the world camouflages in part a deeper thrust toward electronic protectionism that is shattering the international free-trade system. The laws and regulations on individual privacy passed in recent years in France, Britain, Germany, Sweden and Brazil are increasingly used for purely commercial goals, as a way of circumventing the established rules of the Western Alliance that demand free movement of goods and capital. These rules have governed international behavior for forty years. They grew out of the Second World War, a war that Roosevelt, Churchill and others believed had its roots in the protectionist, beggar-thy-neighbor trading policies of the 1930s.

Yet today, countries around the world, especially in Europe, are using the popular issue of privacy to embark on a new form of protectionism. In a desperate bid to restructure their economies away from heavy industry toward new high-tech products of the twenty-first century, politicians everywhere are threatening to fracture the essential economic framework of the modern era. Although formal tariffs are barred by established international codes, government officials are creating nontariff barriers to trade and investment. Behind these new walls, they hope to revitalize their economies and catch up with Japan and America. Along the way, they hope to break the dominance of the United States and Japan over the world's high-tech industries.

•

THE PRIVACY–PROTECTIONISM CONNECTION

Measuring the growth of electronic mercantilism is quite easy. Just check on the stringency of national privacy laws and codes and you will find an almost perfect match with protectionism. The greater the publicly voiced concern over individual privacy, the higher the number of restrictions on data flow and the more quietly mercantilist will be the government policies on telecommunications. Take Sweden, for example. The Swedes are so concerned about privacy that they won't allow computerized data to be shipped overseas for processing. Yet while Stockholm is making privacy policy by stopping Swedes from sending information abroad, it is also making industrial policy. If Swedish companies and agencies cannot export the processing of data, they must do it at home. And if they don't have computers to process the information properly, they have to develop them. In Sweden, as elsewhere, the issue of computer privacy is completely intertwined with the policy of promoting the telecommunications industry. Unlike the electronics behemoths of Germany or Britain or the Netherlands, the Swedes have found a formula for flexibility and ingenuity for their corporations that is putting them among the top players in global markets. But they are using their protected home markets as a base from which to begin the process of developing high-tech products. It should come as no surprise that Swedish companies are particularly expert in the data-processing and telecommunications fields. Data-Saab, now part of Volvo, today can hold its own anywhere. L. M. Ericsson is one of the top players in the multibillion-dollar market for advanced computerized telephone-switching equipment. By preventing the data on its citizens from being sent abroad for processing and storage, the Data Inspektionen is also giving local companies the work and the experience with which to create new equipment, amass profits and then move out into the international marketplace. Behind a protected home market, they sally forth to fight the Americans, Japanese and other Europeans. Privacy, protectionism and high technology go hand in hand.

•

THE FRENCH TELE-CONNECTION

The supreme player in the emerging electronic mercantilism game, however, is France. The French over the decades have managed to "outprotection" the Japanese without bringing down the wrath of Washington or their neighbors. In the 1970s, to aid its own companies, France threw up barriers against foreign steel and autos. In the 1980s, it is putting up barriers against foreign computers, semiconductors, robots, consumer electronics and virtually every other high-tech product of the post-OPEC era.

The creation of the Common Market in 1957 was supposed to open up the Western European continent as a single mass market. Yet the various governments never really gave up their control over communications. All Western European PTTs (post office, telephone and telegraph authorities) are state-controlled. Indeed, these were all created and nurtured in the late nineteenth century after the invention of the telegraph and telephone.

What this means for Europe, and for Americans doing business in Europe, is that there is no single market for telecommunication on the Continent. There are only national markets, each one in itself much smaller than either the United States or Japan. Each is too small to nurture a global telecommunications giant capable of taking on IBM or Fujitsu. Thus, Germany's Siemens, France's Thomson-Brandt, Britain's Plessey are all big, but not big enough to win, because they don't have the Continental-market size to grow and mature in.

Every European government, often under the guise of protecting its own citizens' privacy, insists that contracts for building PTT equipment be given to domestic companies. Thus, Paris recently stopped a local hospital board from buying Siemens equipment and "recommended" that it buy the machines from the Thomson-Brandt electronics group. Of course, that kind of action is unlawful under both the rules of the Common Market and GATT. But they did it anyway in this new era of high-tech protection.

Siemens is not usually the target of discrimination. IBM, the giant of the industry with 60 percent of the European market for computers, is the normal target. In Britain, the government has consistently pushed its own internal revenue service to turn down IBM bids on computers, even though nearly everyone agrees that the equipment is the best and cheapest available. Instead, London "persuades" the tax collectors to buy from ICL, the national computer company. ICL is only about a decade old. It was stitched together by the government from the remnants of several failing British computing companies and has never managed to fuse the parts into a successful whole. ICL can't even take on Siemens, much less IBM. Only with government help can ICL hope to get contracts. Only by noncompetitive bidding, by breaking the rules of free trade, is it surviving. And ironically, the decision to bypass IBM for ICL was made in 1981, under the laissez-faire regime of Margaret Thatcher.

In Germany, a nation that prides itself on its free-trade principles, the government clearly puts major telecommunications contracts in Siemens' way. After spending $250 million in the 1970s with Siemens in an abortive attempt to build an advanced mechanical telephone-switching system, Germany's own PTT abandoned the project when the Swedes, Canadians, French and Americans came out with computerized, electronic telephone equipment. And then, rather than buy this more sophisticated stuff from abroad, the PTT proceeded to set up a second telephone contract with Siemens to make a similar computerized device. So far, Siemens has been only marginally successful. Its only major market is in Germany, and it has to team up with the French to sell overseas. When Italy decided in 1982 to modernize its entire telephone network, it turned to General Telephone and Electronics Corporation of the United States. Only L. M. Ericsson had been a major contender for what will turn out to be a multibillion-dollar project. The telephone system the Italians want to replace is a mechanical system put in by Siemens after the war.

Paradoxically, even with enormous government subsidies and protected markets, none of the major European companies will be a match any time soon for the Americans or the Japanese in telecommunications. For the government supports that are being offered are at the same time crippling them on the world markets. Without a Continent-wide market base for telecommunications there isn't enough business to build big enough factories and to make the investments that can drive down prices fast enough to compete overseas. The economies of scale just aren't there in manufacturing for middle-size markets, which is exactly what France, Germany, Britain and Italy are today with populations varying around 50 to 60 million people. The Japanese have 110 million people and the Americans 225 million. A truly European market for telecommunications of 300 million would be the critical mass for a European takeoff in the industry.

But, alas, the Europeans are unwilling to open up their telecommunications markets in the same way they have opened up their more traditional markets under the rules of the Common Market. Each country is unwilling to risk having its own corporations fail in a truly competitive environment. In a free market Siemens, for example, could prove to be better at making computers than France's Cii-Honeywell-Bull or L. M. Ericsson could win most of the orders for advanced telephone equipment from Siemens. No country wants to risk losing out in the high-tech markets of the future, so each government protects its own domestic markets while trying to invade its neighbors'.

The French are leaders at this game of high-tech mercantilism. They are the most unwilling to open up their electronics market to foreign competitors, be they Asian, American or European. In December 1981, when the Common Market tried to pry open up a mere 10 percent of all public telecommunication contracts for free, competitive European bidding, Paris firmly said no. The French complained that all the IBM subsidiaries in Europe would then be able to compete, and their own companies would be smashed. More than that, they were afraid that the Swedes would win significant contracts and perhaps even the British. Paris wasn't worried about the Japanese. They aren't even allowed into the French market. In late 1982, the Socialist government told Tokyo that all Japanese videotape recorders (VTRs) imported into France would have to be cleared through a customs post in Poitiers. There are only four customs officials in this tiny town and, consequently, Japanese VTR exports to France plummeted. To emphasize their point, Paris officials reminded the Japanese that Poitiers was the site of a French victory against the invading Arabs in the eighth century. To no avail, the Japanese took out full-page ads declaring "We are not Saracens." High technology is reviving the nationalism that poisoned the world a half century ago, and it is reversing decades of progress in furthering free trade and investment.

•

RECIPROCITY—A NEW U.S. HIGH-TECH POLICY

Until 1982, the United States had the most open borders for both the transmission of data and the sale of high-tech products. There was no licensing of data banks, no "inspectorate" of information, no information police. European and Japanese companies were free to buy into any high-tech company, except for the big defense corporations, and were free to bid on nearly all private and public contracts. To be sure, a "Buy American" sentiment existed, AT&T purchased 80 percent of its communications equipment from captive Western Electric, and there were restrictions against exporting some defense-related goods to the Eastern bloc. And, of course, Washington, under previous Administrations, had managed to impose import limitations on Japanese color TVs and on autos and steel from Europe and the developing countries. But given all that, the American market for foreign high-tech goods remained huge, as evidenced by the flood of Japanese consumer electronics, semiconductors and machine tools. When the Europeans can compete, they have found a market for French helicopters and Swedish and Italian robots. They have offered Western Union and other American companies lower prices for their French-built Ariane rocket that can send telecommunications satellites into space. And Eastern Airlines has bought dozens of Airbus commercial jets.

But with the election of Ronald Reagan, a man not from the Eastern Establishment—which has favored free trade over the decades—but from the more isolationalist West, America's commitment to free trade at any cost is eroding. In fact, fair trade, not free trade, is the clarion call in Washington these days. And increasingly, the focus is very much on high technology.

The ostensible issue for Washington is defense, not privacy. And like Brazil, where the National Security Council plays a role in data control, so too in the United States it is the CIA and the Pentagon that are leading the attempt to control technology transfer.

The first hint that a dramatic change was in the works came in the very first year of the Reagan Administration. The CIA, under "Bobby" Inman before he resigned, launched a major blitz against academia's right to freely publish any and all research. Inman's goal was simple—to deny the Soviets data that could be used for military purposes. At a conference on optics and lasers, the Pentagon prevented dozens of papers from being given because there were Soviet observers in the audience. Congress now has before it legislation that would, in effect, restrict the publication of scientific and technical data that it decides could be helpful to the Soviet Union. In its broadest form, this legislation could mean that data on such toys as Speak and Spell or Pac-Man might have to be cleared with either the Commerce or State Department. For the first time, America is proposing curbs on the free flow of data.

The second step taken by Washington was to expand the notion of what is technologically useful to the Soviet military. In the past, only those items of a direct military value were restricted. Thus the export of computers and semiconductors had to be approved by COCOM, the Coordinating Committee on Export Controls set up by the United States, Europe and Japan to oversee technology transfer to the Eastern bloc. But COCOM is like a sieve, and the Soviets have gotten virtually anything they wanted. Advanced computers, microprocessors and chips, all move easily eastward.

Now the Administration is trying to expand the concept of technology that should be barred to include anything that might help the Soviet economy. The change is extremely significant, for it moves the issue of technology exports away from a narrow definition of what is militarily useful towards economic warfare. If the Reagan Administration wins out on this issue, it will signify a radical step in U.S. foreign policy. Nothing that can possibly aid the Soviet economy, from U.S. grain to Unimation robots for welding cars, would be freely exportable to the Eastern bloc.

The third and final step in Washington's policy change toward protectionism came in late 1981 and early 1982. AT&T, a short time before, had put out for bidding a contract for a 404-mile portion of a 776-mile fiber-optic communications network. The glass cable would run down the Northeast Corridor between Cambridge, Massachusetts, and Moseley, Virginia, passing through New York City. In the past, Ma Bell bought all of its fiber-optic cable and equipment from its subsidiary electronics manufacturer, Western Electric. This time, however, it opened up the bidding and received offers from

Fujitsu, Hitachi, NEC, Sumitomo Electric, the Dutch Philips and Compagnie Générale d'Électricité of France and Harris Corporation of the United States. Fujitsu came in with the lowest bid, nearly 33 percent below the Western Electric offer. Fujitsu would have built the electronic hardware for the system and would have bought the fiber cable from Siecor, a joint venture of Corning Glass, the leading producer of fiber cable, and Siemens.

Everything went smoothly for Fujitsu, and it appeared to have won the contract. This warmed the hearts of the Japanese, since fiber optics is one of their target technologies for the 1980s—they hope it will replace copper cable and eventually knit together all telephone and computer lines into a single system; for them, it is an immense international market.

A few months before announcing Fujitsu as winner of the contract, AT&T began to get a lot of heat from Washington. In September Senator Strom Thurmond, chairman of the Senate Judiciary Committee, and a strong defense advocate, sent a memo to the White House saying that he opposed awarding the bid to Fujitsu because it would allow a foreign company to be an "essential operator of our sensitive communications network." Other congressmen began to worry about the loss of jobs to the Japanese. Bernard J. Wunder, Jr., Assistant Secretary of State for Communications and Information, began discussing the bid with AT&T officials and expressing concern about helping the U.S. fiber-optic industry. Finally, in October, Congressman Timothy E. Wirth, chairman of the House Subcommittee for Telecommunications, wrote a letter to FCC Chairman Mark Fowler warning that the national security of the nation would be damaged if the contract went to the Japanese. The FCC asked the Defense Department for its opinion, and it sent back a vague report saying that if the American telecommunications network became dependent on foreign corporations, the United States might have a difficult time rebuilding after a war. Within weeks AT&T rejected the Fujitsu bid and opted for

Western Electric. To add insult to injury, FCC Commissioner Joseph Fogarty then accused Fujitsu of submitting an illegally low bid, a charge he subsequently withdrew.

The circle is now complete. National-security issues are becoming intertwined with high-technology business problems. After years of pressuring the Japanese to open up their own government-controlled National Telegraph & Telephone Company (NTT) for competitive bidding—indeed, only months after Japan signed an agreement doing just that in exchange for permission to bid on high-tech Ma Bell projects such as the fiber-optics deal—America began moving away from its free-trade policy toward protectionism. The United States has stopped trying to keep high-tech trade free against the budding protectionism of its trading partners. It is now joining the game.

The Fujitsu case is quickly leading to others. On January 4, 1982, the U.S. Commerce Department filed a preliminary suit against NEC for "dumping" its high-power microwave amplifiers for satellite ground stations at 13 to 39 percent below the price in Japan. This $3-million sale was Japan's first in the United States of advanced telecommunications equipment for linking satellites to earth stations. Just as Fujitsu is an acknowledged leader in fiber-optic technology, so is NEC an acknowledged leader around the world in microwave ground satellite equipment.

The drumbeat against Japanese technology is now picking up to a march. One bandmaster is Lionel Olmer, Commerce Undersecretary for International Trade. Olmer was for years an executive at Motorola, one of the biggest American semiconductor and electronics companies. And he is pressing to block certain imports of Japanese electronics. His major pitch is that the United States has to curb its use of foreign electronics to prevent growing military dependence on foreign sources of supply. In particular, Olmer wants to cut back on United States dependence on Japanese semiconductors. This is one area of Japanese market supremacy. In the latest generation of semiconductors, the 64k RAM, Japan has 60 percent of the world market.

Earlier, however, they had 80 percent of the market, and the Justice Department launched a formal investigation into whether six Japanese companies conspired to control supply and determine prices in the United States. In the summer of 1982, Justice notified Tokyo's Foreign Ministry that it was looking into price-fixing by Hitachi, Nippon Electric, Toshiba, Fujitsu, Mitsubishi Electric and Oki Electric. The investigation came just months after the Japscam case, in which employees of Hitachi and Mitsubishi Electric were arrested for paying $600,000 for computer secrets stolen from IBM. No one in Tokyo believed that it was a coincidence.

American semiconductor companies, led by Motorola and Advanced Micro Devices, are saying that no one can make profits at the low prices at which the Japanese are selling their 64k chips. They are lobbying Washington for import restrictions or an end to Japanese dumping, and the Defense Department is chiming in with concern over U.S. military contractors becoming too dependent on foreign suppliers of crucial electronic components.

Olmer wants to change American antitrust law to allow U.S. companies to combine so that they will be able to compete with the Japanese, particularly in electronics. "Semiconductors have become the 'crude oil' of U.S. industry," he explains, because advances in so many industries now depend on America's capability in this one field, a field increasingly dominated by Japan.

Right now Congress is flooded with bills to protect American technology and open up foreign markets to U.S. high-tech exports. And for the first time there is an "or else" clause in all of these bills—a threat. The California delegation, representing the heartland of American electronics and computer producers, is pushing for the High Technology Trade Act of 1982—a bill focusing on opening up a world market for computers, especially in Japan.

While most of the legislation offers positive incentives to U.S. manufacturers, there is a dark, protectionist side as well. The buzz word is *reciprocity*. The Congress and the Reagan Administration are quickly shifting to a high-technology protectionist stance that is the very opposite of free trade. The High Technology Trade Act of 1982 authorizes the President to enter into agreements with other countries to open up access to foreign markets for U.S. high-tech exports. The bill defines high technology as including semiconductors, computers, robots, and CAD-CAM equipment. If the United States can't get free access, the President is then empowered to close U.S. markets to foreign high-tech goods. A separate Senate bill specifically focuses on reciprocity in telecommunications. Free trade is becoming fair trade, which is becoming reciprocity. If Washington implements this policy, the effect will be devastating—especially for Japan. The open-trade markets, which have been closing down in recent years, will begin to slam shut. The U.S. market, the largest in the world, would become forbidden territory to foreigners. And the Japanese would suffer most of all. America takes the largest portion of Japanese exports, especially high-tech equipment. Closing it to Japan would be the equivalent of the pre–World War II act of cutting that country off from steel and oil. And the consequences might be just as dramatic.

•

UNESCO—BATTLEGROUND OVER INFORMATION POLICY

The free flow of data is not only an issue among industrial nations, but is becoming a major North–South problem as well. As with the industrial countries, the developing world is defining the issue in moral terms, while camouflaging its real concern—economic and political power.

The arena for this increasingly bitter dispute is UNESCO, the United Nations Education, Scientific and Cultural Organization. Over the past three years, Third World countries have protested that all the major news organizations that report on their countries—AP, UPI, Reuters and Agence France Presse—are owned and operated by the West. They charge that these Western-owned organizations slant their news and write biased, negative, unfair stories. They want it to stop.

Through the UNESCO-backed International Program for Development of Communications group, the developing countries are trying to build a "new information order" that would permit much greater government control over the media. A Pan-Africa News Agency and an Asia-Pacific News Agency are to be set up as soon as UNESCO finds the money.

Washington, of course, opposes the whole notion of government control over the media. The American delegation argues that when the Communications Program was set up, it focused on strengthening free journalism in the Third World. Now the Program concentrates on government control.

The United States also suspects the Third World nations of wanting control over more than just the news media. Indeed, another UNESCO group, the Intergovernmental Bureau for Informatics (IBI), in Rome, is trying to raise $1 billion for a telecommunications program for the Third World. It is hoping to get 40 percent of the money from OPEC, and it has thirty members. France is a major participant; in fact, France is setting up its own organization to spread telecommunications technology to developing countries.

An IBI conference on "informatics" will be held in Havana in 1983 to discuss the new disequilibrium between North and South based not just on wealth but on an unequal distribution of data and telecommunications technology. At a preparatory session in 1982, the IBI called for an international debate "on transborder data flow and its impact on the international division of labor." This is far afield from reporters covering their beats properly. It gets to the heart of the UNESCO debate over information control.

Washington doesn't think the IBI's goals are legitimate, and it isn't very happy about Fidel Castro hosting the conference. It sees France as using the organization as a sales agent for its own electronics exports. But most importantly, Washington fears that a UN regulatory blanket could be thrown over all transborder data flow. It strikes the same fear as the Law of the Sea Treaty, which would make the UN the regulator of deep-sea mining. In both cases, Third World governments would prevail over private corporations, bureaucracies would dominate markets, cartels would set prices, and the United States would lose out to weaker Third World nations and their Western allies.

Washington has a tough fight ahead. By 1979, African countries were already challenging U.S. multinationals on the security of their data banks. One group at an IBI conference that year said that all African governments should have privileged access to information held in foreign computers that involves their national security, however they define it. Data control around the world will increasingly become a major international policy issue. The fate of the world's economy is at stake and, with it, dominance of the balance of power.

•

HIGH-TECH NATIONALISM

Telecommunications is not the only industry of the future that is leading the world back to the past. In fact, the renewed rise of nationalism and the breakdown in free trade are being fed by governments trying to harness all the major locomotive technologies of the twenty-first century.

Once again the French are pointing the way in Europe. But whereas the French rationalize breaking free-trade rules in telecommunications by focusing on individual privacy, they make no excuses for themselves in other industries. Even under the conservative government of Giscard d'Estaing, Paris had decided on the industries of the future—and began restructuring the entire corporate network to make France a leader in them. Government officials decided that there are six locomotive technologies of the future—consumer electronics, military electronics, robots, machine tools, biotechnology and data processing, or telecommunications. Giscard set national goals, poured billions of public dollars into them and, most importantly, closed French borders to high-tech competitors. It was as if the Common Market didn't exist. It was as if free trade was no longer the guiding value among the industrial nations of the West. It was as if France were returning to the Golden Age of Mercantilism, with a high-tech gloss.

In fact, so strong was this "statist" approach, this *dirigisme*, among the conservative Giscardists that, when the Socialists took power in 1981, their policies were barely distinguishable from their right-wing predecessors. For example, under Giscard, the government's telecommunications monopoly, the Direction Générale des Telecommunications (DGT), decided that it was in the national interest to have a mostly French company produce optic fibers. Now the DGT is a formidable organization in France. It has an annual budget of $6 billion, and it plays a major role in industrial policy. Gérard Théry was the DGT's director under Giscard and he alone decided that the optic-fiber producer in France should be a three-way joint venture involving Saint Gobain, the $10-billion conglomerate specializing in pipe, glass, construction, electronics and computers; Thomson-Brandt, France's biggest electronics group; and Corning Glass of the United States, the world's leader in optic-fiber technology.

The DGT pushed this merger through—even though Corning Glass already had an exclusive technology agreement with another French company, Cables de Lyon. To make his point, Théry simply froze out Cables de Lyon from all DGT contracts. Thomson-Brandt, at the same time, suddenly began receiving DGT money. Corning, against its wishes, decided to leave Cables de Lyon and join the new consortium led by Saint Gobain. The French state had made its point. *Dirigisme* won the day.

The Socialists have taken the strategies developed by the Gaullists one step further. They have nationalized virtually all the high-tech corporations in France not previously controlled by the government. In addition, they have taken over nearly all the banks, putting billions of dollars in capital under their control. The Socialists have set up a new Ministry of Research and Technology, and added billions to R & D spending. They plan to funnel the capital from the nationalized banks into the high-tech corporations.

The other key phrase among the Socialists is "reconquering the domestic markets"—which officials in Europe, Japan and America regard as a euphemism for protectionism. They have good reason. As an industrial policy, reconquering the domestic markets means providing government financial aid and import protection for particular industries and corporations.

For example, the Socialists are furious that France's once powerful tool industry is being destroyed by the Japanese. The French have lost nearly 50 percent of their market to the Japanese, and a good chunk of the rest to the Germans. Armed with computer-controlled electronic machines, the Japanese have been able to offer more sophisticated and cheaper machines to French manufacturers.

The Socialists are now offering $700 million in a four-year plan to save the domestic machine-tool industry from annihilation. They are combining the dozens of small machine-tool companies into two or three giants. Paris is going about "persuading" corporations, many of them under its control now through nationalization, to buy the new machining equipment that the reorganized French companies will produce. And it will also put new capital into the companies and help in R & D. By 1985, the government expects to double domestic production.

In microelectronics, the Socialists are working on a four-year, $500-million R & D program that is four times the size of the previous plan under the conservative Gaullists. On top of that, the money the government will spend for computer data processing is nearly as impressive—$350 million for research and development. The Socialists are also expanding the Gaullists' program for creating the first "telematique" society in the world in France. Under Giscard, Paris announced that it would spend several billion dollars on equipping each and every household in the nation that has a telephone with a computerized electronic directory. These data terminals would be installed by 1992. That means putting thirty million terminals into French homes. This plan is far more ambitious than AT&T's electronic Yellow Pages and makes even the Japanese ideas pale in comparison.

In 1981, right after the Socialists won power, they chose CIT-Alcatel, a subsidiary of the giant Compagnie Générale d'Électricité group (which they also nationalized), to begin producing cheap computer terminals. By 1983, CIT-Alcatel will be manufacturing 1.5 million computer terminals annually. And by providing it with an enormous protected home market, the French government is encouraging the corporation to take advantage of its economies of scale and to begin exporting. Indeed, CIT-Alcatel has already lined up a U.S. distributor to sell 250,000 of its cheap terminals every year for the next three years. The French government's policy of electronic mercantilism appears to be working—for France. In the United States, Source Telecomputing Corporation, a subsidiary of *Reader's Digest*, will be CIT-Alcatel's agent.

In robots, Paris is relying on Renault's good track record. Like Toyota and GM, and other car companies, Renault has been active in using certain types of robots, especially welders, for years.

In biotechnology, the French have the same advantage as the Japanese—they are leaders in fermentation. The United States is clearly in the forefront of the key procedure in biotechnology—using microsurgery to take out nuclei from one type of cell to put into another and thus creating "bug factories" that produce highly valued pharmaceuticals or chemicals. But the French are masters at making the "broth" in which these bugs must live and grow and produce their highly valued products in commercial quantities. This is a very different type of technology. And France's centuries-old experience in making wine and cheese, processes that use fermentation, may well be transferred to making interferon or insulin if the French can make the switch. The state oil company Elf-Aquitaine, the cement maker Lafarge-Coppé and the chemical and textile maker Rhône-Poulenc, are all coordinating efforts in biotechnology.

•

MARKETS FOR TECHNOLOGY—THE NEW TRADEOFF

The man who has best explained Europe's high-tech strategy for the 1980s is Carlo de Benedetti, chairman of giant Olivetti. He has single-handedly revived that once-moribund Italian office-equipment company and is firmly placing it in the "office-of-the-future" market. Not only is he pushing Olivetti away from mechanical typewriters into electronic machines, he is pouring millions into developing Olivetti electronic word processors, bank terminals and copiers. By the end of 1982, Olivetti was even selling its own small personal computers, one of the few European companies to do so.

De Benedetti is a quiet man. Composed. Even when excited, his expressions are contained, his motions fluid and brief. He is from Turin in the northwest and is one of the few Jews in Catholic Italy to attain power and high office in the closed, often secret world of Italian business, Masonic lodges, and quiet ties to the military, the Vatican and often the underworld.

De Benedetti first made his name when he took control of Fiat after Giovanni Agnelli bought out his auto parts company. At Fiat, he demanded sharp changes in labor and management practices to turn the ailing auto company around. Agnelli and the unions refused, and de Benedetti left after only three months. Last year Fiat put into place practically all of his recommendations and is now turning profitable for the first time in years.

De Benedetti left for Olivetti for the same purpose, to turn an ailing giant around. He sold his Fiat stock and bought into Olivetti, making him the largest private shareholder. This, in turn, gave de Benedetti the power he could never have at the Agnelli-dominated Fiat. And his prescriptions are being followed, with success. De Benedetti's strategy for saving Olivetti is very simple. He has spent $40 million to buy into some twenty-five small American high-technology companies. He then extracts the technology Olivetti needs for new electronic products and ships it home. In exchange for American technology, Olivetti arranges market access for the U.S. firms in Europe. The tactic is exquisite in its simplicity. It is also based on a single solid fact. To work, it assumes that Italy, France, and nearly all the other European markets are closed to free trade—and, of course, they are. Europeans are speeding to close their borders, erecting barriers to outside high-tech products and then using these same barriers as bargaining chips to get technology. In short, they are trading access to their domestic markets for access to crucial technology. "We want their technology and we provide them with markets," says de Benedetti.

For de Benedetti and Olivetti the payoff is already quite clear. Olivetti's new personal computer was not designed in Italy. It wasn't developed in Europe at all. Cupertino, California, in America's very own Silicon Valley, is the birthplace of Olivetti's new machine.

EUROPE TILTS TO THE PACIFIC BASIN

Olivetti's high-tech linkups are among a hundred such ties between European corporations and United States or Japanese groups. Many of Europe's oldest and proudest names are scrambling into joint ventures to bring in critical technology from overseas. Nothing illustrates the global tilt toward the Pacific Basin in the post-OPEC era more than the incredible number of ties now being created as European companies reach out to U.S. and Japanese corporations. Siemens alone has invested in twenty-two American companies, and its links with Japan's Fujitsu go so deep that the German company would be without computers or copiers to sell if it were not for the Japanese. Fujitsu has just agreed to put up a manless factory in Germany to turn out robots, and Siemens will sell these too under its own label. Siemens also sells optic-fiber cable produced jointly with Corning Glass under its own name. Without Corning, Siemens, the once proud German telecommunications giant, would be unable to lay the cable of the future—glass.

While the Italians are looking to the Americans for help in remaking their telecommunications network, they are turning to the Japanese for help in semiconductors. The only major Italian chip maker, SGS, has just signed a licensing agreement with Toshiba to import technology for local production. In Great Britain, Hitachi and NEC are setting up factories to produce the latest 64k RAM memory chips—to compete with the Americans. Siemens is just starting its own 64k production. In autos, of course, the weaker European companies are turning to the Japanese, with their proven technology. Britain's nationalized BL—British Leland—is assembling the Honda Acclaim automobile, while Italy's Alfa Romeo is signing up with Nissan.

•

THE FRENCH MILITARY-INDUSTRIAL COMPLEX

In getting access to foreign technology one European nation has a card not available to the others. Paris can offer the Americans something Germany, Italy, Britain and even Japan cannot—the second-largest military-industrial complex in the West after the United States. It was no coincidence that the Argentine fighter-bomber that sank the British destroyer HMS *Sheffield* in the Falklands fighting in May 1982 was the Super Etendard, built by France's Dassault-Breguet aircraft company. The missile that completely destroyed the ship was the Exocet, a French-built weapon made by Aerospatiale. Both companies, of course, are now nationalized under the Socialists. In fact, François Mitterrand's brother, Jacques Mitterand, is the head of Aerospatiale. France today is the third-largest exporter of modern arms in the world, and its $6 billion in annual shipments places it third behind the United States and the Soviet Union. And France's exports are not simply pistols or boots; they are all high-technology equipment. In fact, France's military electronics are among the best in the world. Military electronics are crucial to France's weapons programs—programs that employ 300,000 people; programs that the Socialists would not change once they came to power despite strong pressures to cut back France's exports of arms from its own left wing and Communist Party allies.

This huge military market, and of course the giant PTT telecommunications market, are the ones that U.S. companies are granted access to if they play France's high-tech protectionist game. In 1980, the central government offered up to $23 billion in contracts for the Defense Department. That came to 46 percent of all central government procurement. The PTT offered about $10 billion, or 20 percent of all the buying. Between the two departments, they ate up a huge percentage of the entire procurement pie. These enormous markets are controlled by skilled French technocrats who can guarantee set portions of it for U.S. high-tech manufacturers—but only if they play the game of technology transfer and joint venture.

Take Cii-Honeywell-Bull, for example. In 1976 France was desperate to build a national computer company that could compete both domestically and on world markets against IBM. Its own efforts at building computers had failed miserably. Paris went to a Minneapolis company, Honeywell, and offered a deal. If Honeywell would merge with Cii and transfer advanced technology to the French joint venture, it would provide government contracts to the new French company of up to 5 billion francs over a five-year period. This was a guarantee that IBM or Fujitsu or Siemens would not get those contracts, even if they offered better computers at lower prices. Honeywell agreed. Ironically, the government offer wasn't enough. Cii-Honeywell-Bull lost money continuously despite Paris's help. In 1982, Honeywell decided that the red ink on its own balance sheets wasn't worth the effort, so it sold most of its share in the joint venture back to the government.

The Cii-Honeywell-Bull joint venture is just one of dozens of business deals between French and American companies that involve trading access to a closed but huge French electronics market in exchange for advanced technology. With the Socialists now in power, that market may grow even faster than under the conservatives. A few U.S. corporations are pulling back from joint ventures with the French, because they fear the heavy hand of French bureaucracy. Continental Telephone, for example, broke off a project with Thomson-Brandt after the Socialist victory. But others are forging ahead, trading their expertise for profits. One of the biggest companies taken over by the Socialists was Matra, an electronics giant famous for its missiles, but also big in consumer electronics. Matra has a joint project with Harris Corporation, from which it gets semiconductor technology. In 1981, it enticed Intel Corporation, perhaps the leading American semiconductor maker, to join in a Matra-Harris-Intel project. So willing was Intel that it actually paid Matra to get into the new deal. And in October 1981, Tandy Corporation, maker of the popular TRS 80 minicomputer that it sells in Radio Shack stores around the United States, signed up with Matra to build personal computers for the French market.

•

VISION OF THE FUTURE

Matra's deals highlight France's special position in Europe. If any one European country manages to make the big leap from pre-OPEC heavy-industry to a post-OPEC high-tech economy, it will probably be France. For unlike anyone else in Europe, the French have a vision of the future; they know where they want to go and they are making every effort to get there. So far, they have had mixed success, but when compared to the British, German and Italian efforts, they are far ahead. Supported by their advanced military programs, helped by heavy government aid to the PTT, and tough enough to extract technology from foreign sources, the French are making a good showing for themselves in the fight for the technological heights of the '80s.

What they must now overcome is the heavy hand of Socialist bureaucracy, which could stifle innovation and kill growth. The new locomotive technologies require extreme flexibility and fast response to change—characteristics that hardly describe government bureaucracies. With most of the high-tech industry now under Paris's direct control, the French will have to allow them wide leeway in making decisions or they will fall further behind the Japanese and Americans. Without the winds of the marketplace to direct capital flow and product innovation, the technocrats will have a hard time succeeding.

The Concorde, of course, shows what could go wrong when bureaucrats, rather than the marketplace, rule. But the French can also point to the success of their Aerospatiale, the nationalized aerospace company that is one of the world leaders in helicopters. Aerospatiale is also the French member of the European Airbus consortium and the head of the Ariane rocket group that is challenging the U.S. space shuttle for the telecommunications satellite business.

•

SILICON FJORDS

While the behemoths of European industry, Germany's Siemens, Holland's Philips, Britain's Plessey, struggle to make the switch to high technology by linking up with the Americans and Japanese, there is a small group of companies across the Atlantic that are successfully innovating on their own. Right now a Silicon Fjord is being built in Scandinavia that may one day match the Silicon Valley of the West Coast. This little-known leap into the future for Europe at its icy, northern fringes may show the way for the entire continent.

In Sweden, Norway and Denmark, about a dozen private companies are breaking new ground in robots, telecommunications and biotechnology. They are competing with the likes of Fujitsu, ITT and General Telephone and Electronics and are winning huge contracts worth billions of dollars around the world. It was L. M. Ericsson's push into computerized telephone exchange in the middle 1970s that revolutionized all telephone systems around the world. Teamed up with the Dutch Philips for marketing clout, Ericsson has won a $5-billion contract—the biggest in the world—from Saudi Arabia to modernize its phone system. Yet this is just the icing on the cake. Some thirty countries now have Ericsson computerized telephone exchanges.

And L. M. Ericsson is not alone. Sweden's ASEA makes some of the finest industrial robots in the world. Many U.S. companies license them. The Japanese have copied them. And Volkswagen buys a third of the Swedish company's output every year. The Germans are even paying ASEA the same compliment the Japanese paid it—they are copying the robot.

To the south, in Denmark, Novo Industries is carving out a major name for itself in advanced drugs. It is a leader in enzyme research and is one of a dozen corporations at the leading edge of the biotechnology revolution.

In Norway, among the fjords, Norsk Data is growing at a 45 percent rate every year. It is a minicomputer company set up just years ago that can compete with any of the giants.

Indeed, that may be the secret behind Scandinavia's surprising success in technology. Scandinavian companies have home markets that are tiny compared to Germany, Italy, France or Britain. Companies in the middle-sized European countries have lulled themselves to sleep over the years thinking that they had safe, monopoly markets. But these markets are proving to be too small to generate world-class corporate competition. The Americans and the Japanese have markets big enough to provide the growth for success around the world. The European nations just aren't big enough.

The Swedes, Norwegians and Danes have always known that their tiny economies could not support large-scale companies. They have always had to export, to move into other markets. They have always had to be innovative and extremely flexible.

In some cases, individual entrepreneurs have started up their own companies in Scandinavia, a practice rather rare in most of Europe. Norsk Data was founded by three engineers on $500,000, much like Apple, the American personal-computer maker. In 1967, it developed a minicomputer. Since much of the seed money for Norsk Data came from Norway's wealthy shipping companies, it was natural for Norsk to first sell a collision-avoidance system. In 1972, the company came out with another computer, and sales have doubled annually since then. In 1981, Norsk won a $7.5-million contract to provide computers to Hughes Aircraft for the command-and-control system for NATO's northern European region.

Even the bigger Scandinavian companies like L. M. Ericsson have received much smaller amounts of government aid compared with the giants of the Continent. True, they have benefited from protectionist data policies, but so have dozens of other European companies. The key is in using the safety of a protected market to innovate, and selling those new products around the world. The French were leaders in semiconductor technology back in the 1950s but did nothing with it. The British have been in the forefront of jet planes, radar, CAT scanners and computers, yet they have failed at selling them. And the Germans are falling very far behind in virtually all the new technologies despite being pioneers in the old nineteenth-century innovations. By translating new inventions into new products and by moving quickly into the international markets with their high-tech wares, the tiny Scandinavian companies may be providing the pathways for the rest of Europe.

•

BALKANIZATION OF EUROPE

Yet, if there is some hope for France and a handful of small Scandinavian countries, the outlook for the rest of Europe remains very gloomy. None other than Otmar Emminger, head of Germany's Bundesbank for years and one of the great central bankers of the postwar era, says that "Europe is now a second-rate economic power. It is definitely number two in technology behind the United States and Japan. For the next fifteen years, it will be behind."

The closing-down of the world trade and investment lanes is far more advanced than politicians on either side of the Atlantic will admit. High-tech protectionism is building barriers around nations at a speed that hasn't been seen since the 1930s. In fact, so fast and so far has this new high-tech nationalism gone that people would be devastated if the evidence were shown to them.

If the Japanese would take time from basking in their own momentary technological glory, they might discover that nearly half their exports are already restricted formally or informally by governments. Autos, consumer electronics, machine tools, textiles, steel, ships and now semiconductors are all limited. Americans, Europeans and even developing nations around the world are curbing imports from Japan because of the enormous trade deficits they are running with that Pacific juggernaut. And it doesn't really matter that most of these restrictions are illegal. They are being implemented. It is not something that is supposed to happen in a world built on the principles of free trade and competition, a world built on the ashes of World War II.

Yet while all eyes are focused on the protectionist barriers being thrown up against the Japanese, it is within the Common Market itself that the worst damage is being done. It is now just as difficult in terms of border taxes and customs fees to ship from France to Germany as it is to ship from Germany to Australia. At a critical time, when tremendous resources are needed to make the switch to a whole new series of technologies, the Common Market is developing rigor mortis. It is drying up, caking over with brittle barriers.

With unemployment now reaching ten million people and with some estimates suggesting that by 1985 Europe may have as many as fifteen million out of work, politicians are frantically turning inward to save their countries and their own skins. They are worried because everywhere European politicians are being turned out by the voters. If the incumbents are to the Left, the voters go to the Right. This has happened in Britain, the Netherlands, Sweden, Belgium and elsewhere. If the incumbents are on the Right, the voters go Left. France, Greece and Spain are the best examples. But everywhere people are frightened as jobs are lost in obsolete industries and new jobs are not created in high-tech ones.

At its worst, the Common Market will become increasingly irrelevant. It is an organization that spends 80 percent of its money and 90 percent of its time on agricultural matters—an absurdity in the present context of high technology. If the

Common Market cannot move ahead, if it cannot create a genuinely united European market for the high-tech goods of the twenty-first century, then it will most surely break apart. Perhaps Greenland's decision in 1982 to leave the Common Market is far more apocryphal than people thought at the time. It is not improbable that by the year 2000, France will have led Spain, Portugal, Italy and Greece away to form a new Mediterranean Community while Germany takes the Netherlands, Denmark, and Austria into a separate orbit, perhaps closer to the East.

7

CRIMES OF THE '90s

AT THIS MOMENT, THERE ARE UP TO 300 KGB AGENTS ROAMING America on a special mission for Moscow—to ferret out the most advanced U.S. technology and get it back to the Soviet Union. Most of them ply their trade inside a triangle that fits within the Silicon Valley of the San Francisco Bay area, the "Silicon Prairie" around Dallas and the "Silicon Desert" near Phoenix. About two dozen or so KGB spies are stationed in the East to penetrate Route 128 in Boston and such companies as IBM, Loral and McDonnell Douglas in New York State. Like the world itself these days, the KGB presence tilts away from the Atlantic toward the Pacific.

The KGB is interested in all types of American technology, from the electronics that go into spy-in-the-sky satellites to the mysterious materials that mask Stealth bombers from radar. But they are especially keen to get their hands on one item, VHSIC (pronounced VISIK), the very high-speed integrated circuit that may determine the military and economic balance of power in the world for the next generation.

The Soviet spies are not alone. The French Ministry of Defense has a man with a Ph.D. in engineering in charge of a program to keep track of all advanced computer developments in America. This man, who holds a green card that allows him to work in the country, also has instructions to be especially sensitive to a particular project—VHSIC. The French have a long history of technology "adventures" in the United States. In 1974, Vernon Edler, an aerospace executive from Newport Beach, California, was convicted of selling rocket technology to Paris. He signed a contract with Société Européenne de Propulsion to provide advanced rocket gear and advice. But when the State Department turned down his request for permission to proceed with the contract, Edler went ahead anyway, and was convicted for it.

Of course, the Japanese are around as well. In the 1960s they set up dozens of "listening posts" in California to gather intelligence about American electronics companies. The data they gathered were critical in establishing Japan's early semiconductor and computer industries. In the 1970s, dozens of Japanese swept through the Silicon Valley like a plague of chip-eating locusts. Offering millions of dollars in cash, they scooped up thousands of the most advanced semiconductor chips then available. Most of the purchases were legal. Many were not. Once home, Japanese scientists reverse-engineered the chips and began building on the American invention to the point where they now are the equals of any in the world.

Today, however, the Japanese are especially worried. They know their laboratories can push any known electronic invention to its limits. But they also realize that Japan has yet to move to the point of creating its own technology. The Japanese are copycat manufacturers, buying and borrowing brand-new innovations from abroad and improving them for export. Any foreign innovation threatens to leapfrog them. Today, the United States is forging ahead faster than ever in computer technology, and the Japanese are scrambling to keep up. In 1982, in what has come to be called "Japscam," the FBI caught a number of Hitachi and Mitsubishi Electric employees trying to buy stolen IBM computer secrets. The aim was to gain early access to IBM technology, copy it, and sell it abroad for a lower price. Ironically, the FBI "sting" that caught the Japanese was originally set up to snare KGB industrial spies. The Japanese simply walked into the trap first.

Governments have been spying ever since people banded together to create governments. Spying, or data gathering, is an essential component of all statecraft. In the past, the usual targets were military installations and contingency plans. Nations have also been interested in the actual machines of war. The Soviets used spies to get their hands on the hydrogen bomb. And the Israeli Kfir fighter-bomber is a near-duplicate of the French Mirage.

At the same time, industrial espionage has been around for centuries as well. The British made every effort to stop competitors from getting their new technology at the beginning of the Industrial Revolution: The spinning jenny had to be smuggled into the United States as memorized blueprints in the brains of skilled English workers. The machines themselves couldn't be exported from the country. Today, "patent infringement" is a common cry in America. Apple Computer has taken other companies to court for copying its software. And IBM spends $50 million a year to field a small, private corporate army of former FBI agents to look after its secrets and ensure the loyalty of its employees.

Occasionally military spying and commercial espionage even come together and overlap, as when the Germans needed the secret of synthetic rubber in World War II and I. G. Farben became involved in it. But usually, foreign spies tend to turn up in places like Langley, Virginia, headquarters for the CIA, or in military bases in Germany. Industrial spies tend to spend their time breaking into safes and looking for the secret of Coca-Cola's syrup, or hanging out in the Bay area, at bars frequented by engineers. The two spying fraternities have not generally mingled in the past.

THE TECHNOLOGY DISJUNCTION

A good part of the reason why political and commercial spies don't mix is that for the past century most industrial nations have had just about the same kinds of industries based on the same kinds of technology. Man's machines haven't changed a whole lot in recent years. The technology of the world's industrial base was invented in the nineteenth century, and the past decades have been periods of refinement, not dramatic change. The cars, electric motors, chemicals, plastics, steel, telephones, telegraphs, heavy machines—all go back many, many decades.

There are exceptions, of course—aviation and nuclear power. Indeed, one of the best examples of military espionage involved the passing of American nuclear secrets to Moscow. And that did change the balance of power to a degree. Yet even so, the people of the United States, Japan, Europe and the Soviet Union have continued, until recently, to live on the same technological plateau, producing very similar products.

This has now all changed. Periodically, the world undergoes a technological disjunction that kicks everything out of place and rearranges how we all relate to one another. When, centuries ago, the world moved from agriculture to industry, new empires were born and old empires were destroyed, nations rose and fell, classes disintegrated, and the very structure of the family changed. None of it could have been foreseen. Britain became the most powerful country in Europe, and Europe came to dominate agrarian China and the rest of the globe. Power shifted away from the Pacific Basin to the Atlantic Ocean and remained there for the next three or four centuries. The second phase of the Industrial Revolution in the mid-nineteenth century produced another dramatic shift. Within Europe, power shifted away from Britain to Germany, setting the stage for two world wars and the emergence of a bipolar world dominated by the United States and the USSR.

Today, another technological disjunction is taking place. The world is poised to take a quantum leap to a higher technological plateau. We are in the midst of a massive, all-enveloping whirlwind of change occurring in all spheres of life at once. It is like nothing before it. It is completely different from the introduction of the airplane or the beginning of television. For it is an all-pervasive, powerful and penetrating blast of change that is affecting homes, workplaces, governments, and international politics, all at the same time.

•

TECHNO-ASSETS AND CRIME

The fate of this century and the century to come is being decided now. Success in high technology in the 1980s will determine the balance of power in the world for the 1990s and the early twenty-first century. Government leaders aware of what is taking place know that those left behind now will become second-class global citizens tomorrow.

This is why high-tech crime is exploding. This is why the stealing of information, of data, of technology itself is becoming the crime of the future. Technology is becoming the most valued commodity in all the world. Every government, every corporation, every individual needs it to make the transition to the twenty-first century.

But, like the natural resources of the past—iron, coal and oil—technology is not evenly distributed around the globe. Only a tiny number of countries can produce it, only a handful of people can make it. These individuals, these companies, these nations now hold destiny in their hands. And everyone wants a piece of that future. If they can't create technology themselves, then they want to buy it. If they can't buy it, they want to steal it. They must get technology or perish. A pool of technology is now the most important asset a country can have, and it is becoming increasingly clear that for America, as for every other nation, "techno-assets" cannot be allowed to be sold cheaply, leaked or stolen away. In an era of technology supremacy, technology transfer has become a major political-, social- and economic-policy issue.

This is why high-tech crime will soon supersede street crime in America as the most serious type of injury. In an era of fantastic industrial upheaval, in a time of dramatic changes in military weapons, the future course of history will be determined by what is being invented and how it is being used.

This is why military spies and industrial spies are beginning to trip over one another as they go about their business. Industrial espionage is becoming a *modus operandi* not only for the KGB but also for Japanese computer makers, French semiconductor manufacturers and probably not a few American corporations as well.

Military needs for high-tech goods are becoming identical with commercial needs for high-tech goods. Chips that go into jet-fighter aircraft also go into toys, appliances, machine tools. Military competition and commercial competition are beginning to overlap. Everyone is getting into industrial espionage. Today, the KGB has more to worry about than just the FBI as it hunts about the United States. The men of Hitachi or Mitsubishi may get to the laboratories before them!

In fact, it is likely that dozens of Japanese and Europeans are graduating every year from supersecret corporate-espionage schools. So intense is the drive for industrial espionage that Herschell Britton, executive vice-president of Burns International Security Services, believes that there are now two such schools in operation in Japan and another one in Switzerland. These schools are privately owned and operated, although they could not possibly exist without the governments of both those countries knowing about who runs them and what they do.

•

"ONE-EYED JACK"

With political and commercial spies tripping over one another in an increasingly competitive business, it is little wonder that they are beginning to look for help. It is now clear that the masters of the KGB, the cream of Soviet society, and Japanese corporate moguls, the cream of Japanese society, are both turning to ordinary American hoods for help. Crooks are becoming the middlemen, stealing high-technology items to sell to the highest bidder, be it a local American company desperately short of supplies, a Japanese or German corporation wanting to compete with the United States, or the KGB, looking for ways to improve the accuracy of Russia's missiles. High technology is the most valued item in America today and everyone wants it—including local crooks who need to make a buck, domestic corporate rivals, foreign economic competitors, and the sworn enemies of the United States.

Nothing better illustrates this new configuration where the line between old-fashioned crime and espionage disappears than the bizarre story of "one-eyed" John Henry Jackson, a petty thief with a bad eye, who would be king of the high-tech outlaws. John Henry was never really big in the crime business. He has been convicted of passing bad checks, forgery and burglary. In the middle of 1982, he was facing charges of grand larceny, or "conspiracy in the buying, receiving and possessing of stolen and altered property," as they say in the courts. But the property so mentioned is not gold coins, fancy hi-fi equipment or sterling silver. It is microchips and rather fancy microchips at that.

In San Jose, California, John Henry is being accused of leading a crime ring that stole ten thousand 32k Eprom chips from Intel Corporation, the inventor of the "computer on the chip" microprocessor and one of Silicon Valley's biggest manufacturers. Like so many of today's technological innovations, Intel's Eproms can be plopped down into arcade video games to make space blasters work. And they can also be plugged into electronic guidance systems for supersonic jet fighters.

The people of San Jose are saying that John Henry bribed a security guard at Intel to get around the closed-circuit TV, sign-in logs, fenced-in storage room and twenty-four-hour guard system. He also had an "inside" man at the executive level of Intel, according to the police. This insider set up the paperwork to get ten thousand extra chips manufactured, then destroyed the papers and allowed the chips to be stolen without any record of their manufacture or their disappearance.

The chips were taken from Intel's Santa Clara factory to Sunnyvale, where John Henry had a distribution company called Dyno Electronics. Dyno, it is alleged, then sold the Intel chips to Space Age Metals in Gardenia, California. Space Age denies this. The police also say that Jackson told them Space Age then sold the chips to Mormac Technology, Inc., of Tarzana, California, and to Republic Electronics, Inc., of Arlington, Virginia. Mormac and Republic are known in the trade as "schlockers"—chip brokers, or middlemen, who provide chips to needy customers caught short of the precious little devices. Where they obtain the chips is of little concern to their desperate clients, who usually don't ask too many questions.

According to the court documents, Mormac and Republic then sold the stolen Intel chips to another broker, this one in West Germany. It is called E.D.V. Elektronik. E.D.V. Elektronik turned around and sold Intel's Eproms to Germany's electronics giant Siemens. Siemens was already receiving about one thousand Eproms a month from Intel, but it wasn't enough; it needed a lot more.

But this is only part of the story. While a German corporate competitor was getting the stolen chips, another rival to the United States is alleged to have received them—Moscow. In addition to John Henry Jackson, Patrick Ketchum is being charged in San Jose in the same case. Ketchum is an officer with Mormac, and John Henry has told the police that Ketchum sold some of his stolen chips to Anatoli T. Maluta and Werner J. Bruchhausen. Maluta is a naturalized United States citizen born in Russia and Bruchhausen is a West German. Charges were later dropped against Ketchum, because the government couldn't prove he knew that John Henry was peddling hot chips.

There is good reason to believe that those fancy stolen Intel chips made their way not only into Siemens consumer products, but perhaps into Soviet "reverse-engineering" laboratories, or even directly into MIG jet fighters. Bruchhausen has made a business of selling U.S. high technology to the Russians. In mid-1982, he was at large in Europe while the United States tried to extradite him. He has houses in Monte Carlo and Vienna, a traditional Soviet transit point, as well as in Germany. A federal grand jury accused him in late 1980 of using seven front companies in the United States to acquire advanced chips and other electronic gear for illegal export to the Eastern bloc. He is charged with getting to Russia at least two Data General computer systems, three microwave receivers and other electronic surveillance equipment and a number of Xincom semiconductor–memory-test systems made by Fairchild Camera and Instruments Corporation. The federal prosecutors say that Bruchhausen used a front called Consolidated Protection Development Corporation to buy equipment that is used by the U.S. Navy for submarine reconnaissance, and to ship it to the East. The crates were labeled "electrical meters." While it is legal to export meters, it is not legal to export microwaves. Bruchhausen remains at large, but his partner Maluta was convicted of income-tax evasion and thirteen other felonies in relation to the illegal exports.

•

JAPSCAM

The "one-eyed Jack" operation highlights several major trends coming together in the crimes of the 1980s: the targeting by both commercial and political rivals of the same type of high-tech goods; the use of local gangsters as providers of these goods; the concentration on the Western region of the United States for high-tech espionage.

The stolen-chips crime also highlights one other major fact of life in the Silicon Valley: everybody is in the market for high-technology information. The existence of dozens of "consultants," of middlemen, of industry "analysts," indicates that information about rival companies and their products is critical, and always for sale, not especially to the Japanese but to the hundreds of local American companies doing business there.

The buying and selling of high-tech information is part of the corporate culture in California. It stems in large part from the high mobility of the scientists and engineers who work there. It is part of the tradition of Silicon Valley for people who work for major electronics companies to defect and set up their own tiny companies. In fact, this is how such established giants as Intel and National Semiconductor got their start. But the very mobility of the people means that they bring with them information, if not in written form, then in their heads. These engineers carry with them the modern equivalent of the spinning jenny.

In this explosive environment, intense rivalry often pushes companies to extremes. "Buying" product managers and engineers from competitors with hot tubs, cars and sexual favors, not to mention money, is common in California. It is a lot cheaper to try to get a look at a new product or a new set of designs, but if that fails, buying the man or team behind the project is another way of beating the competition.

In this game, consulting firms are major players. They bring together the money men, the venture capitalists, and the engineers with the innovations. They also sell detailed intelligence on companies and their products. Sometimes, they will even put together a whole corporation for a foreigner. Integrated Circuit Engineering, out of Arizona, has stitched together entire teams of semiconductor engineers and production managers plus the actual manufacturing plants for Japanese clients.

But this is all part of the game in Silicon Valley—a game everyone plays. What is not common at all is the federal agents' arrest at the San Francisco airport of an employee of one of Japan's biggest electronics companies just as he was boarding a flight to Tokyo carrying out stolen documents on advanced IBM computers. What is not common is for the FBI to deliberately set up a "sting" operation that aims to catch KGB spies and winds up with senior Japanese engineers from Hitachi and Mitsubishi. What is not common is for huge sums of money, perhaps up to three quarters of a million dollars, to change hands during the course of the Japanese intelligence gathering.

"Japscam," as it was called in mid-1982 when the scandal splashed across the papers on all continents, marked a new level of industrial espionage—and counterespionage. Eighteen Japanese businessmen, many of them top officials, were charged with conspiring to steal confidential IBM technology. Six were arrested by the FBI, and warrants were issued for the rest of them in Japan, including Kenji Hayashi, senior engineer for Hitachi.

Both Hitachi and Mitsubishi admitted that their officials paid cash to obtain secrets on new IBM computers. They argued, however, that they did not know that the secrets were stolen. Yet such sums of money could not have been authorized without senior people in both companies knowing about it. An FBI affidavit filed in court in San Francisco said that a source working with an undercover agent made it a point to tell a senior Hitachi engineer that the people who stole the

IBM documents "risk disgrace and perhaps imprisonment" if they were apprehended. The response was "the risk involved in obtaining the IBM products is not important to Hitachi."

The Japanese objective was to get intelligence about IBM's biggest machines, the 3081s, hundreds of which have already been shipped to customers. IBM has made significant changes in the architecture of this new series of computers. These changes increase the power of the computers far above anything yet in existence, including competing Japanese computers. But IBM has not yet given its customers the software to activate the new features of the 3081 family of computers. That is in the "microcode," the detailed program instructions that tell the computer what to do. With the microcode in their hands, the Japanese would be able to know just what the new generation of IBM computers was capable of doing and how it did it.

Like the Soviets, both Hitachi and Mitsubishi make copycat IBM computers that operate very much like IBM originals and use the same programming. In fact, nearly all the Japanese computer makers, from Fujitsu, the leader, to Mitsubishi, the smallest, make IBM "plug-compatible" computers. Only Nippon Electric Corporation (NEC) makes a different type of machine. The Japanese computer makers know that IBM dominates the global market. Their strategy is to wait for IBM to come out with a powerful new model, reverse-engineer it, copy it, and offer their own brands to customers at lower prices. In addition, they make peripheral devices, such as printers, memory disks, and terminals, that can be plugged right into the IBM.

In the 1970s, the Japanese companies grew very quickly. IBM was slow in upgrading its technology and waited five years or so before moving on to more complex computers. This allowed the Japanese plenty of time to copy them. Recently, IBM changed policy and deliberately began to increase the frequency of technological changes it introduced into its computers. Now the changes are occurring much faster, and

IBM's rivals are racing to keep up. The attempt to buy the stolen documents and equipment parts was an attempt to shortcut the copying process. The Japanese wanted a peek at the new generation of computers so they could produce their own as quickly as possible. In fact, there is a real risk that unless they get that information, Hitachi and Mitsubishi might not be able to keep up with IBM. Only Fujitsu appears able to compete with IBM on nearly equal terms.

Hitachi is number four among computer makers in Japan, behind Fujitsu, IBM-Japan and NEC. It is by far the most ambitious to catch up, and it is no coincidence that it was Hitachi and Mitsubushi that got involved in Japscam.

In September 1981, the FBI set up their Operation Pengem —"Penetrate the Gray Electronics Market"—to catch Soviet spies stealing U.S. high technology. A month later, one of their own former agents, working for IBM, went to it with news that the Japanese had already bought confidential computer documents and were shopping for more. In August, IBM found out that certain volumes of its "Adirondack Hardware Design Workbook" had found their way to Hitachi.

Later it would turn out that an Iranian national, Barry Saffaie, working as a product manager for National Semiconductor Corporation's National Advanced Systems unit, had delivered eleven volumes of the Adirondack material to a Hitachi official. National has very close business ties to Hitachi. National sells Hitachi's big IBM-compatible computers in the United States. It would also turn out that Saffaie had hired for his assistant an IBM alumnus, Raymond J. Cadet. Finally, it would turn out that the thirty-eight-year-old Mr. Saffaie was something of a charlatan. His Ph.D. from the University of Southern California was a fake. But National had never checked him out. Nor had Amdahl, Magnusun Computer and Xerox, all of which had employed him as an engineer and product manager. Nor had the Defense Department. National is a major producer of microchips for the Pentagon.

After being shown the evidence, the FBI reluctantly agreed

to shift the focus of Operation Pengem away from Moscow to the Japanese. Following the procedures set up in the congressional Abscam case, the FBI, along with IBM's own security staff, began coordinating a "sting" operation. A dummy corporation called Glenmar was set up to look like a typical Silicon Valley technology brokerage firm. An agent, Alan J. Garretson, led the operation. He met with Kenji Hayashi, a senior engineer at Hitachi, several times in Las Vegas, Honolulu, Hartford, and elsewhere. Hayashi's requests for information continually escalated. In the end, the Japanese wanted more than just the microcode and other data on the new 3081 computer series. They wanted Garretson to recruit retiring IBM employees to serve as "consultants" to Hitachi. Hitachi had a kitty of $1 million for these retirees and was willing to pay up to $40,000 for a month's "debriefing."

At one point, Garretson gained entrance for another senior Hitachi engineer, Jun Naruse, into the Pratt and Whitney Aircraft Group's building in Hartford in order to see a working 3380 computer disk drive. Fat envelopes were exchanged for badges that allowed them to pass armed guards into the computer room.

The trap was finally sprung in June, when Hitachi sent a half-million dollars over the bank wire to an account in Garretson's name. Several Japanese were led off in handcuffs, a terrible dishonor. After denials, both Hitachi and Mitsubishi admitted paying the money but insisted they did not know they were doing anything illegal. On February 8, 1983, Hitachi pleaded guilty to conspiring to steal IBM secrets.

•

IBM—THE "DARTH VADER" OF COMPUTER COMPANIES

"Japscam" highlighted one of the major new crimes of the '80s —technology theft—and lifted the secrecy on IBM's own efforts at protecting its valuable secrets. In September 1982 it sued three of its own engineers, charging that they were selling secret information on the popular new IBM personal computer. The three had been in charge of developing the small computer and were offering data that would permit other companies to build plug-compatible peripheral equipment for the computers. In fact, they were planning to leave IBM, set up their own company and begin building the peripherals themselves.

Had the three waited to offer the information until they had left IBM, their action might have been legal. Silicon Valley is awash with lawsuits by companies against former employees who left to establish their own competing businesses. Most of the lawsuits fail because the information is in the minds of the people involved. It is very difficult to distinguish between proprietary information and knowledge carried around in a person's brain. But the IBM three appear to have been greedy and couldn't wait before selling their secrets.

They also went up against one of the biggest, well-trained and aggressive private police forces in the world—IBM's $50-million security system. Led by former FBI and Treasury agents who retain close ties to the government, the private guards are organized under the euphemistic name of Information Systems and Communications Group, within IBM. The Group has more than four hundred people working on security matters, and it uses IBM's own superiority in computers to keep track of data and personnel. IBM's security force matches the power of the company itself. In California's Silicon Valley, IBM is known as "Darth Vader."

•

REACH OUT AND TOUCH THAT PERSONAL FILE

Not only is the current technological revolution changing who is involved in crime and what is being stolen, but the way crime is being committed is undergoing a vast change. America is fast becoming a "wired" society where activities of all types are taking place electronically. The switch from a paper culture filed away in drawers to an electronic society where computers store information and transmit data is occurring much faster than any of us really imagines. And the consequences are incredible.

Think for a moment what it means for the IRS to have your financial life stored in computers instead of paper files. With files, a few people had access to your personal information. It probably took a lot of time to call out your particular papers in Washington. It took hours to write new information down on you, days to mail it, and perhaps weeks to put it all together.

When the IRS went "hot," that all changed. All the data on your financial life was centralized in a single computer. Adding to and subtracting from that file became virtually instantaneous. And most important of all, anyone who could tap into that IRS computer could tap into your file as well. Anyone with a terminal and a phone hookup can now "reach out and touch that file" in the IRS computer. Anyone with the right code can pass the security system of that computer and enter your very own IRS file. When the government tax men went electronic, information became incredibly centralized; yet, at the same time, access to that information became more available. Both in terms of numbers and geography, the potential number of people who can tap into any computer anywhere depends simply on the phone lines in this country—in the world, for that matter—and the number of computer terminals available.

What does that mean? The potential for government abuse of the right of privacy is growing tremendously. Washington is into its second year of the Computer Matching Project, a massive attempt to track down deadbeats by comparing computers' spools. That goal is something we can all applaud. The procedure is simple. Two spools of data about individuals are cross-checked for contradictions. And the contradictions can be anything the government wants to investigate. For example, the Veterans Administration ran tapes listing people on the federal payroll against tapes listing people owing the government money. It discovered thousands of people who owed a total of nearly $40 million and immediately began taking cash out of their paychecks. In New York, Albany is running tapes of welfare recipients and matching them against wage information filed with the Department of Taxation to find out if they are working or not. A saving of nearly $70 million has been reported by curbing "double-dipping," or the drawing of salaries as well as welfare.

But the government wants to go beyond checking up on welfare cheats. It also wants to use IRS data to help the Selective Service track down draft evaders. That would involve using, for totally different purposes, data submitted by individuals for tax purposes. The government also wants to curb cheating by checking on the interest income of Social Security recipients. Yet such data are submitted by banks solely for the purpose of taxes and have nothing to do with the Social Security Administration. At the same time, Washington is trying to save money and raise efficiency by reducing the "redundant" number of computers and data files flowing around the government by centralizing many of them. It's a laudable goal, but it threatens individual privacy. The Computer Matching Project is looking into a central federal computer service, although opposition from the ACLU and other groups has kept it all in the study stage so far. But it may be that one day we will be stopped for a broken taillight and, after waiting a few moments while the police check into the federal computer, find ourselves being dunned for some overdue taxes or questioned about a nephew who hasn't registered for the draft.

•

THE TAPPING OF HOME COMPUTERS

The potential for computer abuse at the government level is clearly growing. But it still lags light-years behind what is taking place right in our own homes. With personal computers now costing as little as $100, they are invading the households of America and Japan like the TVs of the 1950s. And the children are leading the computer revolution in both countries. Go into any video store in either country and you will see kids taking their fathers by the hand to model after model. In America, they often go first to the video games—Atari or Intellivision. But soon afterward they are back for the real thing—personal computers that have the power of the behemoths of twenty years ago, the giants that took up whole rooms.

Right now computers are becoming the home appliance of the 1980s. In 1980, only a few thousand home computers could be found scattered around the country. By 1981, one half of one percent of all U.S. homes had them. A year later 2 percent had them. By the end of the decade, over 25 percent of all American homes will have small computers to play on, work on, design on—and steal with. Where once people talked about their Zeniths or Sonys or RCA color TVs, they now discuss their Apples, their IBMs, their Commodores, their Tandys and their Sinclairs.

Computer classes are spreading throughout the nation's school system, and computer literacy is becoming as important as reading, writing and arithmetic. Computer camps and computer schools are popping up all over. Where once only specialists knew how to manipulate computers, now millions of kids are into "data diddling," "superzapping" and "logic bombs." Even prisons are teaching computer programming, to the horror of many police authorities. And computerized operations are sweeping through corporate America, as the "office of the future" tries to do away with paper. Pretty soon, every secretary, every manager will know how to use one.

What this means is that access to computer-based information is increasing tremendously. The equipment to tap into corporate or military or government computers is spreading quickly along with the skills in using the new electronic machines.

This will have tremendous consequences for all kinds of things in America, including crime. Some of the biggest crimes of the past five years involved computers. The pioneers in computerizing their operations were, of course, the banks. "Electronic funds transfer," or EFT, has been around for years. In fact, all money transactions today go over a complex electronic wire system that connects the banks in this country and a good many foreign banks as well. It isn't any surprise that the first "computer crimes" have involved robbing these banks electronically.

But we are going far beyond banking today. Nearly all the designing of products, ranging from airplanes to missiles to automobiles to Nike running shoes, is being done on computers. Electronic "pens" are being used to trace intricate designs right on terminal screens. And the technology isn't so esoteric as to be used only by engineers. Anyone can buy an Apple and pick up an electronic "pen" to design toys, clothes, a new Rubik's cube perhaps. Even computers are being designed on computers. CAD—computer-aided design—is designing America's tomorrow.

U.S. microchip companies such as Intel and Motorola are setting up design facilities in Europe and Israel to take advantage of their excellent and less expensive engineers. Communication is done through satellite. That means that anyone who wants to know what his competitor is planning for the future will have to change his mode of operation. In the past, a thief would have to steal the large number of paper pages the designs were drawn on, be they designs for a new Detroit car or designs for a new fighter guidance system. Now the thief has to tap into the computer on which the engineer is designing his new creation. Or intercept the satellite transmission of a company factory with headquarters.

•

THE VULNERABLE ARPANET

In fact, the more the United States gets wired, the more vulnerable it is to high-tech crime. Already the Post Office is experimenting with an electronic mail system, E/Com, that uses computers to send private messages. Unfortunately they are more like open postcards than closed letters, for anyone with access can read the message. And anyone who really wants to intercept will be able to "mailtap" the telephone wires along which the electronic mail runs.

But we don't have to wait a few years to experience this new electronic vulnerability. The supersecret VHSIC project is a concrete example. The VHSIC chip will have one hundred times the data-processing power of existing chips. It is at the heart of the Pentagon's strategy of technological superiority over the Soviets. It will provide a whole new generation of chips that will be the foundation of the nation's electronic warfare. And it may become the heart of America's commercial counterattack against the Japanese in consumer electronics as well.

The VHSIC project is being funded by the Department of Defense and coordinated by the Defense Advanced Research Projects Agency (DARPA), but nearly all the actual work is being done by private U.S. corporations and universities. To hasten the goal of building new microcircuits that can handle information at speeds of one hundred times that of present chips, DARPA has set up a separate electronic network called the Arpanet that transmits classified data among twenty Defense Department installations around the world and forty U.S. universities and technical institutions. This allows the Pentagon to have access to the widest pool of talent available.

Satellite communications permit both military and civilian chip designers to sit in front of their CAD terminals, call up special software, create new chip-circuit designs, transmit them to colleagues for discussion and eventually pass on completed chip matrices to the University of Southern California's Information Sciences Institute. When USC is satisfied, it sends the designs to a silicon "foundry" for production.

It's a marvelous way of cutting time and speeding production. It could also be an electronic nightmare if the Soviets, the Japanese, the French or anyone else finds a way to tap into the system and copy the data flowing along. In fact, one of the KGB's prime espionage targets in America today is the Arpanet and the vital information on VHSIC that flows through it. The Pentagon insists that the network lines are secure. But in fact, teen-agers have been tapping into Arpanet for years, using the network as an electronic bulletin board. And if the kids can get into Arpanet, so can America's commercial and military rivals.

•

HIGH-TECH IMMIGRANT LABOR

VHSIC also highlights another vulnerability of America's techno-assets—a problem common to the entire semiconductor-chip industry. From a quarter to a third of all designing engineers in the United States are foreigners. It is one of America's great strengths that it can tap the entire brain pool of the world in this great race for the technological heights of the 1980s. No other nation is as open to the scientists and engineers of other countries. And no other nation is benefiting as much. Clearly, the Japanese, with their closed society, even the French or the Germans and certainly the Russians, could never hope to bring together the mind power of so many diverse peoples.

But there may yet be a price to pay for all this. Thousands of students from abroad have finished their engineering degrees at MIT, Stanford and Berkeley to go to jobs as chip designers or product engineers in the most advanced U.S. corporations. Many come from Europe. Hundreds come from Pakistan and India. Hundreds more come from Libya and Iran. Often they are debriefed when they go back home. Often this information gets back to Moscow. Often they are more open to bribery or blackmail, less committed to the United States and their companies than are American citizens.

Corporate officials insist that they are excluding foreign nationals from classified and sensitive semiconductor and computer work while moving quickly ahead on VHSIC and other programs. Perhaps they can succeed. But it may be no coincidence that in the IBM spy case, an Iranian, Barry Saffaie, working for a U.S. computer company, National Advanced Systems, a unit of National Semiconductor, which has close business ties to a competing Japanese electronics giant, Hitachi, was instrumental in getting the high-tech secrets.

•

THE FRENCH CONNECTION AGAIN

The problem of vulnerability to foreign tapping of high-tech secrets does not end with personnel. Many of the U.S. high-tech companies involved with the Pentagon in VHSIC are also linked to foreign corporations and foreign governments. As yet there is no evidence that technology is being transferred out of America through the foreign connections of any U.S. companies. But the possibility grows every day, and an increasing number of Washington officials are contemplating legislation to block technology flows of this type.

Exchanging market access for technology is one of the most common strategies of the Europeans and Third World countries. Without forking over significant kinds of technology, U.S. companies could not operate in France or Brazil, Singapore or South Korea.

Right now Harris Corporation is deeply involved with Matra, the French electronics giant, in designing and producing semiconductor chips. Intel is also intimately involved in chip design and production with Matra. Recently nationalized by the Socialists, Matra is also one of France's premier missile makers and sophisticated arms producers. Harris Corporation is one of about a dozen U.S. companies deeply involved in VHSIC. It is part of a Westinghouse-led team of companies that includes Control Data and National Semiconductor.

Many officials in the government believe that Moscow, through agents and the local Communist Party, has access to virtually all of France's technology. They had access before the Socialists in alliance with the Communists took power in 1981, and that access has improved since. Already there is fear that certain technology designed in the United States that lends itself to be radiation-hardened against nuclear attack may pass to the Soviets because, under recent contracts, Matra will be able to buy it. One close observer of this scene says, "The Soviets will have access to this technology and in the next two or three years will reverse-engineer it." But the big prize is VHSIC. If the French gain access to VHSIC? "The more the French know about VHSIC, the more the Russians will know about VHSIC."

•

ELECTRONIC WARFARE

For the Soviets, VHSIC is just one of the parts that go into a larger concept—electronic warfare. Israel's total destruction of Russian-built SAM missiles in the Lebanon war in 1982 sent a deadening chill down the backs of the Soviet Union's military leaders. In one day, Israel destroyed nearly ninety MIGs without a single loss to their own U.S.-made jets. They took out not only all the old SAM-6 antiaircraft missiles that had done so much damage to them in the 1973 war against

Egypt but also the more advanced SAM-8s and SAM-9s as well.

The Israeli victory was based on electronics. Small, inexpensive drone planes were sent into the Bekaa Valley of Lebanon where the Syrian SAMs were stationed and beamed down signals that persuaded the Syrians they were jet planes. The Syrians then switched on their radar to attack them. This allowed the Israelis to "fingerprint" the radar. This information was then beamed to U.S.-made E-2C command planes jam-packed with computers. It coordinated the radar jammers on board Israeli attack planes and also directed artillery barrages on the SAM sites. As the Israeli jets came in, they sent out small rockets; these dispersed aluminum chaff, which helped to confuse the ground radar, already under pressure from jamming. F-4 Phantom planes with Wild Weasel jammers came in low and fired missiles that homed right in on the radar frequencies of the SAM missiles. When the Syrians realized that their own radar was the vector for the attacking jets, they shut them down. The Israelis then attacked with old-fashioned iron bombs and wiped them out. When the Syrians sent up a hundred MIGs to counter the Israeli jets, the E-2C command plane sent the Israeli F-16s and F-15s out to a point where they could fire their long-range air-to-air missiles before the Syrian jets could detect them.

It was a masterful display of the war of the future—a war that the Soviets now realize they cannot win without electronics. To get these electronics, Moscow is beefing up its high-tech spy network. It has nearly doubled its technology collection agents to five thousand and is targeting VHSIC and computers. Just as important, the agents are going to the corporate source for many of these innovations, and they are looking for the actual manufacturing equipment to take home and copy.

Such major companies as IBM are always a focus of industrial espionage, as the Japscam spying episode shows. But the most vulnerable companies appear to be the smallest. One of

America's strengths in technology is the ability of individual engineers and scientists to translate their inventions into small businesses. Very often, these shoestring firms are among the most advanced in the world, technologically—and the most backward financially. Scientists only sometimes make good businessmen. When they find themselves in trouble, some do not ask too many questions from people offering "help."

Today, the nine hundred small high-tech companies ranging throughout the West and Southwest plus the one hundred or so in the East are the main targets of foreign industrial espionage. The Soviets are also targeting the big Japanese high-tech corporations as well as the dozens of tiny companies in Britain, Scandinavia and France.

Moscow has a standardized method of operation in collecting high-tech data. The State Committee for Science and Technology (GKNT) coordinates the program. First it identifies a specific technology or piece of equipment that is new and potentially useful to Russia. The Soviets are specially set up on the West Coast for this type of thing. The Consul General in San Francisco is Aleksandr Chikvaidze, an engineer and former chairman of the Soviet Union's Committee for Science and Technology.

The first option is to buy the data or the equipment legally on the open market. Nearly 90 percent of all the high-tech items the Soviets want can be purchased legally. With so few barriers to technology transfer and with toys and appliances often containing more advanced electronics than fighter planes or missiles, Moscow can usually satisfy its needs simply by putting up hard cash.

When the Soviets cannot buy high technology freely, they proceed to the second step—setting up a local "front" business either in America or in Europe. The front begins to buy non-sensitive equipment and advice from the small, targeted company that also makes the new technology. The goal is to build up a financial dependency gradually.

At some point the Soviets pull the string taut. In the past, this has occurred most often during bad economic times. The recession of 1974–1975 and the most recent one were periods of very high activity. Now, with the push into a new era of high-tech development, industrial espionage will continue on a new high level of frequency for the rest of the decade.

Once the string is pulled on a target company, the demand for that "special" high-tech product is made. The Soviet or Eastern bloc front company buys it, but since it is illegal to export such goods to the East, the item must first be exported to a third-party company outside the borders of the United States. From there it can be forwarded. Canada is a favorite country for this purpose, because you don't need an export license to ship to Canada if the goods are for local use. Once there, however, these goods are repacked and sent East. Another favorite funnel is Finland. The Soviets have received hundreds of Apple personal computers and electronics through Finland. Switzerland, Liechtenstein, Austria and Sweden quite frequently are used for third-country "drops" before high-tech U.S. goods are sent to the Soviet Union.

All these countries have one thing in common: they are not members of COCOM, which was set up after the war to limit the export of sensitive goods to the Communist bloc. They are free to export whatever they want to the East.

But all NATO countries and Japan are not. They do belong to COCOM, which is supposed to pull together all attempts to restrict the flow of technology East. Unfortunately, COCOM is something of a failure and a growing bone of contention between a more aggressive Washington and its European allies. After the Soviet invasion of Afghanistan the United States under Jimmy Carter declared a total high-tech embargo on Moscow. Europe and Japan demurred. They needed the exports for profits and jobs. Under the Reagan Administration, a major attempt is under way to expand COCOM and curb nearly all technology transfers to the Soviets and their Eastern European allies. But again, the Europeans are holding back.

OPERATION EXODUS

Under the best of circumstances, the non-American members of COCOM are reluctant partners. When Caterpillar Tractor was told to stop its shipment of gas- and oil-pipe layers to the Soviets, Japan's Komatsu picked up the contracts. The French have made it a practice to venture into Eastern-bloc business deals if the U.S. connection is cut. Less than a year ago, the Japanese sold special silicon-on-sapphire logic chips to the Russians. These little wonders have terrific applications in ICBM guidance systems and satellites. To many people overseas, trade is far more important than East-West politics. If there was any doubt, the European insistence on going ahead with the Siberian gas pipeline despite the destruction of Solidarity in Poland should erase it.

The United States is now trying to expand the COCOM embargo list to include entire technologies rather than specific products. Right now even robots are allowed to be exported to the Soviet Union. And many types of electronic-grade silicon, printed circuit-board technologies, small computers and software, are free to be shipped to Moscow. But without cooperation from overseas, it will be extremely difficult to stop the transfer of technology to the Soviets. With advanced electronics found not only in military weapons but in toys, only a multilateral effort can hope to succeed. It is no accident that thousands of "Speak and Spell" educational toys manufactured by Texas Instruments, the U.S. semiconductor giant, are imported into the Soviet Union every year. The microprocessors within the toys can be used for military purposes.

The U.S. Customs Service has set up its own Operation Exodus which aims to crack down on illegal exports of high-tech goods to Eastern Europe. Since it began, arrests have shot up tenfold. In the middle of 1982, customs agents stopped shipment of four computers en route to West Germany because they feared the machines were destined for the Soviet

Union. The seizure was made after an investigation by U.S., Canadian and German agents tracked the papers of the deal. The four minicomputers were made by Digital Equipment Corporation and are favorites of the Soviets.

•

VICTIMS AND PERPETRATORS

The policy issues of national security, corporate secrecy and individual privacy are all coming together as America and the world move toward the "wired society." The crimes of the '80s and '90s will increasingly involve theft of high technology through tapping electronic transmissions. People, companies and the government itself will be both victim and perpetrator in this new twenty-first-century electronic landscape. The glitter of a new, computerized life style will be tarnished by the simple fact that the coming world of high technology is opening up a whole new era of espionage, crime and just plain snooping.

8

JAPAN LEADS THE PACIFIC BASIN

•

Of all the nations in the world, Japan is making the fastest transition to the twenty-first-century society of high technology. Its incredible growth and momentum, coming at a time of stagnation and decay in Europe, in most of the Third World and in much of America, are already causing a seismic tilt in the economic axis of the planet. And with that is coming an even more remarkable shift in the balance of power.

Japan today is the center of an economic whirlwind in the Pacific, and around it swirls the booming societies of Hong Kong, Taiwan, South Korea and Singapore, and perhaps the West Coast of the United States. So powerful is the Japanese commercial thrust that only a revitalized America has a chance of challenging it in the near future. Europe is simply not in the game—and won't be for the rest of this century.

Throughout the industrial world, Japan's explosive thrust is leaving a trail of economic destruction and despair unseen since the early days of the Industrial Revolution, when Britain flooded the world with cheap, machine-made cotton and threw millions out of work. Today, the Japanese, the leaders of another technological revolution, are invading the internal economies of countries everywhere, capturing huge shares of domestic markets on every continent.

Before the death of the old Industrial Age, Japan had already emerged as the ultimate victor in the international economic game. By the middle 1970s it had caught up with, and finally surpassed, the West in the manufacture of steel, ships, machines and, of course, cars. In the new high technology age of the 1980s, Japan is one of the great leaders in robots, bioengineering and microelectronics. Its consumer-electronics industry dominates America and Europe. Its semiconductor industry controls the biggest chunk of the global market. And its computer makers have already pushed IBM out of first place at home, making Japan the only country ever to do so.

How did this come to pass? How did Japan capture nearly a third of the American car market before "voluntarily" cutting back under tremendous political pressure from Washington? How did it grab two thirds of the new 64k RAM semiconductor market, even though semiconductors were invented in the United States? How did it insinuate itself into the hearts of tens of millions of American consumers who automatically think of Sony or Panasonic when they buy radios, cameras, TVs, or videotape recorders.

These questions rose from the deep belly of America in the early 1980s, when Japan's tremendous success became the envy of a nation facing the economic devastation of its industrial heartland. To many Americans, Japan's success was the cause of this country's failure. They were one and the same. Everywhere came the great question: What is their secret and how can they do it while we can't?

•

JAPANOPHOBIA

The answer created a mini-industry in the United States and in Europe. Dozens and dozens of books were rushed into print to "explain" Japan to the country. Academic experts came running, pipe smoke trailing, to show how the Japanese were succeeding in an era of rising oil prices and soaring inflation, while everyone else was not. The explanations of Japan's success flooded America in much the same way as Japan's products swamped the country. A deluge of reasons poured forth—quality control (QC) circles; lifetime employment; homogeneous population; workaholics; mysterious government-business ties; cheap labor; dumping; manipulating their currency. Even the destruction of World War II was seen as an added advantage, because it forced Japan to rebuild, thus giving the country up-to-date factories and equipment.

To a nation suffering from a growing case of "Japanophobia," we received a massive dose of *Shōgun*-like explanations that dipped here, there, everywhere into Japanese society for reasons for its success. In the end, all the books, all the explanations came down to two prevailing themes: "The Japanese cheat," and "Their culture is unique."

Both explanations have the virtue of totally absolving America for any of its economic problems. There isn't much anyone can do against cheaters except beat up on them enough to curb their cheating. And if a country has a unique culture that permits it to do things that other societies find impossible, there isn't much that can be done about that either—except, perhaps, isolate it from the family of nations.

The Japanese do cheat. They departed from the international rules of free trade and free exchange of capital from the very beginning of their reconstruction after World War II. They closed off their economy from outside competition, restricted capital flows and used the government to aid industry in ways not possible in the United States.

In addition, two of Japan's biggest corporations have recently been caught with their hands in the computer cookie jar. Hitachi and Mitsubishi Electric will go down as participants in one of the greatest international high-tech crimes of the century after the FBI caught them buying secret IBM documents.

Yet none of that explains Tokyo's success. Hitachi and Mitsubishi are also-rans in the computer business in Japan. They are both trying to catch up not only with IBM, but also with Fujitsu, the most powerful computer company in that country. It is Fujitsu that dominates the computer business in Japan. It was not Fujitsu that was caught in the act of high-tech crime in America. It was the second string.

Every major nation in the world has cheated on the global rules of the game to some degree. Have the Japanese cheated more than the others then? Yes. But not much more than the French, who often make the Japanese appear to be virtual disciples of Adam Smith. Compared to the Americans, even to the Germans, the Japanese do have more protected home markets, and they do have greater government financial subsidies.

But all that is still very marginal. Only an exercise in Western xenophobia and racism could attribute Japan's incredible success to cheating. It's possible that an outraged American car-assembly worker who has just lost his job might want to put up a sign outlawing Toyotas from the company parking lot because he believes they are being "dumped" in this country, but he won't get much support from the average consumer, who likes the lower price and higher quality of the foreign car after years of getting stuck with "Monday lemons" put together by hungover workers with sledge hammers.

It is plausible that a distraught retailer selling U.S. radios and TVs should call for a boycott of all Japanese consumer electronics because they "exploit" made-in-the-USA technology and take away profits and jobs. But are the Japanese really to blame for applying technology in such a way as to make attractive new products that fit the lives of millions of Americans—who, we should be reminded, voluntarily jump at the chance to spend their dollars to buy Sony Walkmans and Betamaxes.

Cheating cannot explain Japan's tremendous success, and neither can "uniqueness." It is quite true that Japan has a very special culture that is more alien to Westerners than even the Chinese or the Indian or the Arab. Certainly, Japan is far more different from the United States than is France or Germany. And it is quite true that Japanese culture does strongly affect that nation's economy, as do the cultures of all countries. What is not true is that Japan is winning the fight for the technological heights of the 1980s because it is some kind of homogeneously pure nation of workaholics who labor together in perfect harmony. And Japan's success is not attributable to some hidden government-corporate partnership or to any willingness of the Japanese people to work for low wages for the greater glory of the motherland.

The "lifetime" employment pattern that American unions point to as proof of the innate, traditional "family" nature of Japanese corporations was imposed by none other than Douglas MacArthur after the war. He wanted to put people back to work as fast as possible to curb the growing Communist presence in the labor unions, and he virtually commanded the Japanese corporations to hire and retrain workers.

The "harmony" of industrial life is a two-decades-old phenomenon that followed tremendous union strikes led by the Communists in the fifties and enormous conflict between industrialists and right-wing militarists during the 1930s. Even the novel and TV movie *Shōgun* has brought home to millions of Americans the enormous conflict that was part of everyday Japanese life in the past.

As for the special government-business alliance, it is there, and it has helped tremendously. But it is perhaps less pervasive than Paris's role in the French economy under both conservatives and Socialists. And the famed tuning of the economy by the Japanese Ministry of International Trade and Industry (MITI) is tremendously effective, but it has its counterpart in Britain, in France and, perhaps most important of all, in the United States, where the Pentagon plays a major role in our economic life. MITI's influence on high technology in Japan has been no more nor less than the Pentagon's influence on technology in the United States. Without the Minuteman missile, there would have been no early market for semiconductors. With the Japanese focusing on commercial success while the Pentagon emphasized military application, the economic consequences of the two institutions' actions have, of course, been very different.

•

BACK TO BASICS

What, then, has been behind Japan's phenomenal economic success at a time when Europe sinks into commercial torpidity and America wavers between moving forward to the electronic future and staying behind, mired in the heavy-industry past? As in many complicated questions, the answer is simple. The Japanese have returned to the basics of production; they have gone back to the early principles of capitalism to propel themselves into the future of high technology. They have rediscovered the importance of the factory, the assembly line and the worker as the true keys to higher productivity. They have given new life to the concept of competition as the furnace in which companies fight for market share and, in the process, lower prices and raise quality. And most important of all, they have relearned the basic tenet about all production —it is the job of the producer to add value to raw materials to create better, cheaper and newer products that people will want and be willing to buy. *Value added* is the key to all successful production, whether it is General Motors turning out a new car from steel plates or an office worker using a minicomputer to make charts out of masses of data. The concept is the same. Value added is the social component of capitalism as well as its crucial economic underpinning.

Without value added to products, consumers won't buy, profits will fall and jobs will be lost. When Kodak came out with its new disk camera, which uses a flat, circular disk instead of regular film, it added value to its camera line, generated higher profits and hired several thousand additional people for its Rochester plants. When Akio Morita, the co-founder and president of Sony, went against all his market research people and decided to mass-produce a personal stereo player, made from existing parts, he added value. When Apple put together the first personal computer from available circuits, it added value. When Detroit continued to mass-produce gas-guzzlers after the OPEC oil shocks, it added nothing. Japanese imports, offering consumers 25 to 30 miles to the gallon, or two to three times as much efficiency as Detroit's products, won the day—and the market and the profits and the jobs.

In Japan everyone—worker, manager, government official—knows that the way to survive and prosper is to import raw materials and change them into products with enough value added to attract consumers around the world. The amount of value added put into a product determines the wealth of the country. For this reason, as well as others, Japan knew years before anyone else that the key to future commercial success lay in high technology. It realized, perhaps five years before the United States, that the OPEC oil shocks and the resulting surge in energy prices would open up enormous global markets in energy-efficient, high-technology products. They understood that the switch from cheap energy to expensive energy would translate into the need to transform modern society from an energy-guzzling machine culture to an energy-sipping electronic culture. The Japanese were the first to see that robots and automation would be in great demand in such an economic environment, as well as computers and "bug factories."

•

FACTORY FOCUS

The Japanese use the assembly line as their main focus for adding value. Whereas the laboratory or the office appears to be the main arena of change and innovation in the United States and in Europe, the line itself, the very lowest level of production, is where the Japanese put their efforts.

It is at this level that the Japanese can bring to bear some of their strongest social and cultural traits. For example, Japanese workers are the most educated and literate of any in the world. Compared to Detroit line workers, who often do not have high-school diplomas, the men putting together Hondas and Toyotas have four to five years of additional schooling in institutions that insist on rigorous testing and grades. This education is used in the factory in two ways. First, Japanese workers are given many more tasks to do at their station than are the Americans. They are expected to think for themselves in operating complex machines. They change jobs often. Their level of skills is higher and their boredom much lower. "In my view, the Japanese advantage is in the factory. The quality of blue collars is much better in Japan than in the U.S.," says Naohiro Amaya, adviser to MITI. "Japanese workers have the strong will—even passion—to make good things. They have pride in making high-quality products."

Also, blue collars are consulted much more often when it comes to change. Japan, with half the population, produces twice as many engineers as does the United States. More than half these engineers work long periods of time right on the shop floor. Their innovations, their changes are small, but continuous. They are in constant contact with the workers, asking their advice, offering their own.

Indeed, most research and development in Japan occur on the assembly line and are not the exclusive preserve of a separate breed of scientists and engineers working in far-off labs. By focusing on the shop floor, the Japanese can bring one of their strongest cultural traits to bear—the ability to accept and improve on foreign ideas. Ever since the Meiji Restoration in 1868, Japan has been playing "catch-up" with the West. To do that, it has used a single strategy over and over again—import foreign technology and adapt it to make new products more efficiently for sale at home and abroad. Adaptation means small, incremental steps, and there is no place better than the assembly line for this process. In fact, so advanced is Japan in incremental innovation on the line that the country has already become the world's leader of process and production technology. "At the top, where creativity is most important, U.S. and U.K. are ahead of Japan," says Amaya. "But when you go to the process of applying this creative device to engineering, Japan is more advanced."

This explains why quality control is so high in Japan. It is not the special quality control circles that cause the higher quality in Japanese semiconductors. QCs are merely part of a larger process of innovating on the assembly line and using engineers and workers to continuously make changes in the product and the manufacturing process.

Quality control is built into the drive for error-free work that is the goal of Japanese assembly lines. There are very few defect checkers in Japan's factories. In the United States, they are a major part of the production process. As many as one in eight automobile-line workers check for errors. In America quality is considered an expense that raises production costs. Volume is emphasized over quality in many cases, much as it is in the Soviet Union. In the United States, there is an underlying assumption that defects will occur and must be caught. In Japan, the assumption is that defects must not occur and if they do, they must be corrected immediately by the people on the spot. This difference in attitude is a major reason why the "yields" of defect-free semiconductors are much higher for Japanese producers than for American manufacturers. And it is one major reason, in addition to price, why the Japanese have captured such a large share of the U.S. semiconductor market. They are more reliable.

There is one cultural factor that does come into play strongly in the factory setting—cleanliness. Most American shop floors are sloppy, if not dirty. "Clean" tools and a "clean" workbench seem to have become forgotten virtues, although it is every bit as much a part of American culture as it is of Japan's. No Japanese assembly line is anything but immaculate. The same value system that gave birth to taking off one's shoes before entering a house now offers a major edge commercially. Cleanliness is a significant part of quality control. This was true for the industrial era, when cars were manufactured in tremendous volume, and it is doubly true for the electronic era, where even the tiniest piece of dust can contaminate the intricate parts of a computer-on-a-chip. It is another reason for the high "yields" of error-free Japanese chips.

The Japanese have rediscovered still another major tenet of basic production, flexibility. Japanese factories are nothing more than shells. Visiting American businessmen are often shocked by their unsubstantial nature, and many have been known to refer to them as "sheds." The Japanese don't put much time or energy into the physical housing of their workplaces, because they are forever changing. The *factory* in the conceptual sense is a constantly evolving thing in Japan. It is continuously being remade by small innovations, additions of new machinery, adaptations. The inside changes every five to seven years, allowing the factory to be constantly at the edge of whatever technology is available. With the introduction of robots and automation, factories will soon be able to change within hours.

This is not something that emanates solely out of Japan's social or cultural makeup. The government actively promotes it through its tax policies. Japan has one of the fastest depreciation rates in the world, and companies can practically write off entire factories within five years. In contrast, before the Reagan Administration passed its reforms in 1980, the United States required a full 15 years before equipment could be written off. And even with the Reagan changes, American companies still have to wait years to get the full tax benefits.

Japan's flexibility in the manufacturing process also makes itself felt in the mobility of its workers. In Japan, it is work, not the particular job, that is important. People move from job to job within the factory and within the organization as a matter of course. Given the lifetime job security that about 40 percent of the workers now have, leaving one job because of the introduction of automation is not nearly as threatening as it is in America. Another job will be made available. This flexibility within a cocoon of security has allowed Japan to introduce massive robotization in many plants, without any significant opposition from labor. As long as alternative slots are available, workers will freely move about.

The emphasis on the factory, the assembly line, the worker and the line engineer gives Japan tremendous strength in the mass production of quality products. That includes items ranging from cars to optic fibers. So-called "commodity" products made by the millions are the Japanese forte, including high-tech "commodity" products. It is this advanced basic production technology that allowed Japan to capture the automobile, steel and shipbuilding industries back in the 1970s and early 1980s. The same basic production factors are putting Japan at the head of the pack in the rush toward high technology.

•

A LITTLE THING LIKE SAVING

But if the Japanese have rediscovered some basic truths about the manufacturing process, they have also returned to another basic truth about investment: you cannot build anything without capital. To fuel its tremendous economic machine, Japan has built an organizational structure that draws out savings from its people and redirects it to industry. Japan has the highest savings rate in the industrialized world. At 18 percent it is three times the average U.S. rate of 6 percent, although lower than the incredible 24 percent rate of 1975.

It is true that the Japanese people have a tradition of saving a very large share of their income. But so do the Europeans.

What has distinguished Japan from other countries in saving is the government policies that have been implemented to encourage and reinforce those habits.

The government uses the Postal Savings system, once common in the United States, as a national drainage system for capital. By allowing tax-free interest on several accounts held in several names in a family, the government actively encourages people to put their cash into this national trust fund. At the same time, interest on time deposits at commercial banks, is taxed at a 35 percent rate. Moreover, the government is deliberately lax in its enforcement codes when it comes to the postal system. The bureaucracy simply doesn't try to track down people using more than their legal share of family names, for example. Institutionalized cheating is permitted by Tokyo for the sake of generating more capital.

This funneling of savings provides about $40 billion a year to the government, which then converts it into long-term, low-interest loans to industry for growth and exports. About half the money goes to financing small businesses. The Export-Import Bank, which provides subsidized financing for exports, gets about $5 billion. And the Japan Development Bank gets another $5 billion. On top of this, the government directly spends about $2 billion every year for science and technology research.

This savings structure was created by the Japanese after World War II to insure a steady flow of cheap credit to its companies, which were then rebuilding. It has since provided an extra edge to Japan in world competition. For the past thirty-five years Japanese corporations have had access to extremely cheap, low-interest capital for modernizing their plants and equipment. Until very recently some U.S. car factories were nearly fifty years old. Japanese factories are two, three, four years old. They are constantly being rebuilt from the inside out.

Just as important, Japanese companies haven't had to worry about the vagaries of the stock market when making their investment plans. They always have lots of debt capital to make them run and very few stockholders demanding a quick return on investment. The Japanese, through their savings and credit-allocation system, could plan for the future. And they did.

•

VISION OF THE FUTURE

But what future? For about 120 years now, Japan has been playing a game of "catch-up" with the West. It has had a single goal—parity with Europe and America. This has been its driving force, and it has served the nation well. Japan has not only reached equality, it may even have gone beyond.

Within that single-minded pursuit of parity, the Japanese are constantly setting themselves shorter-range goals. They do this for specific industries, particular companies and individual technologies. The Japanese see themselves as a small island people struggling to move ahead one step at a time against tremendous odds. They are on an unfamiliar sea, and they must take extra-special care to keep pointing their bow forward or they will get swamped. They feel they must have an excellent intelligence network set up to tell them what unfamiliar things await them, and what new things they can borrow to adapt and sell. And always, they must keep moving forward.

This vision of where Japan should be in the future is a constant preoccupation. It is not the standard five-year plan of the Communist countries, but rather an idea of where Japanese society will be in 1990 or 2000. The vision is a long-term concept of where the nation must go. It is a long-term goal to achieve. It allows the government, industry and the people in general to focus their energies. And it sensitizes the entire country to sharp changes that, in the international arena, will have a strong impact domestically. It was Japan's vision of itself and where it was going in the world that allowed it to become the very first nation to truly understand the deep meaning behind the OPEC oil-price hikes. It was Japan's vision of itself that permitted it to see that the era of cheap energy was ending and was giving way to a new period that would give tremendous value to high-tech products.

•

MADE IN JAPAN

It was not always so for Japan. Only three decades ago, "made in Japan" meant cheap, shoddy toys and little umbrellas that children stuck on top of their ice-cream sundaes. For the Japanese, however, even that achievement was important. For the first vision the Japanese had after the war was to rebuild the economy. And the way they did it was to focus on light industry—textiles, toys, cheap machines. It was the fastest and easiest way back from destruction. Douglas MacArthur's edict that unemployment should be ended by ordering the big corporations to keep all their employees on the payroll, even if they had nothing to do, gave Japan its lifetime employment pattern. To get the money to pay their employees and to get the factories back to a civilian mode of production, the Japanese decided on light industry. They were "helped" in their decision by pressure from the Americans to keep away from anything that would provide the economic foundation for rearming. That meant nearly all heavy industry.

The American occupation of Japan lasted a very long time —thirteen years—until 1958. When it ended, the Japanese quickly changed the direction of their economy. Their new vision was of heavy industry. There was a lot more value added to be gained in the products of heavy industry, and the Japanese went after it once the Americans were gone from their shores. They had moderate success in the sixties in bringing their country up to world standards. By the beginning of the seventies, their exports of heavy-industry products were comparable to those of the nations of the West in price and quality. But Japan was hardly the superpower that it is today.

It took the OPEC oil-price hikes to launch Japan on its upward spiral of economic success. The 1973 OPEC shock hit Japan harder than it hit any other industrial country. Inflation soared to 30 percent, a sharp recession set in, profits plummeted. Before anyone else realized what was taking place, the Japanese were changing their national vision once again. They knew that everything made with energy and everything that used energy would go up tremendously in price because of the OPEC action.

Immediately, the Japanese began an energy-conservation program. Within a year after 1973, Sony had redesigned its Trinitron color TV set to consume less power. Months later, it changed the entire chassis to use fewer parts and less metal. The automobile companies started turning out additional quantities of gas-saving cars for export to the United States. Steel and cement factories changed their processes and heating systems to cut back consumption by 20 to 30 percent, making Japanese steel much more competitive on world markets. The vision for Japan in the middle 1970s was to produce energy-efficient industrial products that the world desperately needed. In addition, the country began laying the groundwork for an eventual shift into high technology.

The country's vision changed once again after the second oil shock in 1979. This convinced the Japanese that the entire industrial era was going to pass because of the rise in energy prices. And with its passing eventually would go the whole machine age and the entire chemical era. The new vision for Japan, born in a report by the MITI in 1980, was for a high-tech future of electronics, robots, automation, bioengineering, computers and telecommunications.

For the future, the greatest "value added" to be gained would be in these energy-efficient new technologies. A new technological plateau was about to be breached and an old one left behind. This vision of the future gave Japan a head start on all its competitors.

Japan's big corporations immediately began shifting resources. Electrical companies that, like Hitachi, had concentrated on massive power turbines stuffed huge sums of money into computers and semiconductors. Fujitsu, which had been founded by Germany's Siemens to build heavy-industry electrical gear, moved to become Japan's number-one computer maker. Kawasaki Heavy Industries, one of the biggest shipbuilders in the world in the 1960s and 1970s, became the country's largest maker of robots. Toray, one of the nation's biggest chemical companies making synthetic fibers, moved into pharmaceuticals and biotechnology. Even Ajinomoto, the food-additive specialist that gave the world MSG, moved into biotechnology. The entire economy shifted toward the new vision of a high-technology society—a twenty-first-century society.

In their technological research, the Japanese are guided by strong cultural norms. Simplicity and detail have always been a major factor in Japanese aesthetics. Their prints, paintings, and especially rock gardens, so unfathomable to Westerners, emphasize the absence of undue complication while focusing on the simplicity of beauty.

The attention to detail pays great economic dividends when it comes to quality control and the manufacture of consumer items. The hundreds of Japanese exports to the United States fit the lives of its consumers in ways made-in-America products do not. The smallness, the compactness and the high quality are all appealing to Americans.

So is their simplicity. In making robots or designing chips, the Japanese keep it very simple—and very inexpensive. While Americans go about making the most sophisticated technology possible, pushing it to its furthest extremes to see if it can be done, the Japanese are keeping their eye on function. The first machine tools exported to the United States were welcomed because they did the job at a much lower cost.

Japan's robots are built in a modular way, with basic models kept very simple and additional equipment available for new, more complex tasks. Japan's chip designs are less complicated —and less prone to failure—than those of the United States. The emphasis on simplicity and detail fits right into the Japanese emphasis on the basics of production.

•

THE MIRACLE OF MITI

How the changing vision of Japan and its future becomes implemented through specific policies is a job for the Ministry of International Trade and Industry (MITI). In fact, MITI plays a major role in crystallizing the vision in the first place.

The government of Japan has always been very involved in the society. Defense of the island nation against the more advanced West is a constant theme in Japanese history. It was the major reason for Japan's expulsion of all the Portuguese in the sixteenth century and its killing of hundreds of thousands of Christian converts. And it was the reason behind Japan's intense drive toward modernization after Admiral Perry insistently knocked on its door again two hundred years later.

The first iron mines, steel mills and cannon factories were owned and operated by the government, financed by heavy taxes on the peasant population. In the early years of modernization in the mid-nineteenth century, the government sent thousands of young Japanese abroad to Germany and the rest of Europe to learn the "secret" of industrialization. Between the world wars, a Ministry of Commerce and Industry existed to coordinate growth. After the war, MITI was formed.

It is MITI's job to set industrial policy in Japan. It determines which industries will shrink and which will grow. In the late 1950s, it was MITI that decided that consumer electronics would power Japan through the late 1960s as the wave of the future. It was MITI in the late 1970s that emphasized the need for advanced semiconductors and sharply pared back the oil-intensive aluminum and chemical industries. And it is MITI that has now decided that Japan should have a national goal of winning for its new computer industry 30 percent of the worldwide market share and 18 percent of the U.S. market by 1990.

Through JETRO, the Japan External Trade Organization, MITI has eighty offices around the world, with nine in the United States. The job of JETRO is to read all the technical material coming out of foreign countries, digest it and send it back to Japan. High MITI officials are always passing through their JETRO offices, talking with American and foreign businessmen, politicians and local journalists about political and economic trends affecting trade with Japan. All this too is condensed and sent back home.

But the hundreds of Japanese working overseas gathering industrial, economic and political information is just the beginning. In Japan itself, an informal process of intense communication between MITI, the biggest corporations and the government goes on continuously. Nearly all high Japanese executives meet after work, nearly every day of the week, with their counterparts in industry and in government to discuss events and trends. There are "Monday clubs," "Tuesday clubs," clubs for all the days of the week. On the weekends, there is golf, and the discussion continues on the fairway.

There is also a great deal of job switching between government and private sectors, with people moving between the two constantly. And finally, there are the university classes. Classmates have extremely tight bonds and move through life in tandem. Classmates who wind up in MITI never stop talking with classmates in industry or the government.

Are any of these institutions radically different from the private city clubs, country clubs, Ivy League ties so common in the United States? Less, perhaps, than one might think.

But Japan is so group-oriented that the ties are much more intense and the communication far more important than in the West.

MITI is at the heart of all this discussion, this debate. It distills the common themes and makes very hard decisions on where the country must move in the future in order to keep growing. By the time MITI decides on a new industrial policy for Japan, the companies that dominate the economy have agreed to shift their corporate strategies to fit the new direction. After long discussion, a partnership develops between the government's new industrial policy and the corporate world's separate, narrower tactics.

MITI then publishes a general policy paper pointing the way to the future. It outlines the technologies the country will attempt to develop and starts pumping money into research. The usual pattern is for MITI, through the Japan Development Bank, to put up $200 million to $300 million for a project and invite a select group of companies to join in. The companies also put up their own funds.

In 1970, for example, when IBM came out with its 370 series of big computers, MITI decided to make computers a priority industry for the country. In 1972, a year before the OPEC price hike, it launched a four-year program to bring Japanese technology up to the standards of the world leader, IBM. Once the energy-price hike hit, it became clear that MITI was on the right track. Computers were pushed much harder after 1973 for several reasons:

1. It was a high-tech industry, which added great value (the difference between what companies paid for the raw materials and the price they demanded for the finished product was extremely high).
2. It was an energy-saving, resource-saving industry.
3. It contributed to other industries' saving energy and resources.

4. It had a major ripple effect on the entire industrial base, driving it toward high technology.

MITI organized six companies into three groups. All six at the time were heavily into electrical-power equipment. Hitachi and Fujitsu were scheduled to make large copycat IBM-compatible computers. Mitsubishi Electric Company and Oki Electric Industry Company went ahead with small IBM-compatible computers. NEC and Toshiba were given their heads and allowed to develop their own distinctive computer architecture different from IBM's. MITI put up $300 million for the project, which was to run between 1971 and 1976.

MITI's projects always focus on basic research, never on merchandising any specific product. There is no product division, no market division involved. Only R & D. The companies, for their part, proceed to scour the United States and Europe for information on the new technology. MITI helps through JETRO. But the thousands of Japanese who manned the listening posts of Silicon Valley during the early 1970s worked for the big companies, not the government. The hundreds of licensing agreements and dozens of joint ventures entered into with American companies to get the required technology was done on a private basis. But once this stage is passed, MITI's role begins to recede. For what happens next would make the heart of Adam Smith beat with joy. Once there is a sufficient pool of advanced technology available, it is shared among the participants. And then each company goes into the marketplace and tries to blast its competitors to pieces.

An orgy of intense competition then takes place as new products using the new technology are brought out, and each corporation tries to make its products cheaper, better, and more innovative than anyone else's. Dozens of other companies often jump in at this stage, when access to the technology becomes more available. The slugfest lasts several years, and when it is over only a handful of companies remain. In computers, Fujitsu has completely dominated the market, sending Hitachi into the illegal world of buying IBM trade secrets. In semiconductors, NEC is a clear winner. MITI launched a project between 1972 and 1979 to bring Japan up to the highest technology in semiconductors. Its goal was to win control of the world computer market by taking control of the chips that make up the hearts of computers. NEC, Hitachi, Fujitsu and Toshiba joined in the VLSIC (very large-scale integrated circuit) program. Recently, Japan became the first to mass-produce 64k RAM memory chips, ahead of the United States. NEC is in the lead, with Hitachi right behind.

Throughout the entire competitive process, MITI stays in the background. But it does occasionally play a public role. To stimulate the production and sale of a specific type of high-tech product, it will sometimes set up a special company that buys that product from the manufacturers and leases it out at low rates to consumers. MITI uses the Japan Development Bank to provide the funds. In this way, MITI offers the makers of the new product a minimum market and, in turn, offers consumers a break on the pricing.

For example, MITI designated robots as one of the "strategic industries" for Japan's future in the late 1970s. In April 1980 it helped set up the Japan Robot Lease Company (JAROL), which is made up of twenty-four members of the Japan Industrial Robot Association (JIRA) and ten insurance companies. JAROL specifically encourages the spread of robots to small and medium-size companies. It buys robots from the manufacturers and then leases them out at very low prices to small businessmen. JAROL gets nearly all its funds from the government at very low rates of interest and is therefore able to lease its robots for incredibly low prices. In effect, JAROL is creating a mass market for the robots while encouraging production.

MITI has also used this leasing system with computers. In 1980 it provided $263 million to the Japan Electronic Computer Company, which buys the computers and then leases them out to customers. This fell to $218 million in 1981 and to about $100 million in 1982. As the computer manufacturers are weaned off the government subsidy they are setting up their own leasing companies. The robot makers will be doing this in the years to come.

All this occurs years before MITI moves on to the next step in implementing Japan's vision for the future. When the most efficient companies emerge from the competition in the domestic economy, they begin to move abroad. Japan has managed to keep its huge domestic market hermetically sealed against any foreign company that it wishes to keep at bay. Those companies invited in possess technology that Japan cannot license or purchase abroad. IBM is the best example. And even then, Japan, using the same strategy as France and other European countries, insists on trading access to its internal market for technology. IBM must share a good deal of its advanced research with Japan for the privilege of doing business there. This was critical in the early years of launching the Japanese computer industry. Other companies that get into Japan, like Coca-Cola or Kentucky Fried Chicken, are basically marginal to the economic core of the country. It would be unthinkable for a foreign company to buy any significant Japanese corporation. There is no way Fujitsu would ever be sold—or Honda, for that matter.

By keeping the domestic market closed, the Japanese are able to raise the production volume on their new products sharply and thereby lower prices significantly. With that, they hit the docks and after detailed market research, begin exporting. "The Japanese export like they conduct a war," says one British trade official. The export effort of Japanese companies is nothing less than a blitz. A narrow market niche is found abroad through market research, and high-quality, low-cost items are poured into it. Unless stopped by countervailing pressures, the Japanese aim to capture 100 percent of that narrow market. They then move on and expand that niche, moving to capture ever more of the larger market, building greater sophistication and value-added into their products. Sony began with cheap transistor radios, moved on to high-quality color TVs, then introduced its Betamax VTRs, which use a large number of semiconductor chips. Honda began with motorcycles, then tiny Civics and now normal-sized sub-compacts.

The target is always greater market share and the time frame is always the long term. The Japanese are ferocious discounters, willing to buy their way into markets, thus opening themselves up to charges of "dumping."

With their highly productive manufacturing technology, their literate and skilled blue-collar workers and their vision of the future, the Japanese march into foreign domestic markets with the full intent of capturing as much as possible before meeting opposition, either commercial or political. At that point, the Japanese strategy calls for accommodation, and they will pull back and negotiate over market share. Part of that accommodation is the building of factories overseas to satisfy local markets. By providing jobs domestically and by getting under the tariff wires, the Japanese hope to circumvent rising protectionism against them. But this is the last resort. Japan prefers to export and keep the jobs and profits at home.

•

MITI'S VISION OF THE FUTURE

For the immediate future, MITI has already targeted several major new areas for Japan. Japan, or at least Fujitsu, the leading computer maker, has come abreast of the United States in computer hardware technology—the making of intricate computer architecture. IBM still sets the pace, directing the global computer market, but as long as it sticks with its current architecture, the Japanese can reproduce it.

Where the Japanese are way behind is in software, the instructions that tell the computers what to do. Software is the key to the success of any computer manufacturer. It took the writing of a single software program called VisiCalc (which allowed people to plot their finances) to get the Apple personal computer and the entire industry off the ground. Writing software in the United States right now is almost a cottage industry. It is not uncommon for 1960s dropouts up in mountain cabins to write them. Software writing is something the Japanese have not yet mastered, and because of that their computer exports have suffered.

To encourage software writing, MITI is providing $150 million to the nation's leading computer makers and $30 million to independent companies being set up. It is also offering a 40 percent tax break on software revenues to companies for the first four years of a program's life. Highlighting how anxious MITI is to get Japan producing its own software, the program is only for three years, not the usual eight or ten.

As always, the private companies are taking their cues from MITI but are moving ahead independently. They have hired 1,500 American software specialists to write programs and train their people. They are all over Silicon Valley once again with their "listening posts." They are hiring thousands of Japanese, especially women, to write programs at home. And they are bankrolling over a hundred "independent" software companies.

MITI also has just launched programs in robotics and biotechnology. It is about to begin a $140-million, seven-year plan to push research into developing the next generation of intelligent robots that can see and feel. MITI wants to build a universal robot to assemble almost anything anywhere. With the right kind of sight and a more powerful computer brain, these robots will be able to replace millions of skilled workers. Right now, Hitachi is putting together a five-hundred-man task force to build a standardized robot that has both visual and tactile senses, a powerful microcomputer brain and some form of mobility. It will be able to travel around from assembly line to assembly line. Hitachi plans to have the new robot ready by 1985 and to have 60 percent of the total assembly operations throughout the huge multibillion-dollar corporation robotized by 1986.

MITI is pushing biotechnology with a ten-year, $110-million program. Chosen companies are being grouped into three teams, one concentrating on the new gene-splicing techniques, one on building new types of "pots" to grow the new bacteria in, and another focusing on new "soups" to grow the cultures in. Each of the two dozen companies involved is linking up with one or more U.S. or European company to get their hands on the new technology.

But the strangest project now being put forth by MITI, and potentially the most far-reaching, is Japan's Fifth Generation Computer Project. Over a ten-year period, it aims at nothing less than building computers with artificial intelligence.

The Fifth Generation Computer will be much more humanlike than anything yet built. It will use speech instead of the usual programming, make judgments and decisions. It will process nonnumerical information such as pictures in nonlinear ways—totally different from today's data processors. The machines will be intelligent "pals" to people at home, at work or on the golf course. They'll give tax advice and make suggestions on where to build factories.

To do all that, the Japanese are betting on technological breakthroughs in software, in speech-recognition semiconductors and in a science-fiction-sounding something called the Josephson junction—high-speed integrated circuits that must be supercooled. The new machines will be not only faster but smaller than today's personal computer, perhaps the size of this book.

This is the first project that attempts to put Japan ahead of the technology of the West. All the others have been games of catch-up. It is Japan's biggest challenge, and its biggest test.

•

CAN THE JAPANESE CREATE?

In fact, the great question now confronting the Japanese is: Can they create? Businessmen and political leaders around the world are asking what may soon become one of the most important questions of our time: Will Japan be able to invent? For the Japanese have now come abreast of most Western technologies and may no longer be able to use the adoption of superior foreign ideas as a device for commercial success. Since they are as good as their competitors technologically, the Japanese are now faced with a task that they, as a culture, have not had to deal with for most of their history—inventing totally new things that can be made into products sold at home and abroad.

So far, nearly everyone watching the Japanese challenge to the United States and Europe agrees that it will be difficult for that insular nation to change its culture to be able to innovate. Standing squarely in the way is the group nature of Japan's social organization. The need for group conformity and consensus before acting and the desire never to be ahead of anyone else acts as a major deterrent to individual creativity. Just as important, the group is usually dominated by the *sensei*, the leader or teacher who must be followed. In Japanese laboratories and university classrooms, the *sensei* is often a man who has simply been around longer than his colleagues. Personal accomplishment is second to seniority. For an individualist, this can be deadening. Naohiro Amaya of MITI puts it very bluntly: "Japanese work as a group, not as individuals. The creative individual leaves Japan and goes to the United States, where he feels more comfortable." That has cost Japan dearly. In the entire history of the Nobel Prize, only five Japanese have ever won.

Think for a moment of the tremendous commercial successes the Japanese have had in the past decade. Autos, steel, shipping, and now consumer electronics, semiconductors and computers. None of these involved Japanese invention or original thought. All had their roots in American or European laboratories or machine shops. The transistor and silicon chip came out of American laboratories. The video tape recorder came out of RCA. Japan succeeded in taking Western technology, raising productivity tremendously, boosting quality, adapting to foreign markets and selling below competing prices. It did so with incredible success, but not with original innovation. Many Japanese admit this is a cultural fact of life. Even Keiichi Takeoka, president of Matsushita Electric Corporation of America, which sells products in America under the Panasonic and Quasar labels, agrees: "Japanese engineers cannot develop something from nothing, but they can build if they have something."

The Japanese education system itself highlights some of the heavy cultural restraints on innovation. Deference to elder faculty members and memorization by students are the twin norms in Japan, and both are antithetic to originality. In fact, the entire system of education may have to be radically altered before Japan can even hope to begin creating new technologies and new products. From the earliest grades on, Japanese students are geared to pass the critical university exams. These exams do test vast stores of knowledge, but not original thinking. Because of the sheer number of applicants, the examinations are composed of easy-to-grade questions requiring short, simple answers. There is no emphasis on originality of thought. According to Matsushita's Takeoka, "Japanese education is discouraging in developing something from nothing. We have to retrain graduates from universities."

Of course, the Japanese themselves may be wrong about their culture's ability to invent. Not everyone believes that Japan will not be able to make the cultural leap from adaptation of technology to innovation. The Japanese are building an entire "Science City," where 10,000 scientists and engineers are trying to create a center that will generate huge amounts of new inventions.

More than that, the giant Japanese corporations for the first time are spending large sums of money on basic research. Research and development expenditures in private industry have doubled in the past five years, with more and more of them going into basic, not applied, research. R & D spending is up 169 percent since 1977 at Sony, 179 percent at Toyota, and 110 percent at Hitachi. If the Japanese fail in their new quest for creativity, it will not be for lack of trying.

Indeed, it may just be that the new technology itself breeds a new, innovative type of Japanese. I had lunch in mid-1982 with several officials from Nippon Electric Corp., one of Japan's leading high-tech companies. After a six-course lunch of sushi, tempura, eel and other tasty exotica, plus several Japanese beers, we began talking about the social implications of the new technology. One of the Japanese sitting across from me burst out, "You should see the new ones coming to work now! The ones brought up on computers! Their faces have no expression. They have no emotion. They don't want to work with anybody. Only their own terminal!" Here, perhaps, is the beginning of a new kind of Japanese, one who prefers to be outside the group, to work alone and, perhaps, if Japan is lucky, to be able to chart his own way and create.

•

AGING

But if Japan can overcome this most serious of problems, it will still have to deal with many others. So far, it has been able to push forth a vast automation program within its factories without having to fire anyone. People have been moved around within corporations without much trouble.

Yet that labor mobility took place at a time of high economic growth, which now appears to be ending. Even when Japan's domestic economy slowed down in the early 1980s, along with that of every other country around the world, it still was able to grow by exporting. But in the first quarter of 1982, for the first time in thirty years, GNP actually dropped and by a large amount, 3.5 percent. The export strategy was no longer working, growth was slowing, and Japanese labor was getting nervous about steel-collar workers. So far, the government has tried to avoid the entire problem by simply repeating again and again that new, better jobs will be found for those who lose their old ones to robots. But it hasn't any plan for them.

Just as unemployment begins to cloud the horizon, so does another social problem—aging. For the past thirty years, Japan has enjoyed an unusual advantage over the rest of the industrialized nations. It has possessed two or three times as many young, productive workers per retired person as the United States or Europe. This has relieved the government and private corporations from a huge burden of social-welfare payments. It has also generated much of the savings as people prepared for their old age.

In the decade ahead, the ratio will change, and Japan will come to have the same proportion of workers to retired people as anyone else. The added burden on the government will be heavy. If the timing is right, the two problems of unemployment and retirement may cancel themselves out as people losing jobs to robots simply leave the work force because of age. If they don't, and if there is a time lag, there could be trouble.

Another internal problem facing Japan already is a runaway government budget deficit. Until the first OPEC oil shock, Japan ran a budget surplus almost every year. Afterward, the government began borrowing heavily. That deficit is larger per capita than America's. And while Japan's sky-high savings rate more than pays for the deficit without igniting inflation, capital that could go into more productive pursuits has been sopped up.

To curb that trend, the government of Prime Minister Suzuki, before it fell in late 1982, pledged to balance the budget and end heavy government borrowing by 1984. His successor, Yasuhiro Nakasone, is keeping to the same policies. But to do that Nakasone is trying to cap social-security payments, cut health-care costs and, above all, end the hemorrhage of the Japanese National Railroad system that absorbs a whopping 18 percent of the government deficit. To dismember the JNR, Nakasone will have to break its Communist-controlled union, the most militant and powerful of Japan's unions. If Nakasone proceeds, it means a period of harsh labor conflict for the nation and an end to the harmony that has kept it going for these past three decades.

Finally, Japan will soon have to come to terms with the rising tide of protectionism now directly threatening it. More than half of all Japanese exports are now limited by formal or informal agreements, and this is one reason for the decline in the nation's growth. Japan doesn't make anything any other nation desperately needs. Its inability to innovate has turned the country into an export giant of products that all other advanced countries can manufacture if they have to or do without if they choose to. Certainly the Japanese make lower-priced, higher-quality goods. But who, after all, really needs a Sony Walkman?

The solution, of course, is for Tokyo to open up its domestic market in a way that will help balance the huge deficits the United States and Europe now run with Japan. The strategy of keeping the local market closed while exporting abroad will have to change if Japan expects to keep exporting at all.

Despite its problems, Japan is clearly in the lead for the race to the high-tech society of the twenty-first century. The West has habitually underestimated Japan since the Russo-Japanese War of 1905, and to concentrate on the country's difficulties now would be foolish. To be sure, Japan has problems that will grow as the decade wears on. But no nation has shown the vision of the future that Japan has shown. Only one other country has exhibited comparable economic vigor in the high-technology fields—America.

9

AMERICAN RENAISSANCE

STAN T. LIVES IN YOUNGSTOWN, OHIO, WITH HIS WIFE AND four kids. He never finished high school, and he went directly into the steel mills when he turned eighteen. Stan spent the next thirty years working at a skilled craft that paid him good wages. His union bargained well for him, and in 1977 he owned a house, two cars and a camper. In 1981, he lost his job. The mill shut down and won't open again—ever. Stan got unemployment compensation for a year plus union benefits. He went on welfare for a few months and now works pumping gas at a neighborhood gas station. His wife took the first full-time job in her life last year in a McDonald's. His two sons also work part-time at McDonald's. They are joining the Army to escape Youngstown, and they hope to learn some new skills that will get them jobs.

Stan T. is a "de-skilled" American, one of millions thrown out of work by the 1970s surge in energy prices and the technological revolution that it unleashed. His craft is obsolete, his income has been cut by two thirds, his job security is gone, and his union ties with fellow workers are shattered. The camper was sold and the cars are both over ten years old. Stan T. is forty-eight years old.

Bob T. lives in Sunnyvale, California, in the San Francisco Bay area, with his wife and two kids. After doing graduate work in engineering, he joined one of the biggest semiconductor makers in the nation. To keep him happy and loyal, the company offered Bob the use of a $2-million sports complex, complete with Nautilus machines, a running track and Jacuzzis. He also received big stock options. Last year Bob came up with a new idea that holds great promise in the telecommunications area. He is now negotiating with two venture-capital firms to get the money to set up his own company. Bob wants to make a million dollars—just like his neighbor down the road, who started his own company after coming up with an invention four years ago. Bob wants a yacht, a house in Bel Air and a Ferrari—just like his neighbor. Bob's kids want that also. One is so impatient that he dropped out of Stanford to write computer game programs, hoping to come up with a new hit like "Pac-Man." Bob T. is thirty-nine.

•

THE NEW PACIFIC FRONTIER

These prototypical families represent the most important trend in American life today—the decline of the Northeast-Midwest industrial hegemony over the country and the tilting of the economic and political axis toward the West and Southwest. The United States has always sat astride two great ocean basins, but never before has the rise of one and the decline of the other been so striking. Just as the industrial heartland of Europe is now in a period of stagnation, so too is the old industrial base of America, the Northeast-Midwest region, in decay. As the Pacific Basin is exploding in growth, technology and optimism for the future, so too is America's West and Southwest bursting with the dynamism of this country's new high-tech Pacific frontier.

This Pacific frontier is the nation's only chance for catching Japan in the high-tech sweepstakes of the next decade. Europe, the Soviet Union and most of the Third World have little chance in catching up in the years ahead. This corner of America provides the only road to prosperity that we have.

But its growth will inevitably mean pain. The switch from heavy industry to high technology means the death of communities, the destruction of jobs, the breaking of many proud men and women. While new industries are being built by scientists and engineers in California and Texas, while the dream of tremendous wealth is being realized by thousands of people in the Pacific region, half a country is being broken on the wheel of technological change. How to manage the pain, how to ease it, alleviate it and finally end it by taking America through this difficult transitional period to the future will soon be the most important policy agenda of any Administration in Washington. Without clear plans and programs, it is quite possible that the dynamism and drive of the new high-tech Pacific frontier will be smothered in the angry reaction of displaced workers and the dispossessed poor.

For there is nothing inevitable about the current shift of economic and political power toward the Pacific. Change—especially change unleashed by a technological revolution—is always messy. Critical choices must be made in the months and years ahead if the United States is to scale the technological heights of the 1980s. How the transition is made from a heavy-industry country drawing its leaders and policies from the Northeast and Midwest to a high-tech economy based in the West and Southwest will determine who gets hurt and who gains, which regions prosper and which suffer, which groups gain power and which lose it. A second "war between the states" is already more than just cocktail talk.

A footnote is needed here to distinguish what is commonly called the Sunbelt from the new high-tech Pacific frontier. In the 1960s, Northern corporations began pouring huge amounts of capital into such states as Alabama, Georgia, Tennessee, the Carolinas and other Southern areas. Attracted by low taxes and the absence of unions, hundreds of factories opened up. Millions of people moved South for these jobs, reversing postwar migration patterns. Millions more went South seeking the sun for their retirement.

But the manufacturing jobs opened in the Sunbelt were from heavy industry. Steel, auto parts, chemicals and rubber made up much of the industries leaving the North. In many ways, a good portion of the South, especially the Southeast, became an industrial appendage of the Northeast-Midwest heartland of America.

Today, the Sunbelt is beginning to suffer the same fate. Unemployment rates are higher than the national average, factories are closing down, people are moving away. The jump in oil prices will make much of the South's brand-new industry just as obsolete as Ohio's or Illinois's—or the Ruhr's, for that matter. Its hope for the future lay in high tech, just like the Frostbelt's. And already such states as North Carolina are focusing on technology to build for the 1980s.

•

LOST RENDEZVOUS WITH DESTINY

For a while, it appeared that America didn't have any real choice about that future. It seemed that we were caught up in a Spenglerian decline of power and spirit. The 1970s were a shattering period. The terrible domestic conflict over Vietnam and the awful defeat left people numb and full of self-doubt about themselves and their country. The Watergate scandal and the resignation of Richard Nixon just before the impeachment barn door was closed behind him shattered the institutional framework of the polity. Inflation and the plummeting dollar led people to give up their traditional values of thrift and saving to plunge into speculation and debt. Crime continued to worsen, the cities never really recovered from the riots of the 1960s, blacks remained outside the mainstream of American life, and all the expensive social experiments of the Great Society appeared to fizzle.

Beneath the surface, an even worse erosion was taking place, rotting the very foundation of the nation. The first OPEC oil shock in 1973, tragically underestimated in Washington by a dying Nixon-Kissinger Administration obsessed with Vietnam, was soon drawing out the very life of industrial America, draining the Midwest and Northeast.

To be sure, there were earlier hints of erosion. The Sunbelt began drawing industry south in the 1960s. But in 1973, Detroit was still the center of the world automotive industry, Ohio was still the steel capital of America, and the great waterways of the Great Lakes and the Ohio and Mississippi rivers carried enormous supplies of steel, cars, rubber, chemicals and other industrial goods to the rest of the country and the rest of the world.

The fifteenfold jump in energy prices over the next decade ended all that. The 110-year reign of American heavy industry was finished so quickly that even now historians are only preparing to analyze the event. The assembly lines that poured forth tens of millions of cars began to shut down. In just three years—between 1979 and 1982—a depression settled over the towns and cities that had carried the country to greatness.

The first hints began to appear as Japanese cars started showing up on the roads. Japanese TVs, cameras, hi-fis, radios were in the stores. Machine tools began arriving, and ships and steel. Then electronic calculators, watches—a flood of goods from Japan washed over America's basic industries, drowning them in lower prices and higher quality.

Suddenly everyone knew that something was wrong. Had the U.S. economy continued to grow at a high 5 to 6 percent rate in the 1970s, the imports wouldn't have mattered. An expanding economic pie provides for everyone, including foreigners. But OPEC was extracting a heavy price for its oil. In the 1970s an energy "tax" of nearly $200 billion was levied on America. So bad was this new drain on the United States that real incomes remained virtually stagnant for the entire decade —for the first time in the history of the country. So the economic pie didn't expand, and the Japanese export onslaught conquered huge sectors of the domestic market of America.

•

HARVARD HURTS AMERICA

Paradoxically, the OPEC-induced decline of heavy industry in America was aided and abetted by a home-grown virus: the failure of U.S. corporate management. When the soaring price of energy began to make the industrial base of much of corporate America obsolete, our managers proved to be totally incompetent.

The shock was startling. For two decades after the war, American management was the envy of the world. Thousands of Europeans flocked to American business schools to learn the secrets of managing big corporations.

But when the biggest challenge to American industry in a century came in the 1970s with OPEC, its managers choked. They showed themselves to be incapable of the same kind of hard decision making that allowed Japan to adapt and thrive during these very same years.

What went wrong? Quite simply, corporate managers lost sight of the fact that they were in the business of producing things for people to consume. They forgot about products, and quality, and became obsessed with short-term finance. Their perspective of the future began to shrink. Instead of planning investments for three or five years down the road, spending money on research and development, and opening up new markets, these managers of corporate America turned their gaze on the quarterly earnings reports put out by their accounting departments. Decisions began to revolve around how much more those quarterly earnings reports would show. The stock market began to reward companies with continuously growing quarterly earnings statements. Managers began to link their own compensation to improvements in short-term earnings. Even retirement pay was tied to quarterly reports.

Now, quarterly reports mean just that—four times a year or every three months. Imagine huge multibillion-dollar corporations acting on the basis of a three-month time perspective! The "future" meant next quarter. Not only could the managers of corporate America not see the forest for the trees, they couldn't even see the trees for the leaves.

To make matters worse, these giants of American capitalism increasingly turned away from the nitty-gritty of the assembly line to the cool crisp numbers of the finance sheet. Big corporations were run like investment portfolios. Each manufacturing division had to show a rising return on investment or it was chopped. Older units producing large profits were "milked," and the cash was used to fund new projects that had to produce profits very quickly or be chopped in turn. Pseudoscientific formulas were applied to the decisions that went into investing. "Discounted cash flow" was the most common. The net result of all this financial flimflam was an inherent bias against capital spending for the future. Money became too precious for long-term investment. It had to be squeezed out of the company quickly for those quarterly earnings statements.

The financial focus of management during the 1970s meant that financial people began taking the helms of many big corporations. To be sure, there was some reason to have people with a financial background around at that time. The dollar was plummeting, interest rates were bouncing around all over while continuing on an ever-upward trajectory. Inflation was heating up. But replacing managers with backgrounds in engineering, science, and sales, with superaccountants was a terrible mistake. And the country's business schools made it worse. Harvard Business School in particular was enamored of "numbers crunching" and investment-portfolio analysis. Other schools tried to turn out "managers" who could handle either government bureaucracies or corporate bureaucracies —as if they were exactly the same.

In the end, the nation's industry was run by men who knew nothing about building their own companies from scratch. When a fundamental shift in the economics of their production took place as energy prices soared in the 1970s, these businessmen were totally unprepared. The decline of America's industrial heartland was hastened by the incompetence of its corporate managerial elite.

Nothing illustrates this more than the tragic case of U.S. Steel. The company is by far the largest steel producer in America. As the 1970s progressed, it began losing big shares of the domestic steel market to lower-priced European, Japanese and Third World manufacturers. Its mills were antiques compared to the modern plants overseas. Instead of modernizing, U.S. Steel went to Washington for help. It argued that steel was needed for national defense and, if only it got some temporary help, it would update its equipment and become competitive again. Washington complied, gave the steel industry tariff protection through a trigger-price mechanism that kept imports low and even gave the industry more cash by speeding up depreciation allowances on old plant and equipment. U.S. Steel was very thankful for Washington's help. One of the first things it did was to take most of its new profits and go out and buy an oil company, Marathon Oil, for $6 billion.

The president of U.S. Steel has argued that the higher cash flow from oil profits will help steel production. Yet by purchasing the company, U.S. Steel now has 62 percent of its assets outside the steel business. In addition to oil, it is into shopping centers and real estate, and the suspicion cannot be allayed that it plans to move further and further away from its core business in search of "cash flow." In essence, U.S. Steel is liquidating itself as a steel company—with help from the taxpayer, who is giving it tax breaks, and the consumer, who is paying more for everything made from steel.

•

THE HOT MIX

While the decline of American basic industry was taking place throughout the Northeast and Midwest an economic miracle of sorts was beginning across the continent. There, in the 250-square-mile area of Santa Clara County, in the Bay area of San Francisco, a confluence of people, ideas, money and markets suddenly came together to reignite the "animal spirit" of American capitalism—and to take the nation forward into the twenty-first century. These elements had been there for years, in isolation from one another. It took the OPEC price hikes of 1973–74 and 1979–80 to catalyze them into action and to create the Silicon Valley syndrome. For the first time ever, the higher price of energy made their innovations and new concepts economical. For the first time, their energy-sipping devices were in tremendous demand. For the first time, fantastic fortunes could be made in the practical application of the high-tech inventions that they were creating.

What took root in California in the late 1970s and early 1980s is unique. There is no Silicon Valley in Europe; there is none in Japan. Nothing like it exists in the Soviet Union, and nothing could. For it is a truly American concoction that is basic to our culture. Indeed, it is apple-pie high-tech. In its economic dynamism nothing has been seen like it since the boom of heavy-industry in Germany's Ruhr Valley or America's own bursting Great Lakes–Ohio Valley complex of mammoth smokestacks, blistering ironworks and endless assembly lines.

The Silicon Valley syndrome is a "hot mix" of original ideas, individual innovation, entrepreneurship, venture capitalism and free markets. It is marked by a high-risk culture that is the total antithesis of the risk-avoidance values of Big Business. Building something new by yourself, not managing something old created by another person, is at the heart of the "hot mix." In fact, what is being created in the Western and Southwestern parts of America is a new high-tech Pacific frontier that promises to take the nation forward past the old industrial age based on cheap energy to the new, high-tech twenty-first-century society of expensive energy.

The center of the new Pacific frontier is the university. Where once, in the industrial era, the geographical location of raw materials and transportation determined where factories were built and cities established, the great "raw material" of the post-OPEC high-tech era is the mind. Individual creativity, analytical ability, mental prowess—the muscle of the mind, mind power, is building the industries and companies and communities of the future. And it is in the great universities of America—and in such great corporate laboratories as Bell Labs and IBM—that the scientists and engineers reside. It is where the basic research gets done.

•

THE MUSCLE OF THE MIND

On the West Coast, Stanford University, the University of California at Berkeley and Cal Tech are critical centers for the new high-tech frontier. For example, William Shockley, co-inventor of the transistor, taught electrical engineering at Stanford before he founded Shockley Transistor Corporation. The ripple effect of that action has been incredible. Several Shockley Transistor employees left to found Fairchild Camera and Instrument Corporation, a giant in the semiconductor field. And dozens of Fairchild alumni have left to found additional companies, including Intel. Now Intel is shedding young people who are setting up newer electronic companies.

The new generation of American business pioneers spawned by the universities can be seen in the development of biotechnology. Dr. Charles Boyer of the University of California and Dr. Stanley N. Cohen of Stanford University worked together to make the breakthrough in gene splicing. Their technique opened an entire field to the world—transforming bacteria to produce whole ranges of new products more cheaply than ever before. "Designer genes" made their appearance first in the laboratories of Stanford.

But that was only the beginning. Boyer and Cohen patented part of their discovery in 1980, eight years after their collaboration began. In the past, that would have been the end of the process. Big chemical or pharmaceutical companies would then come in and decide whether to use the new technique for commercial purposes. It didn't happen this time. In 1975, Robert Swanson, then twenty-eight, went to Boyer and persuaded him to join in setting up a new company—Genentech.

•

THE SCIENTIST AND THE CAPITALIST

Swanson was a venture capitalist playing a role that in the "hot mix" of the Silicon Valley is every bit as important as that of the scientist. For, if the European experience shows anything, it is that technological change requires much more than mere inventing—it requires transforming innovations fresh out of the lab into new products that people are willing to buy. Innovation, once it occurs, must grow within a commercial incubator. Without understanding this complex interaction between individual creativity and economic reality, no one can grasp why some nations are succeeding in the fight for the technological heights of the 1980s and others are failing so dismally. For the mere presence of sophisticated technology within a country does not guarantee that it will be able to parlay innovation into economic growth, jobs, exports and international influence. The British can invent jet planes and CAT scanners, but they can't market them. Indeed, the technological foundations of Japan's success came out of U.S. laboratories—the transistor, the semiconductor chip, the microprocessor and now the spliced gene.

The venture capitalist is the crucial link between the university-based inventor and the economy. He provides the seed money for the "baby" company, he acts to transform the scientist into an entrepreneur, he gives advice on hiring experienced business people to run the firm, and sometimes he even takes the adolescent company to the market by selling its new shares to the public. The venture capitalist is the middleman who brings everything together in the Silicon Valley—and no other nation in the world has such people to any great degree.

Without such venture-capital firms as Hambrecht & Quist, Brentwood Associates, and L. F. Rothschild, Unterberg, Towbin, there probably would have been no Apple Computer or Cetus. In fact, without the nurturing hand of the venture capitalist, such scientists as Walter Gilbert, a Harvard Nobel Prize winner for his work on DNA, would probably not be heading the scientific advisory board of Biogen, a new bioengineering company that made one of the first commercial batches of interferon from bacteria. Nor would David Baltimore, an MIT biology professor who won a Nobel Prize for physiology and medicine, be a top scientist for Collaborative Genetics, Inc., a new biotech company.

One final ingredient is required in the "hot mix" of the new high-tech Pacific frontier to make the Silicon Valley syndrome operate. First comes the research by scientists in university labs. Then comes the venture capitalist who helps to transform the scientist into a new entrepreneur with lots of advice and more than a little capital. But the big step, perhaps the most important in the end, is taking the new private company "public" by selling stock. This is where greed comes in. When Hambrecht & Quist took Genentech public in 1980, Dr. Boyer's initial investment of $12,500 blossomed into a $40-million fortune. Demand for the high-tech stock was so great that the shares owned by Boyer in his little company increased tremendously in value, making him an instant multimillionaire.

And the same thing happened to Steven Jobs and Stephen Wozniak, who built their first personal computer in a garage in 1976 and became instant millionaires when Apple Computer sold its first stock on the New York Stock Exchange in

1980. Wozniak used some of his millions in the fall of 1982 to throw a "Woodstock" West high-tech rock party for 200,000 people.

The new capitalism being generated on the Pacific frontier represents an optimistic turn for American technology. Over the past three decades, America has played its strong suit in technology—original innovation—and has left it to others, particularly the Japanese, to transform the inventions into practical items that consumers want to buy.

But this gift for innovation has been allowed to lie fallow when it comes to commercial application. That has resulted in wasted economic growth, jobs and strength. Innovation, not application, has been the thrust of American technology.

•

SILICLONES

The success of the "hot mix" of the Silicon Valley is spurring imitations throughout the country. People with an eye to the future are trying to recreate that critical mass of university research, innovation, venture capitalism, entrepreneurship and fast-growing small businesses. A "Silicon Prairie" has taken root in the Dallas–Fort Worth area of Texas, where such companies as Texas Instruments and National Semiconductor have their headquarters. So does Nippon Electric Company. A "Silicon Desert" is springing up around Phoenix, and North Carolina is pinning its hopes on its Research Triangle in the Raleigh–Durham–Chapel Hill metropolitan area. Boston has its Route 128, which draws on Harvard and MIT for creative inspiration and on the honed instincts of its State Street investment bankers for venture capital. New York State is already home to the facilities of IBM and General Electric, Kodak and Corning Glass. And a growing Long Island complex based on Brookhaven Laboratories is sprouting new companies as well, drawing on such universities as Cornell and Rensselaer Polytechnic Institute.

But just as important, the spirit of Silicon Valley is beginning to seep into the boardrooms of the nation's big corporations. With the automobile and consumer-electronics giants in the lead, a growing number of multibillion-dollar behemoths are heeding the lessons of the Pacific frontier and are turning to high technology for salvation and survival in the '80s. Nothing highlights this trend more than a survey of research and development spending by U.S. companies for 1982. Despite plummeting profits and falling capital-spending plans, corporations planned an incredible 17 percent boost in R & D spending for that year. That came on top of an equally incredible 16 percent jump in 1981. In addition, expenditures of this kind are expected to soar by an additional 35 percent by 1985, to nearly $82 billion. The potential payoff for long-term investments is beginning to sink in among the pencil-pushing corporate managers of America. In fact, there is a discernible trend toward replacing the "numbers crunchers" with people having production or sales experience. People with engineering, not financial, backgrounds are suddenly in demand for executive positions. Technology is suddenly a critical part of manufacturing.

New product development based on high technology is becoming the "in" thing. Whereas Buffalo, New York, sinks into the same depression that is hitting the heavy-industry towns of the Midwest as its steel mills close, Rochester, New York, is having a renaissance. Kodak's new product, the disk camera, has caught on with the public. The smaller, lighter camera is unique in consumer electronics, and Kodak added over six thousand people to its labor force in the area to keep up with demand. Rochester is also attracting lots of other high-tech companies, including Harris Corporation and Xerox.

U.S. companies are also beginning to win high-tech trade wars with Japan—for the first time in a decade. In fact, there is a good chance that the Japanese victories of an earlier industrial era—in cars, steel, ships—may not be repeated in the new high-tech age.

Take computers, for example. The use of personal computers is exploding in this country. Nothing better represents the transformation of the United States from a heavy-industry to a high-tech society than this incredible stampede into computers. They are being rushed into schools, offices and homes at a speed not seen since the introduction of TV in the early 1950s. They are transforming the way we live by bringing enormous computing power right down to the individual where he works and plays. One third of the homes in the United States will have computers by 1990. Computer camps are growing up. Club Med is offering "computer holidays" at its Mexican and Caribbean villages where people can mix sun, sand and programming. Sears is opening forty-five stores around the country just to sell small computers. The revolution wrought by little Apple Computer is spreading, triggering even giant IBM, maker of huge mainframe computers, to enter the personal market with a smashingly successful debut of its own small model.

There is only one other country in the world undergoing the same personal-computer craze—Japan. Not Europe, not Russia, just Japan. And it was to Japan that victory was expected to go in the battle for the personal-computer market. Visions of a great wave of cheap Japanese personal computers smashing the U.S. market and conquering it, as did their TVs and radios, were common. After all, the Japanese were masters at consumer electronics and had defeated U.S. producers in the past.

But this time the Japanese juggernaut floundered. After years of trying, the Japanese have taken a mere 2.5 percent of the market. Its giant producers, dominating the huge Japanese domestic market, failed to compete with American manufacturers. Nippon Electric Company (NEC), with 40 percent of the Japanese market, has had scant success against Apple, IBM, Commodore and Tandy.

The Japanese failed to offer machines any better than those of their U.S. competitors. They weren't as powerful in many cases. They weren't any cheaper. Most important, however, they didn't have the kind of software instructions that are absolutely needed by users of the machines. The Japanese concentration on mass-producing electronic machines has blinded them to the need for individually focused instructions to make those boxes useful. Right now, they are rushing to tie up with U.S. computer companies in order to get their software. Matsushita is trying to link up with IBM. Fujitsu has ties with Siemens in Germany, Amdahl in the United States and ICL in Britain. Hitachi has links to NAS and Germany's BASF. But so far none of these ties has allowed the Japanese to make a strong export push on personal computers. And the same is true of the big mainframe computers. IBM continues to dominate the world market. Japanese manufacturers continue to make mostly copycat versions of IBM machines, and industrial espionage is conducted with the Japanese searching out IBM's trade secrets, not the other way around.

•

THE DE-SKILLING OF AMERICA

But before America can expect to win the fight for the technological heights of the '80s, it is going to have to deal with the ugly problems that technology is bringing with it. The social and political consequences of the high-tech revolution now taking place are immense. Yet few people in Washington are aware of the pain that is confronting the nation, much less prepared to offer solutions. And there is a strong chance that the dynamism unleashed by the new high-tech Pacific frontier will dissipate in the years ahead unless that pain is relieved in a way that is politically acceptable to the vast majority of people in the country.

By far the harshest shock about to hit the country is the march of robots through the communities of America. Across the nation's industrial landscape, a workplace revolution is hitting people, and no one is willing to admit that it is hurting.

Automation will uproot more people in the nation than at any time since the shift from the farms to the cities in the nineteenth century. The same type of technological tornado that swept millions of people out of their rural communities into urban factories will now blow them permanently off the factory floor. Robots and the unmanned factory will transform the nature of work for tens of millions of people—and end all work for millions of others. An army of "techno-casualties" may be growing below the surface of society at this very moment. Millions of people now out of work believe it is because of the recession. Once they discover that their unemployment is structural—perhaps permanent—and derives not from the self-correcting whims of business cycles, but rather from major new changes in the entire post-OPEC economy, there will be trouble.

Right now most automation experts, industrialists, economists and union officials are consoling one another with the belief that automation will create more jobs than it destroys and that people thrown out of one job will be easily retrained for other new roles to come. They argue that the tremendous gains in productivity will encourage economic growth and employment. Data Resources, Inc. (DRI), a world-famous econometric forecasting group, has done projections showing that employment in the booming service sector of America will be increased by 7.5 million people in the 1980s, more than compensating for lost jobs in robot-run factories. A study by the National Commission on Technology, Automation and Economic Progress, set up by Congress in the early 1960s, even found that there are no direct links between unemployment and automation.

But General Electric plans to cut half its 37,000 assembly workers by 1990 by introducing robots. General Motors had 200 robots working in 1978, 425 in 1980, 1,200 in 1981 and will probably have 20,000 by 1990, spot-welding, painting and assembling new cars. Thousands of people now laid off because of the twenty-year low in car production will find their work stations filled by Unimates, Trallfas and other robots when they try to return to their jobs.

Up to 75 percent of all current factory jobs could be done by robots before the end of the decade. Indeed, a study by Carnegie-Mellon University, "The Impact of Robotics on the Workforce and the Workplace," says that 1.3 million assemblers, 750,000 inspectors and testers, 185,000 painters, 713,000 welders, 626,000 packagers, 2.4 million machine operators and another 1 million skilled workers could be replaced by robots in the years ahead. The study says that the current breed of blind and dumb robots is already taking jobs away from hundreds of thousands of unskilled, blue-collar workers. The introduction of the second generation of "smart" robots will have a further devastating impact. There are nearly three quarters of a million arc welders in America who are being displaced at this very moment by the new arc-welding robots being brought in by GM, Ford and Chrysler. They will join the tens of thousands of spot welders who once held jobs in the auto industry—and never will again. Robots will soon be able to do seven million existing factory jobs in America. And by the end of the decade, assembly robots will be able to put together and inspect nearly all kinds of products—threatening an additional 21 million union workers. The strongest unions in the country, the United Auto Workers, the International Brotherhood of Electrical Workers and the International Association of Machinists, will be the first to be hit by the new army of steel-collar workers. These unions are the backbone of the Democratic party, and once they are squashed underfoot by the march of the robots, party politics will never be the same.

Unfortunately, that is just the beginning of the devastation now striking the workplace of America. For the first time, automation is hitting all major sectors of the economy at the same time. In the past, one sector has borne the brunt of automation while others were able to absorb excess labor. This is not true today. Automation is spreading through the office at a pace at least as fast as it is moving on on the factory floor. The office of the future is as much a coming reality as is the factory of the future. While there will not be as dramatic a cut in the number of people in offices as there will be in factories, automation will hit 38 million people in offices, according to the Carnegie-Mellon study, changing their jobs and probably limiting their numbers. And women may be hit the hardest. The entire women's movement of the '70s was based on a huge migration of women from the kitchen to the office. With labor-saving computerized office work stations, there will be millions fewer jobs for the people who now manage paper in America—secretaries. They are all threatened.

Apologists for robotics and automation insist that anyone losing a production job to a robot will easily get another one in the burgeoning service industries of America. After all, they point out, manufacturing jobs have been declining sharply for decades, while service jobs have been exploding. Between 1940 and 1981, for example, employment in service industries as a percentage of all employment rose from 50 percent to 73 percent. Manufacturing has not employed a majority of the work force in decades, and yet jobs have been created at an astounding pace in recent years, especially in the 1970s. McDonald's, for example, employs 350,000 people—far more than the number employed by U.S. Steel.

But what these Pollyannas don't see is that the era of booming service employment in the United States ended in 1980. The greatest source of jobs in recent years has been government, especially state and local government. Government employment hit a high of 16.3 million in October 1980, up from 12.6 million in 1970, 8.6 million in 1960, and 2.6 million way back in 1920. But for the first time in sixty years, 1981 marked a dramatic decline in government jobs. Between October 1980 and early 1982, 600,000 government jobs disappeared. And the end is not in sight. Some percentage of those jobs fell victim to the recession, but most disappeared because of major changes in the economy and society of America. The decline of American wealth and prosperity due to the OPEC oil-price increases and the failure to save and invest for nearly twenty years finally caught up with America in the 1980s. Proposition 13 in California, Proposition 2½ in Massachusetts and, above all, the election of Ronald Reagan symbolized the ground-swell demand to cut back on huge government spending—and government itself. This will not reverse itself quickly in the years ahead.

The other major source of service employment in recent years has been in the fast-food type of businesses and in hospitals. Emma Rothschild at Harvard has pointed out that more jobs were created in fast foods in the 1970s than in any other business in America. But these jobs too are destined for mass destruction. Robots are about to leave the factory and move into McDonald's. Engineers in both Japan and America are hard at work putting language capability into robots—and they will succeed in doing this by the middle of the decade. With language, eyes, fingers and more powerful minicomputer brains, robots will be able to do service operations that are now done by millions of people—mostly in the lower-paid job categories. Nippon Electric (NEC), for example, has an experimental voice-actuated robot that will pour a Coke or a Pepsi and hand it over the counter to you. It's not hard to imagine a robot that cooks the hamburger, shakes the shake and gives change. In fact, it's not hard to imagine an unmanned "McDonald's store of the future" by 1990.

In late 1981, the Japan Industrial Robot Association (JIRA) came out with a report called "Long-Term Outlook on Demand for Industrial Robots in Non-Manufacturing Industries." In a survey of 444 nonmanufacturing companies, the JIRA concluded that by the end of the decade there will be nursing robots in hospitals, sweeping robots cleaning the streets, farming robots milking cows, cutting trees and planting crops. They will almost surely be the gas-pump jockeys of tomorrow, the tellers at thousands of banks, the ticket takers at movies, and the cashiers at grocery counters and the racetrack.

What this adds up to is a de-skilling of America. People with decades of experience doing highly skilled work are going to lose their jobs. Without learning new skills, and perhaps new values, these people will have to turn to the stagnant and declining service industry for work. And even if they are lucky enough to snag a job, the prize may hardly be worth it. A skilled union man who has lost his job will find that his skills are worthless, his income is cut dramatically, his social ties with fellow workers are destroyed, and his pride is shot to hell. "There is no consolation for a skilled autoworker who has to work in a McDonald's," says W. W. Winpisinger, head of the International Association of Machinists.

•

CYBERPHOBIA

Blue-collar workers will not be the only people hurt by automation. The white-collar managers of America, sitting in their air-conditioned offices on their comfortable chairs, are in for a terrible shock. From 10 to 20 percent of them will not be able to adapt to the new computers that are being introduced into their offices because they suffer from a new mysterious affliction—cyberphobia, or the fear of computers.

It invariably strikes an organization just after computers are installed. Anyone who doesn't type, and that includes most senior and middle managers, can get it.

Hostility toward computers stems from a fear of losing control of one's job. It is a fear of not being able to live up to the demands of the machine, and the worry that one's job has been grabbed away by a television screen.

There are very real structural changes in any organization that computerizes. Power does shift dramatically to those controlling the new system. Access to different levels of the system generates a new hierarchy, and a pervasive fear of losing privacy and secrecy immediately spreads among all of the employees.

But cyberphobia does not result from these real situations. It is a neurotic fear, an anxiety that takes hold of managers when confronted with computers. Blood-pressure rates shoot up, people get nauseated, they sweat a lot. They also do irrational things like sabotage. Wires somehow get pulled out. Keys gets jammed. Screens get scratched. Cyberphobia can paralyze an entire business. It can certainly ruin people's careers. And it may take special training to overcome it.

Who takes responsibility for the retraining of America's white- and blue-collar labor forces will become a major policy issue in the years ahead. Should the corporation, the labor union or government bear the burden? Who has the resources? Right now, no one is even thinking about these problems. The Reagan Administration simply refuses to discuss it. Malcolm R. Lovell, Jr., Undersecretary of State for Labor, says that "government cannot preside over worker relocation and worker adjustment. The primary responsibility must be in the hands of labor and management."

•

WAR BETWEEN THE STATES

The last time America found itself with rising and declining sets of regional economies, it became embroiled in the Civil War. The industrializing North required economic and political policies that the plantation South couldn't live with, and while the issue of slavery played a prominent role in the ideologies of the two factions, it was economics that drove them to war.

The North's victory ushered in the golden age of heavy industry. Today, it is this heavy industry that is being surpassed by the new high technology of the post-OPEC era. Regional conflicts are breaking out once again. The high-growth, low-unemployment, capital-rich West and Southwest are vying for economic and political power with the decaying and declining industrial Northeast and Midwest. The same high-tech revolution that is bringing riches to one part of the nation is devastating the other. And the conflict has just begun.

The introduction of robots and automation will not only "de-skill" the nation's industrial workers, it will also realign the economic and political power of the nation. The impact of automation will fall much more heavily on the Northeast and Midwest than on any other part of the country.

The financial burden on state coffers will be tremendous. Already unemployment and welfare costs in the North are leading to major cutbacks in services.

The once-great universities of the Midwest are being starved for money from state capitals. State and local taxes are being raised, negating the positive effects of the Reagan tax cuts and making the Midwest that much less attractive as a place in which to work and live. All this will soon get much worse as unemployment soars. A vicious cycle of declining heavy industry, of automation, unemployment, higher welfare and unemployment costs, and lower economic growth is quite possible. The gutting of the great universities will only mean that the "hot mix" of the Pacific frontier will not move east. The regional dislocation will grow worse.

•

NOSTALGIA AS POLICY

To solve these problems will require major policy decisions by Washington. The new high-tech Pacific frontier is providing the seed of an American renaissance that could send the country to the top of any international power pyramid in the years to come. But that seed must be nurtured through a combination of economic and political policies that leave it sufficiently free to grow and prosper while the country's center of gravity shifts from heavy industry to high technology.

The great debate now taking place on American economic policy is whether the nation should have a specific industrial policy to "reindustrialize" the country. The Reagan Administration appears to have turned its back on such a policy and to favor a big tax-cut program for both business and individuals; this, it hopes, will get the economy moving again. It is hoping that a tight-money policy will kill inflation, and it is shifting federal resources from social programs to military spending. It is betting that macro-economic policies that allow the market forces to operate will generate the growth so sorely needed. That program may yet work. But the odds aren't very good. After years of "Reaganomics," the economy is still soft. Inflation is way down, but any severe recession will do that; you don't need supply-side economics.

In addition, Reagan's program is turning out to have a hidden agenda. It appears that indeed there is an industrial policy in Washington, an unofficial one. The significant parts of the Reagan tax plan are designed more to aid the old, decaying industrial behemoths than to encourage the new high-tech companies of the Pacific frontier. Reagan is turning out to be a closet nostalgic who is looking back to the time of a strong America based on steel and iron. He is not looking forward to the electronic age. Just the idea of "reindustrializing" America is archaic. The country needs to be revitalized, not reindustrialized. The conservatism of the Reagan Administration is itself obsolete.

In the end, the Reagan tax policies will prove to be necessary, but not sufficient. He will get high marks for allowing individuals to keep more of their hard-earned money and for increasing incentives for work. His help for the industrial heartland will ease the transition it must make to a much smaller, more streamlined, but still quite necessary, part of the American economy. His efforts to turn the country away from the years of high consumption and toward a greater capital accumulation are laudable, but not enough.

To guarantee the spread of the "hot mix" of the Silicon Valley throughout the society, a national technology plan may need to be implemented in Washington. It doesn't have to be formally voted on, although that would help. But it might even be easier to simply push each of its segments separately. The United States now does not have either the social or the political consensus to sustain a national debate on the direction of the country. But it is clear that the "magic of the markets" is not going to solve the problem of tens of millions of displaced workers put out of work by robots, of communities overwhelmed with welfare costs, of incompetent companies using taxpayer money not to modernize but to buy other companies and spread their managerial rot. The "magic of the marketplace" will not stop declining corporate behemoths from scooping up tiny high-tech firms and strangling their originality and inventiveness by bureaucratic suffocation. Indeed, the "magic of the markets" will not prevent foreign firms from buying into the most important economic asset this country possesses at the moment—its hundreds of "baby" IBMs.

A technology policy requires focused thought and action. It requires an open agenda that aims to take America forward toward the high-tech future, not backward to a nostalgic past. Today, the debate in Washington centers on an "industrial" policy. In reality, the choice is between the heavy-industry policy of the Reagan Administration and a high-tech policy of some other political faction, be it Republican or Democrat.

For any national technology policy to work, it must begin with the critical resource of the new high-tech era—the mind. The most important part of any technology plan will be not economic or financial policy but something a lot more basic: education.

The shift to a high-tech culture completely changes the skills and values that people are going to need to find work in the future. Mental agility, creativity, analytical abilities—all these are crucial for the new work force. Computer "literacy," programming, logic, a good knowledge of mathematics, foreign languages for competing in the global marketplace, even typing or "keyboarding" are becoming increasingly important.

•

A GROWING *SUPERLUMPENPROLETARIAT*

Right now there is a cataclysmic split in America's education system. Private schools and many public schools in wealthy neighborhoods are installing personal computers by the thousands every day. Instruction in math and science is going up. A renewed emphasis on quality and basic education is taking place. This is especially true of California.

But in most of the public schools of America, people are being graduated who don't even have the skills and values needed to fit into the old industrial society, much less the new high-tech world. Functional illiterates who can't read or write are pouring out of the inner-city schools of the nation to take their place—if they are lucky, at the McDonald's counter; if not, on the unemployment line. Their unskilled labor is not needed today, much less tomorrow, when they will have to compete with robots.

These teen-agers are joining a growing *superlumpenproletariat* that will soon haunt America. They are mostly black and Latin, and they will have no place in the high-tech world of tomorrow unless something drastic is done to help them.

And they are not alone. This new *superlumpenproletariat* will soon be swelled by the millions of skilled workers from the automobile assembly lines of Detroit, the steel mills of Youngstown and the rubber factories of Akron. After decades of holding high-prestige, well-paying jobs, after years of being in the "aristocracy" of the labor movement, they will suddenly find themselves competing with black teen-age dropouts from the Bronx for dead-end employment.

America faces one simple choice with these "techno-casualties"—pay for their retraining or pay for their welfare. The dollars for retraining would be only a fraction of the cost of sustaining them and their families for the rest of their lives. There is perhaps one other choice—pay for their retraining or face a modern-day Luddite rebellion against the robots and computers that are displacing people in factories and offices. If the unemployment rate pushes toward the 20 percent mark, as it might by mid-decade, such a revolt is a distinct possibility.

A massive government program focusing on new skills and values needs to be undertaken. To expand, the economy needs a retooled labor force; to grow, it needs the capital that would otherwise go to welfare. Washington cannot rely on the states to rebuild their education systems to take care of these problems. The Reagan Administration has been cutting back on funding for science and math education in the primary schools, hoping the states would pick up the burden.

But the very states that need it the most are those with the heaviest burdens already. The declining industrial regions of the country face falling revenues and higher welfare costs today. They are cutting back aid to education, not expanding it. This can only exacerbate the conflict that is brewing between regions and states as the country moves toward the high-tech future. Only a federal program can ensure the geographic dispersal of a technologically literate population that in turn can attract their industries of tomorrow. This is absolutely crucial. A technologically skilled labor force is the most important item on the list of things that high-tech companies look for today when they expand. It is more important than taxes, more important than transportation. If declining industrial states allow their education systems to fall apart also, then there is no hope at all for them in the future.

•

THE PACIFIC BASIN STRATEGY

In fact, the mobility of the new industries of the future provides the most promise for the future. There are no geographical reasons to stop a Silicon Valley from growing up anywhere in the country. The requirements are an excellent university, a large number of scientists and engineers, venture capitalists and a culture that is willing to take a chance. There is no need to be within a few miles of coal or iron ore or on a river, for the industries of the future are the industries of the creative mind.

One of the best ways to build new Silicon Valleys is to refurbish our existing university system. Indeed, with Stanford and the University of California profiting from Boyer and Cohen's work on gene splicing, with Harvard linking up with Germany's Hoechst chemical giant to build a $50-million bioengineering department, with Yale conducting research on enzymes for Celanese Corporation, universities are at the very hub of the new technologies and businesses of the future. Their professors are creating new companies, their activities will earn them profits from commercial products and their laboratories are pouring forth the new concepts of the high-tech era.

Right after the Civil War, the government helped to set up a series of land-grant "aggie" colleges around the country to increase research and training in agriculture. They worked extremely well, as the productivity of agriculture can attest today. Some of the biggest universities in America were originally land-grant schools.

What is needed today is the setting up of a series of "techie" institutes. They don't need to be built from the ground up. In fact, they should probably go right on the campuses of those Midwestern aggie schools that have grown into universities. But by geographically dispersing technological expertise throughout the country, and especially in the universities of the declining Northeastern and Midwestern states, Washington could help "seed" the rest of the nation with the "hot mix" that has generated the new high-tech frontier in the West. By extending the Pacific Basin strategy to the rest of America, a national technology policy could prevent a second war between the states by spreading the new industries and jobs of the high-tech era around the country.

•

IMMIGRATION CONTROLS

A national technology policy would also have to deal with the tremendously difficult problem of immigration. Immigration policy is becoming one of the most powerful issues in America today. It strikes at the very soul of this nation of immigrants, and the problem can only get worse as we move into the twenty-first century. For it is a cold, hard, inescapable truth that the last thing America is going to need in the years ahead is a flood of unskilled labor. As techno-casualties mount, a growing number of de-skilled people will be moving into the unskilled-labor pool. At the same time, automation will eliminate a growing number of jobs. Hence a growing number of people, many of them furious at their new lower status in life, will be competing for a shrinking number of jobs. The decade ahead may be one of the most explosive periods in the country's history.

With the shift to high technology, the United States will need highly educated people to man the laboratories and production lines of the new industries. The ability of the country to draw on the brains of the entire world could turn out to be one of its strongest economic assets. No other nation in the world is flexible enough, open enough to do this, certainly not homogeneous Japan. For the most part, educated foreigners come to the United States as legal immigrants or students. The unskilled are illegal immigrants. With the shrinkage of unskilled jobs as automation progresses through the economy, the major motivation for illegal immigration will tend to disappear. But it just may be that to preserve some kind of social harmony as the nation moves through difficult times, it will become necessary to go to extreme measures. Already there is a bill in Congress that would practically force everyone in this country to carry identification papers showing that they were not illegal aliens. No doubt a computer in Washington would keep track of us all. If the pressure to do something about illegal immigration grows under the impact of high-tech change to the point where the bill is passed, we will all have lost something of our freedom. In the end, immigration policy may force us into a painful trade-off between personal liberty and social stability.

•

TECH TRANSFER

If innovative technology is one of America's greatest economic assets, then its leakage or sale abroad might have to be monitored under a national technology policy. Certainly, technology transfers to the Soviet Union must be curbed. As the world moves toward an electronic battlefield, the strengths of the United States will grow. Indeed, the speed with which electronics is changing weapons may eventually allow Washington to parlay the threat of ever-increasing new types of electronic warfare systems into a firm strategic-arms pact with Moscow. With the Soviet Union slow to act in electronic innovation, it is possible that the cost of keeping up will become too much for its deteriorating economy to bear. But that means preventing Moscow from getting U.S. technology.

Just as important, the Europeans and Japanese now have nearly total access to every new high-tech company in America. And they are gobbling them up voraciously. The list of small high-tech firms selling out to needy foreigners is huge, beginning with Fairchild Camera and Instrument going to France's oil-drilling giant Schlumberger. Olivetti's Carlo de

Benedetti says that "it is easy in the United States to find these companies. There is a small club. I just call Hambrecht & Quist and they tell me."

A national technology policy would establish specific quid-pro-quos between the United States and its commercial competitors. Fair trade would be matched by fair trade. Protectionism would be matched by protectionism. For Japan, where the sale of domestic companies to foreigners is unheard of, the United States would make American companies off-limits to Japanese firms looking for software expertise or bioengineering technology.

U.S. companies often turn to foreigners when the stock market is down and they can't get the capital. To prevent the wholesale buying of small high-tech firms, some way of funneling cheap capital to these companies must be found that allows them independence. Of course, the best way would be for the federal government to curb its borrowing, allowing more capital to be made available to high-tech companies. Failing that, a special investment bank could be set up to funnel capital not to the declining industries of steel and autos but to the new "baby" IBMs of tomorrow.

Another way to increase capital flows to high-tech companies might be to do away completely with the capital-gains tax on profits made in the stock market. When Congress raised the capital-gains tax from 25 percent to 49 percent in 1969, the amount of new money going into just-born companies dropped from $171 million in that year to $10 million in 1975. When Congress rolled back the tax to 28 percent in 1978, a venture-capital boom resulted. By 1981, $1.3 billion was available for new start-ups. It is a simple way to "feed" the baby IBMs and the cost to the Treasury is small.

•

HOT-TUB HIGH TECH

The people building the new high-tech America have a very special set of values that sets them far apart from the older Northeast-Midwest heartland of the nation. In fact, they have a lot more in common with the old frontier spirit of the late nineteenth century, with its pioneers and robber barons, than with the corporate managerial style of present-day big-business men. Indeed, they are creating a new Pacific frontier—a frontier based less on the physical geography of the West than on that region's special "hot mix" of bubbling mental creativity, surging economic growth and the "birthing" of hundreds of tiny new companies. The new Pacific frontier is a brand-new frontier of the mind and spirit—of scientific discoveries and engineering innovations, of men at the leading edge of technology joined by a new breed of entrepreneurs creating a form of raging capitalism not seen since the days when Vanderbilt, Rockefeller, Ford and Mellon built the old industrial base of the nation. Their capitalism is the capitalism of the Hong Kong exporter, the Korean industrialist, the Taiwanese businessman and, of course, the murderously effective Japanese corporate commando.

Their optimism is the optimism of the open frontier. For the people building the new high-tech Pacific frontier, the decay of the cities, the massive unemployment and crime are all problems of the "old" industrial base, the rotting Northeast and Midwest. The Pacific frontiersmen see these problems as endemic not only to the older parts of America but to Europe, the "old country," as well—to all the countries bordering the Atlantic. They are turning their backs on this economic and social decline to face the future in the turbulent and exciting Pacific Basin.

For the hot-tub culture of high tech is not one of laid-back passivity, but rather a sizzling striving to create and build as fast as possible. The generation of greater wealth and capital by turning new innovations into practical products for sale in the marketplace is the most important value in Silicon Valley. Making wealth, not redistributing it, is what motivates people in Santa Clara County, California. Growth, high and fast, is what makes people go on the new Pacific frontier. They are possessed by the vision of *more* and *better*, not the defeatism embodied in the "Limits to Growth" document put out by the Club of Rome in 1972 which envisions a static world economic pie that has to be divided up in some kind of equitable fashion by bureaucrats.

The high-tech people are the first generation of builders, the electronic pioneers of the twenty-first century, not the colorless managers of so many failing American corporations. Most of their companies are less than a decade old. Apple was formed in 1976 and sold its first stock in 1980. The granddaddy of modern high-tech companies, Intel, was created by Robert Noyes in the 1960s and went public in 1971. These people have more in common with Byung-Chull Lee, the founder of Samsung Industries in Korea, and Akio Morita, cofounder of Sony, than with the graduates of Harvard's B school, who are taught to manage what other people have created.

Their image of America is one of open markets, open education, open social channels through which individuals can succeed or fail, according to their individual abilities, not their group affinities.

Their image of the international arena is very similar. They want fair, not free, trade. They believe they can win a fair competition. They need foreign markets and trade, but they demand that everyone play by the same rules. There was a lot of celebrating in Silicon Valley when Hitachi and Mitsubishi got caught in an FBI high-tech "sting" operation in mid-1982.

The instincts of the entrepreneurs of the new Pacific frontier when it comes to Washington are similar to those of the earlier pioneers. They want Washington to cut taxes, cut strangling regulations and basically leave them alone. Yet this feeling is increasingly matched by the growing realization that they need Washington more and more to enforce the international trade rules of the game overseas. They also need a whole series of domestic legislation and policy changes from Congress to help them meet foreign competition. And with defense spending surging ahead, they increasingly look to Washington for profits.

At the core of high-tech values is a strong nationalism. To men who have fought and lost many times to the Japanese, the United States is almost an underdog in the global marketplace. It is not the superpower of bygone decades. To them the United States must constantly keep an eye over its shoulder on the few European companies doing well in high technology while keeping a firm bead on the Japanese *zaibatsu* that have declared the twenty-first century "theirs." Moreover, the "techies" are proud that their companies are among the most advanced anywhere. They are expanding, while the older industries are declining, becoming an historical anachronism in the postindustrial epoch. The men building the Pacific frontier identify the America of the future with their own efforts, their endeavors, their advanced technology. The America of the past, the sorry '70s, of lost wars, inflation, economic decline, go with the old economy of the Northeast-Midwest.

Silicon Valley's close ties with the Pentagon reinforce this nationalism. Defense Department spending has always played as critical a role in fostering sophisticated electronics in America as MITI's in Japan.

In addition to individualism, nationalism, progrowth values and anti–big-government feelings, the corporate culture of high technology leaves little room for unions. The engineers and scientists who work there share the same dislike of unions common among all white-collar workers. And they are so much in demand that unions can do very little for them anyhow. Job hopping is a life style in California. The new entrepreneurs have even less use for unions. They run their companies in a paternalistic style that is a lot more like that of

Japanese corporations than like that of General Motors. Profit sharing is common, company swimming pools and Jacuzzis usually go with the job. A sense of family is valued, a sense of mission instilled. It is the "x" company against the world.

•

THE "TECHIES" AND RONALD REAGAN

The values of high-tech America are fundamentally conservative. Ronald Reagan took most of their votes in 1980, and his presidency, in turn, symbolizes the rise to power of the Pacific Basin portion of the country. Reagan attracted their votes by his expression of hope, belief in America, and promise to turn the country around economically at home and politically abroad. Reagan's supply-side policies focused on growth and the accumulation of capital, not the redistribution and consumption of it, and his tax cuts and pare-backs of federal social programs offered to free the markets from government interference. Both appealed to the people of Silicon Valley. So did his push for higher military spending. Perhaps most important of all, Reagan's image of a man on horseback, riding out of the West to do battle with the "bad" guys in the East, from "decadent" liberals to the Soviet Communists, made him, and the Republican party, the repository of the political beliefs of high-tech America. For in many ways, they share the small-businessman, America-first attitudes that have always found a natural home in the Republican party.

But the men on the new Pacific frontier are finding out that the Republican party of the early 1980s is a peculiar ad hoc coalition of groups with which they have very little in common. In fact, the "techies" have every right to be openly hostile to many of their fellow Republicans. For Ronald Reagan was elected by a fragile coalition that includes the fundamentalist Religious New Right of the Reverend Jerry Falwell and the Moral Majority, which is concerned about the cultural and moral decay of America; the Neoconservative Intellectual

Right of Irving Kristol and Norman Podhoretz, former liberals concerned with the analysis and justification of conservative thought; the Economic New Right of the supply-siders, who promised to get the U.S. economy moving again by taking us back to pre-Roosevelt days, plus the traditional forces of the Republican party, big business and small-town America.

The "techies" found that they could live with the creationist ideas of the Religious Right, even though they totally contradicted the rational and scientific basis of what their entire high-tech society was about. But they quickly discovered something a lot more threatening in the Republican party. Ronald Reagan, it turned out, was a conservative who looked backward, not forward—a man on horseback who was nostalgic for the days of Teddy Roosevelt charging up San Juan Hill, not the leader of the future to take us into electronic Star Wars. His conservatism was based on an image of a smokestacks America, a powerful nation pouring forth steel, autos, chemicals—all the products of a bygone industrial era.

His conservative image was translated into his supply-side economic policies, which turned out to favor big business, rather than the burgeoning new companies of the West and Southwest. Worse, when all the political shouting was over, his policies turned out to benefit the ailing, declining industries of the Northeast and Midwest most of all. To be sure, the general tone of the supply-side cuts was applauded, and there were a few token benefits on R & D that helped. But by and large, the tax package that came out of Reagan's Washington was weighted heavily in favor of helping the archaic, obsolete industries of the past. Add to that the incredible \$100–\$200-billion annual federal budget deficits that threaten to gobble up all the capital needed by the hungry entrepreneurs, and disenchantment quickly settled in on the new Pacific frontier.

Suddenly, they realized that it was the Business Roundtable, the Washington lobby for big business, that has the ear of Ronald Reagan. Indeed, it is now clear that high-tech America has no effective voice in Washington at all. On domestic economic policy, neither the Republican nor the Democratic party speaks for it. The high-tech constituency is up for grabs in the grab bag of American politics. It despises the faction of the Republican party that is associated with the decaying industries of the Northeast and Midwest; it has nothing in common with the Religious Right; it indulges the political writings of the New York–based Neoconservatives; and it understands but rebukes the conservative nostalgia of the President himself.

It is entirely possible that the high-tech constituency will bolt the Republican party in 1984 if an alternative can be found. If the "voodoo" economics of the supply-side theorists fail and the coalition of Ronald Reagan begins to split under the strain of soaring unemployment, financial crises and sky-high business failures, Silicon Valley may throw its support behind a moderate conservative—perhaps a Democratic "neoliberal"—who promises to look forward, not backward, in his economic and political policies.

•

A TWENTY-FIRST-CENTURY BALANCE OF POWER

With Europe in decline, Japan in ascendancy, the Soviet empire in disarray and America beginning to distance itself from its Atlantic allies, the balance of power established after World War II is about to be drastically changed. This is one of those moments in history just before maps get rewritten, their colors change, border lines are redrawn. Today, a low, heavy moaning sound of great continental plates pushing up against one another can be heard, but no one knows when the socio-political earthquake will strike and what new realignment will follow.

Two scenarios are possible. They depend in large degree on the speed of technological change, the policy response in political capitals around the world and the amount of disequilibrium they introduce in the balance of power.

The "Dark" scenario develops as Europe sinks very quickly into an economic quagmire in the 1980s. Government officials are unable to put into place policies that foster and strengthen new high-technology industries, and they pour tens of billions of dollars into obsolete heavy industries in order to placate workers and voters. Unemployment rises sharply, there is violence in the streets, and political polarization takes place. The Common Market is split, and NATO becomes a dead letter when Germany refuses to allow the stationing of U.S. Pershing and cruise missiles on its soil. Bonn signs a treaty with Moscow guaranteeing the reunification of the two Germanys by 2000 if West Germany becomes neutral. A "Mediterranean" Common Market led by France emerges.

At the same time, the Soviet economy falls further behind the West. A Solidarity-type organization flourishes briefly in the Ukraine only to be crushed by troops. Similar outbursts occur in the Baltic republics. Moscow becomes embroiled in a military adventure against China or in the Middle East to deflect growing internal unrest with renewed nationalism.

Japan increases its high-tech lead over Europe and the United States with new engineering breakthroughs in computers, telecommunications, biotechnology and consumer electronics. In 1985 its trade surplus soars to $50 billion with America. Tokyo begins to export sophisticated military weapons, and the nation's superiority in electronics gives it a clear edge in the global arms market, taking big contracts away from the United States, France, and the USSR.

In the United States, Washington continues its industrial-nostalgia policy by supporting declining heavy industry. Huge budget deficits continue, double-digit inflation reignites, high interest rates return, and economic growth crawls along at about 1 or 2 percent. Unemployment jumps to 18 percent by 1985 and there are Luddite-type factory riots and a wave of urban violence at the same time. Racism becomes a major political problem again. High-tech industries flourish in the West and Southwest, but at a lower rate of growth than in the early 1980s. Defense spending rises sharply to meet the Soviet challenge, and the Pacific frontier becomes increasingly dependent on the Pentagon.

If the world moves in this direction, we are apt to see a form of corporate authoritarianism take hold in America. A flag-waving nationalism will spread that will give the more extreme New Right groups increasing power. Close ties between the Pacific frontier high-tech companies and the Pentagon and between the old heavy industries of the Northeast and Midwest and Congress will produce state capitalism with Washington playing a growing, not a shrinking, role within a very conservative ideological framework. The regional split within the country will get much worse.

A wave of protectionism will sweep the international trade markets, and a boycott of Japanese goods will be unofficially declared in Washington.

There will be heavy police and Army crackdowns on civilian violence by the *superlumpenproletariat* and the robot-smashers, and civil liberties will suffer. These conditions will last the rest of the century. By then, the transition to the new high-tech society could be over. The country will then return to a more democratic posture as unemployment recedes.

There is, of course, a "Light" scenario for the immediate future, one that has at least as good a chance of being realized as the "Dark." This occurs if Europe muddles through the transition from a heavy-industry to a high-tech economy and begins to recover. Its unemployment rate moves up to 14 percent from the current level of about 10 percent, but there is enough vigor shown in new industries to enable young people to begin to find jobs again. The Common Market holds together, although just barely. Germany allows a limited number of new U.S. missiles to be stationed, and NATO remains intact. France, Germany, Britain and Italy expand their technology ties with U.S. corporations, and increases in their own defense spending spur advances in local electronics industries. France makes the transition to a high-tech society, and power within Europe shifts to Paris.

In Moscow, a new group of leaders is suddenly shocked when a war in the Middle East or Asia shows that the Soviet Union's most advanced weapons are no match for the new electronics-packed hardware of the United States. The group wins an internal power struggle against the KGB and the military-industrial complex, and implements a policy aimed at revitalizing the Soviet economy. It argues that without massive changes in the economy, the Soviet Union will fall victim to capitalism.

In this scenario, Japan remains the most powerful high-tech nation. Its high-tech military exports grow. But its problems begin to catch up with it. An aging labor force, an inability to innovate, growing unemployment start to erode the country's lead. Rising demands from the elderly and consumers lead to a larger redistribution of wealth in the country. Japan continues to lead, but at a slower pace. In all, the Pacific Basin continues to have much faster growth than any other part of the world, and its ties with the United States increase sharply. In America, high technology "reopens" the frontier. A shift in Washington fiscal policies cuts the mammoth budget deficits, and interest rates fall sharply. In addition, major segments of a technology program are passed by Congress. High-tech industries, "seeded" by rebuilt universities in the Northeast and Midwest, begin to spread outside the Pacific Basin region of the country. The robot industry supplants the car industry in Ohio and Michigan. High growth lowers the unemployment rate to 8 percent, and there is a minimum of civilian violence. Government-sponsored programs to retrain de-skilled workers are passed and are successful.

Defense spending levels off and begins to decline. The high-tech companies of the Pacific continue to concentrate on consumer, instead of military, products, and their orientation remains with the market and not the Pentagon. This market orientation makes the companies that much more efficient and competitive against the Japanese.

An explosion of individual creativity takes place and produces a flood of new products. A golden age of invention takes place. The U.S. balance of trade moves into surplus, the dollar rises sharply, and the trend toward protectionism is reversed.

A new balance of power emerges in the world, with America and Japan at the apex. They are the first nations to make the transition to the post-OPEC societies of high technology. A progressive conservatism captures the nation's ideological imagination, and an appreciation for individual creativity is matched by a social responsibility toward the victims of the greatest technological revolution in a hundred years. The transition from one type of economy to another is made peacefully. The curtain on the twenty-first century draws apart, and a new era begins.

Two scenarios for the world—the dark and the light. The odds are 50–50 for each.

NOTES

•

CHAPTER 1 (*pages 17–60*)

In the various discussions on robots, automation and unemployment in the book, I relied on interviews with Paul Aron, executive vice-president of Daiwa Securities America, Inc., one of the leading lights on Japanese and American robotics; William W. Winpisinger, president of the International Association of Machinists and Aerospace Workers; and Harley Shaiken, a management consultant to the United Auto Workers and now research associate, Program in Science, Technology and Society, Massachusetts Institute of Technology. The Japan Society has held a series of conferences on the impact of automation in recent years, and at a particularly good one on April 23, 1982, Shaiken was there along with Winpisinger, and Malcolm R. Lovell, Jr., Undersecretary of Labor in the Reagan Administration.

There is a growing body of writing about automation. For the conventional view that robots will increase jobs, not cut them, see "Robotics and the Economy," March 26, 1982, a staff study prepared for the Subcommittee on Monetary and Fiscal Policy of the Joint Economic Committee, U.S. Congress. For a more realistic perspective, see "The Impact of Robotics on the Workforce and Workplace," Carnegie-Mellon University; "Technical Progress—Impact on the Economy and Labor Market," by Switzerland's Prognos and Britain's MacIntosh Consultants; "Robots Join the Labor Force," *Business*

Week, June 9, 1980; "The Speedup in Automation," *Business Week*, Aug. 3, 1981; "Working with Robots Is a Bore," *New Scientist*, May 28, 1981; and "Microelectronics and Unemployment," *New Scientist*, Jan. 28, 1982.

For the best look at the robotics and automation industries in various countries, see Daiwa Securities America, Inc., "Robotics in Japan," July 3, 1980, and Bache Halsey Stuart Shields, Inc., "Japanese Robotics: The Takeoff," April 22, 1982. Both were prepared with investors in mind.

Not much has been said about Russian robotics. The best over-all piece is "Russian Robots Run to Catch Up," in *Business Week*, Aug. 17, 1981.

For a broad picture on technology and its political and social impact, see David S. Landes, *The Unbound Prometheus—Technological Change and Industrial Development in Western Europe from 1750 to the Present* (Cambridge: University Press, 1969); Christopher Evans, *The Micro Millennium* (New York: Viking, 1979); James Martin, *Telematic Society, a Challenge for Tomorrow* (Englewood Cliffs, N.J.: Prentice-Hall, 1981); John Wicklein, *Electronic Nightmare—The New Communications and Freedom* (New York: Viking, 1979); Ronald Kent Shelp, *Beyond Industrialization—Ascendancy of the Global Service Economy* (New York: Praeger, 1981). And for an overall look at technology in the 1980s, see Colin Norman, *The God That Limps—Science and Technology in the Eighties* (New York: Norton, 1981).

Bioengineering is a field so new that it is difficult to get reliable information on it. I relied on the good sense of an old friend, Dr. Phil Skolnick at the National Institutes of Health, to develop a general idea on the risks and rewards of the new science. Dr. Skolnick is no bioengineer. His work has focused on Valium and other drugs in the brain. But his lab is near a bioengineering laboratory at NIH, and his level-headed advice was most helpful.

For more detailed information on bioengineering, I turned to the following material: "Japanese Biotechnology—Japanese Manufacturers Get the Bug," Sept. 28, 1981, another excellent Bache advisory to investors; "Biotechnology Companies," F. Eberstadt & Company, Inc., Aug. 26, 1981, a list of all U.S. corporations involved in bioengineering; "The Rush to Put Biotechnology to Work," *Industry Week*, Sept. 7, 1981; "Japan Aims to Catch Up in Biotechnology," *Chemical Week*, Dec. 16, 1981; "Securing High Technology Experts Through

Scouting Grows Difficult," *Japan Economic Journal*, Oct. 4, 1981; "Tinkering with Life," *Science*, November 1981; "Biotechnology Puts Zip into Fermentation," *Business Week*, Feb. 23, 1981; "And Now—the Biochip," *New Scientist*, Jan. 14, 1982.

The best coverage of the "C and C" revolution, the joining of computers and communications that is collapsing the audio, visual and data networks of the world into a single system, is being done today by a group of people at *Business Week* magazine, my professional home. In fact, anyone interested in any of the new technologies should look to the pages of this magazine. Led by Bob Henkel, the group includes Otis Port, Robin Grossman and a dozen others who cover technology around the world. I am indebted to them for their ideas and their knowledge.

One of the best-written reports on "C and C" technology is "The Home Information Revolution," *Business Week*, June 29, 1981; see also "The Coming Assault on Communications Markets," *Business Week* Special Report, Dec. 14, 1981; "Toward the 'Wired Society,'" *World Business Weekly*, June 8, 1981; "Wheeling Out Baby Bell to Rattle IBM," *The Economist*, Nov. 14, 1981; "Fiber Optics," *Technology*, March–April 1982; "How Videotex Will Aid Marketing and Management," *Business Europe*, May 7, 1982; "Dawn of the Electronic Newspaper," *New Scientist*, May 13, 1982; "Japan's Information Society," *Far Eastern Economic Review*, Dec. 7, 1979; "Squaring Up for a Fight," *Financial Times*, Jan. 18, 1982; "Japan Takes Aim at IBM's World," *World Business Weekly*, April 20, 1981.

CHAPTER 2 (*pages 61–75*)

Over the years, I have come to rely on Rimmer de Vries, chief economist at the Morgan Guaranty Trust Company, for a clear-sighted view of OPEC and its petrodollar surpluses. De Vries, in his bank's monthly publication, *World Financial Markets*, has for nearly a decade charted the path of OPEC and its tremendous impact on the international financial system and the world's economies. His publication has an underground following on Wall Street and in every financial part of town in every major city of the world, from The City in London to the gray buildings of Frankfurt. I found a young Chinese-banker type reading de Vries's heady and somewhat heavy stuff at the PRC's Bank of China in Hong Kong in 1978.

In addition, I am indebted to Ron Taggiasco, of *Business Week*'s

Rome bureau, which covers OPEC and the Middle East, as well as the strange goings-on in Italy. He was stationed in Cairo for years and knows Sheik Yamani well.

The best source for OPEC and oil has always been the *Petroleum Intelligence Weekly*. It has tracked OPEC production and global energy prices for years and is nearly always ahead of the news that you and I normally get in the morning. For discussions on the end of OPEC's predominance over the world, see *PIW*, May 3, 1982; "The End of the OPEC Era," *Euromony* editorial, October 1981; "An End to OPEC?" a series of articles in *Foreign Affairs*, by S. Fred Singer, former deputy assistant secretary of the Department of the Interior, 1967–1970, and Stephan Stamas, deputy assistant secretary for financial policy in the Commerce Department, 1967–1968; the Bank for International Settlements quarterly reports on global banking developments and cash flows; "Can OPEC Survive the Glut?" *Fortune*, Nov. 30, 1981; "Oil Shale on the Rocks," *New Scientist*, May 13, 1982.

CHAPTER 3 (*pages 76–103*)

The question of Germany's role in Europe is an extremely sensitive one to everyone living there. Germany's search for a role for itself in the modern era has meant great tragedy for millions of people, a good portion of them Germans. Of the dozens of interviews I had with European and American businessmen, central bankers, private investment bankers, union officials and government policy makers, nearly all, particularly the Germans, insisted on anonymity.

That said, Dr. Lawrence G. Franko, now at the Fletcher School after several years at the Center for Education in International Management in Geneva, has been extremely helpful in explaining the changing European political situation. So has Alan Stoga, at the First National Bank of Chicago, and Yves Laulan, chief economist and senior vice-president at Société Générale in Paris.

The public speeches of Arthur F. Burns, former chairman of the Federal Reserve Board and U.S. Ambassador to West Germany, are very useful. "How America Looks at Europe," presented Dec. 1, 1981, before the German Foreign Policy Association in Bonn, is especially insightful about the erosion of the Atlantic Alliance.

Two people, in particular, provided very useful information about Germany. Jean-François Deniau, former cabinet minister for the European Commission under the government of Giscard d'Estaing, gave German current events a powerful postwar perspective. And a Japanese, surprisingly, had a great deal of insightful information as well. Naohiro Amaya, special adviser to the Japanese Ministry of Trade and Industry (MITI) and former vice-minister for international affairs for MITI, offered many interesting observations not only about Germany but about the decline of Europe as well.

One journalist stands out in terms of German coverage—John Vinocur of *The New York Times*. Now head of the *Times*'s Paris bureau, Vinocur's stories are among the best describing the drift and uncertainty prevailing in Germany today. His pieces during 1981 and 1982 on the Greens, on reunification, on political romanticism are superior to those of any of his colleagues. I suggest his piece "The German Malaise," in the *Times*'s *Sunday Magazine*, Nov. 15, 1981, and his commentary "The Silence in Bonn," Dec. 23, 1981, for anyone interested in present-day Germany. *The Economist* has also done a fine job in covering economic and political changes in Germany. "The Return of That Old Nationalneutralismus," Nov. 21, 1981, is excellent.

Dr. Nicolas Krul, an extraordinary investment banker in Geneva, has shared with me his keen observations about the direction of Europe and America over the years. Krul's management of a portion of OPEC's petrobillions forces him to consider both political and economic factors in making his investments. One paper by Krul, "European-U.S. Economic Interdependence: Where Next?" October 1981, is especially useful.

The work of Gordon A. Craig, J. E. Wallace Sterling Professor of Humanities at Stanford University, has been a strong influence on the thoughts expressed in this chapter. Craig's books about German culture, tradition and history are among the best available in English, and his latest was particularly helpful—*The Germans* (New York: Putnam, 1982). I found Edward Crankshaw, *Bismarck* (New York: Viking, 1981), also helpful. Many of the comments about Siemens, the giant German electrical company, come from Sigfrid von Weiher and Herbert Goetzeler, *The Siemens Company—Its Historical Role in the Progress of Electrical Engineering*, an official biography (F. Bruckmann KG: Munich, 1972). Any look at European history requires reading Fernand Braudel's work; his two-volume history, *The Mediterranean & the Mediterranean World in the Age of Philip II* (New York: Harper & Row, 1972–1973), is simply wonderful. His latest book, *The Structures of Everyday Life* (New York: Harper & Row, 1981), follows in that grand tradition. Finally, I used Immanuel

Wallerstein, *The Modern World-System—Capitalist Agriculture and the Origins of the European World Economy in the Sixteenth Century* (New York: Academic Press, 1974). It too is a seminal work.

CHAPTER 4 (*pages 104–133*)

The best information on the Soviet Union, of course, comes out of Washington's intelligence agencies. The most useful declassified document I have come across is entitled "Soviet Acquisition of Western Technology"; it is dated April 1982. It describes in detail Soviet technology needs for both military and civilian economies, how it satisfies them from the West, and what it would cost to deprive them of that high technology.

Comments and conversations with Lionel Olmer, undersecretary of commerce for international trade, have been extremely useful.

I must thank Vladimir Gerasichev, correspondent for Soviet TV and radio, for many of my impressions about life in the Soviet Union. Nearly every New York–based business journalist receives a Soviet "buddy" at one time or another in his professional life. They appear willy-nilly on the phone, and I must assume it is after much effort on the part of Soviet intelligence. I talked with Vladimir every few months for about two years and stopped after the Russian invasion of Afghanistan when our conversations had degenerated into angry shouting matches. But Vladimir did provide me with some insight into the Russian paranoia about both the Germans and the Chinese, their sense of not only economic, but also social, inferiority with the West, their smoldering anti-Semitism, their wonderful dark sense of humor and their ability to laugh at themselves, their need for security, their drive for parity with America, and finally, their deep desire for peace.

For a picture of life in the Soviet Union, I relied on an exceptional piece by George Feifer, "Russian Disorders—The Sick Man of Europe," *Harper's* magazine, February 1981; it chronicles the spread of alcoholism in the Soviet Union and its social and economic impact.

Alex Beam, chief of *Business Week*'s Moscow bureau, who grew up in Moscow when his father, Jacob Beam, was U.S. ambassador, has a better feel for the country than anyone I know. His pieces on Soviet robots, the underground economy and Soviet industry played a major role in this chapter, especially "The Stalled Soviet Economy," *Business Week*, Oct. 19, 1981, and "Cash Woes Haunt the Kremlin," *Business Week*, May 19, 1982.

The Economist has printed several major pieces on the East in recent years, the best being "East-West Trade: An End to Business as Usual," May 22, 1982. "The High Price of Vodka," an editorial in the *Financial Times*, Sept. 16, 1981, was also extremely useful.

CHAPTER 5 (*pages 134–159*)

The best English-language source for information about Asia is the *Far Eastern Economic Review*, published in Hong Kong. I relied heavily on it for this chapter, although the magazine has a decidedly pro-Asian, anti-American bias despite the fact that it is put out mostly by expatriate British and is owned in large part by the *Wall Street Journal*.

For information on the seabed mining treaty, I used the material written by Ruth Pearson, one of the best journalists around covering the United Nations and multilateral negotiation of the seabed variety. Her articles in the *Journal of Commerce* on the seabed treaty are the best by far.

Chase Manhattan Bank publishes a weekly commentary called *International Finance*, which is full of details on Third World economies, as is Morgan Guaranty's *World Financial Markets*.

And, of course, Byung-Chull Lee, chairman of the board of the Samsung Group, was most helpful over tea on March 29, 1982, in highlighting the North-South battle over technology now breaking out.

CHAPTER 6 (*pages 160–195*)

Hans T. works in a world of secrecy that can see $10 billion move from dollars to German marks in a single day, wreaking havoc on global economic policy. The only way to work the international-finance beat as a journalist is to respect that need for secrecy and establish a bond of trust with the men who run the banking networks. With that in mind, I have kept Hans T.'s real identity to myself, although there are a handful of people around the world who might guess the name of this warm, rotund and clever person.

Hans was not the only one with the foresight to begin investing in technologically advanced companies. Ken. E. Mathysen-Gerst, president of Capital International in Geneva, is one of the most sophisticated international investment bankers around. So is Karl Van

Horn, Morgan Guaranty's international pension-fund manager in London. Van Horn was one of the first people to begin investing U.S. money in the Japanese market. Yves Otramare, of the discreet Lombard Odier in Geneva, has provided guidance as to where the big flow of the world's funds was heading over the years, and why.

How Europe is coping with the high-tech revolution and what specific strategies it is using to get access to that technology was the major topic of conversation with Carlo de Benedetti, vice-chairman and chief executive officer of Olivetti, on March 2, 1982. And Naohiro Amaya, again, has shared his thoughts with me on this critical matter. J. Paul Horne, vice-president of the Paris operation of Smith Barney Harris Upham and Company, has been a major source of information on the great French drive toward technological and economic ascendancy. He is perhaps the best nonofficial American observer of France.

There is a little-known publication read only in multinational-business circles called *Business International* that puts out a series of monthly papers of considerable value to anyone interested in what is really happening around the world. Orville L. Freeman, Secretary of Agriculture under President Kennedy, is the head of the organization, which publishes *Business Europe, Business Latin America, Business Asia, Business International*, and other publications.

Business Europe, Nov. 13, 1981, has a big piece, "Tightening the Data Noose," that is one of the best descriptions of privacy laws and their impact on corporations. Its July 31, 1981, piece "Joblessness and Protectionism" is also very good.

One of the best publications dealing with electronics, aerospace and laser technology is *Aviation Week and Space Technology*. In its April 19, 1982, issue, Alton K. Marsh, in "Concern Mounts on Technology," presents a good description of policy changes in Washington. The *New Scientist* magazine, put out in London, is also an excellent way of tapping into the real world of technological change written for the nonscientist. "The World Data War," *New Scientist*, Sept. 3, 1981, is an extremely valuable outline of the issues involved in the fight for the technological heights. I also found the following very useful: "Last-Chance Tactics of Europe's Chip Makers," *Business Week*, June 28, 1982; "Alas, Poor Europe," *Economist*, March 20, 1982; "Why Ma Bell Won't Let a Western Contract Go East," *Economist*, Nov. 7, 1981; "Case of Fujitsu," *Japan Economic Journal*, Nov. 24, 1981.

CHAPTER 7 (*pages 196–223*)

Technology fraud and computer crime are growing issues in America, and a flood of material is beginning to pour out on the problem. I have found that some of the best analyses to date have been in *Aviation Week and Space Technology*. "The Spreading Danger of Computer Crime," *Business Week*, April 20, 1981, is a good introduction to the subject. "How Russia Snares High-Technology Secrets," *Business Week*, April 27, 1981, is very good as well and highlights John D. Shea, president of Technology Analysis Group, Inc., a consultant to the Defense Department on electronic security, and a major figure in the field of technology transfer.

The best description of "One-Eyed Jack" Jackson is in a marvelous piece by Michael S. Malone in *The New York Times*, Sunday, May 30, 1982. See also the *Wall Street Journal*, Jan. 12, 1982, for Caspar W. Weinberger's comments in "Technology Transfers to the Soviet Union"; "The Night They Raided Silicon Valley," *New Scientist*, July 1, 1982; "Killer Electronic Weaponry—Tipping the Balance in Military Power," *Business Week*, Sept. 20, 1982; and "Industrial Espionage—US Companies Are 'Soft Targets,' " *World Business Weekly*, Sept. 28, 1981, for an interview with Herschell Britton, executive vice-president of Burns International Security Services, about private spy schools for business spying. The best description of how the FBI set up the "sting" operation that caught Hitachi and Mitsubishi Electronic in buying stolen IBM computer secrets is in "FBI Wove Elaborate 'Sting' Operation Against Suspects in Theft of IBM Data," *Wall Street Journal*, June 24, 1982.

CHAPTER 8 (*pages 224–253*)

There is no shortage of material available on the Japanese economic miracle. Indeed, there are dozens of books explaining Japan's managerial system, technology, politics and culture. Edwin O. Reischauer has been writing for decades and his work forms the basic foundation for an American understanding of that nation. In recent years, a number of books have come out "explaining" Japan to us in one form or another, including William Ouchi, *Theory Z—How American Business Can Meet the Japanese Challenge* (Reading, Mass.: Addison-Wesley Publishing, 1981); Richard Tanner Pascale and Anthony G. Athos, *The Art of Japanese Management—Applications for American Executives* (New York: Simon and Schuster,

1981); Kenichi Ohmae, *The Mind of the Strategist—The Art of Japanese Business* (New York: McGraw-Hill, 1982); Ezra Vogel, *Japan As Number One* (Cambridge, Mass.: Harvard University Press, 1979); Herman Kahn and Thomas Pepper, *The Japanese Challenge—The Success and Failure of Economic Success* (New York: William Morrow, 1980); and Miyamoto Musashi, *A Book of Five Rings*, a seventeenth-century strategy guide that was put out recently by The Overlook Press and has gained a big cult following on Wall Street.

On the "Back to Basics" managerial theme, I used a pioneering article by Robert Hayes and William Abernathy, "Managing Our Way to Economic Decline," *Harvard Business Review*, July-August 1980.

Most of this chapter on Japan is based on intensive interviews with economists and businessmen, both Japanese and American. I am indebted again to Naohiro Amaya of MITI for his insights into the need for a national, long-range vision and his emphasis on the role of "animal spirit" in economic growth. Talking with him at the JETRO office has been an exciting enterprise over the years. He is one of the most politically astute people I have ever met. Keiichi Takeoki, president of Matsushita Electric Corporation of America, provided important insights into Japanese creativity and adaptability on Nov. 1, 1981. Lew Casanova, of Sperry Univac, was stationed in Japan for many years, and his sophisticated analysis of doing business in that country allowed me to see through the eyes of an American businessman. His ability to see the subtleties of Japanese culture and the interplay between that culture and the business world was extremely valuable to me. In addition, I had many long talks over sushi with Takanori Mizuno, who was senior economist at the New York branch of the Fuji Bank for several years. His analyses of the Japanese economy, international trade and United States–Japan conflicts were excellent.

CHAPTER 9 (*pages 254–294*)

The section on America is the culmination of several years of thought and discussion with many dozens of people, including businessmen, government policy makers, bankers, and foreign observers. These interviews have ranged across the industrial landscape from automobile-company presidents to pioneers in the electronics industry. I have sat through discussions with the top bosses of U.S. Steel as they described how buying an oil company would help them make steel, all the while blaming foreigners for their problems. I have also talked with high government officials from the Departments of Commerce, State and Labor, the U.S. Trade Representatives office, the Senate and the House of Representatives.

For many of my observations on the decline of our managerial class and the need to move away from fancy financing back to the basics of production, I am indebted to Lewis H. Young, editor in chief of *Business Week*, and a trained engineer. It takes courage to tell the readers of your magazine that they are doing things wrong.

For an understanding of the venture-capital business and the crucial role it plays in economic growth, I turned to the Rain Hill Group in New York. Rain Hill screens new inventions and ideas for an international group of corporate clients. The people running it have a thorough understanding of the role of "venturing" in the economy and how it varies from culture to culture. A brief schematic description of this process, called "New Business Opportunity Evolution," printed in April 1981, helped me understand the context within which innovation must take place to have an impact on society.

The best examination of the changing nature of the U.S. economy that I have seen is a special issue of *Business Week*, "America's Restructured Economy," June 1, 1981. I am indebted to the economics group at the magazine, led by deputy editor William Wolman and including Seymour Zucker and Ed Mervosh, for much of my understanding of the tremendous changes now occurring in this country —and for the reminder that they are causing a great deal of pain to the people of this nation. In addition, I recommend "High (Tech) Anxiety" by Rachel Wrege in *Popular Computing*, January 1982, for a wonderful discussion about cyberphobia, the fear of computers.

INDEX

ABOUT THE AUTHOR

Bruce Nussbaum covers international finance and business for *Business Week*. He received his formal education from the City University of New York, Columbia University and the University of Michigan. Nussbaum spent several years in Southeast Asia and currently resides in New York City.